The Stress Management Sourcebook

OTHER BOOKS BY BART CUNNINGHAM:

Action Research and Organizational Development

Quality of Working Life

The Stress Management Sourcebook

by
J. Barton Cunningham, Ph.D.

LOWELL HOUSE

LOS ANGELES

NTC/Contemporary Publishing Group

Library of Congress Cataloging in Publication Data

Cunningham, J. Barton
    The stress management sourcebook by J. Barton Cunningham.
        p. cm.
    Includes biographical references and index.
    ISBN 1-56565-792-6
    ISBN 0-7373-0012-4 (paperback)
    1. Stress management. I. Title.
  RA785.C86 1997
  155.9'042–dc21   97-37447
                                          CIP

Requests for such permissions should be addressed to:
Lowell House
2020 Avenue of the Stars, Suite 300
Los Angeles, CA 90067

Published by Lowell House, a division of NTC/Contemporary Publishing Group, Inc.
4255 West Touhy Avenue, Lincolnwood, Illinois 60646-1975 U.S.A.

Text Design by Nancy Freeborn

Printed and bound in the United States of America
International Standard Book Number: 1-56565-856-6
10 9 8 7 6 5 4 3 2

Contents

Acknowledgments

Over the five years that this book has been a work in progress, I have been grateful for the guidance of a close friend, Dr. Joe Lischeron, a clinical psychologist with whom I often work. He has read many of the chapters and has provided me with a great deal of support and guidance.

The research for this book has been a lifelong pursuit. It has grown from my interviews, research, and personal experiences with people in stressful organizations. It has evolved from my experiences with various cultures when I lived in Singapore from 1991 to 1994. These were people who taught me much about Asian practices like QiGong, Tai Chi Chuan, and yoga.

The book has undergone many changes, based on comments from colleagues and people who are experiencing stress. It was once a very academic book full of footnotes and references. The book's goal is to help people as much as it has helped me focus on my stress management and health.

I would like to thank my editor, Bud Sperry, for his comments on and guidance of the manuscript during preparation. He encouraged me to offer ideas and practices that help people change. This was a very useful suggestion.

Several persons helped me and gave me feedback and support. Maureen Keen and Tom Rippon read several chapters. Tom Whitelaw and Orville White are eighty-year-old models of life who continue to inspire me. I very much appreciate Jonathon and Deano and members of the swim club. John Farquharson continues to provoke me with ideas and visions. My wife, Donna, continues to help me and is an example of patience. Most of all, I would like to thank my three children, Julia, Bret, and Landon, for helping me learn how to be more patient and enjoy life.

Foreword

In over twenty-five years of teaching and consulting in business, government, university, and personal situations, I have come in contact with many individuals who have achieved an incredible degree of outward success, but have found themselves struggling with an inner hunger. They experience a need for personal congruency and effectiveness from a healthy lifestyle and growing relationships with other people.

Here are some problems that these people have shared with me.

- I'm always on a diet. I'm overweight and even though I really want to lose weight, I never seem to have much success.

- I am forty-eight-years old. I do not smoke or drink but may be a little overweight. I have difficulty walking a great distance. I am out of breath from walking down a hallway. If I take the stairs rather than the elevator, I have to stop and rest.

- Over the last two weeks, I have been getting tremendous migraine headaches.

- I had to go on stress leave. I was so angry with what was happening at work that I was unable to work. I could not sleep. I gained 20 pounds. I was drinking. Finally, I went to my doctor. I needed the time off, but now I have to go back to work and face the same situation that I left.

- I have always had clear career goals and have had a certain degree of success. But, it cost me my family. I'm afraid my children have grown up and I do not know them. I hardly spent any time with them. My wife and I rarely do things together anymore.

- There is so much to do and I have no time for anything.

- I've started a new diet. It is called the "grapefruit diet." It says I can eat all I want and all I have to do is to drink grapefruit juice before eating anything.

- I was in the hospital for ten days on traction. Three of my discs have basically disappeared and five vertebrae literally have no protection from those above them. The damage is so bad that I have a constant numbness in my left leg.

In writing this book, I recognize that many of us work in very stressful environments. Mine is no different. Some years ago, three of my fourteen colleagues sought professional help because of the style of one director. Most recently, a university review committee investigated the internal practices of my school's administration. Two staff members are on long-term disability or stress leave and two have been hospitalized for life-threatening illnesses. *Fractious, caustic, divisive*, and *aggressive* are common words used by students and university managers to describe my colleagues. Some faculty members have refused to work with others, and three have arranged to fulfill their obligations outside our department.

I feel a great deal of stress and discomfort because of the anger and hostility expressed in my work environment. I work with people who are proud to describe themselves as forthright, undiplomatic, and caustic. I cannot change them, but I certainly can change the way I deal with them.

Some of these are deep, painful problems—problems that quick solutions in "quick-fix" books cannot solve. The secret to solving such difficulties is to recognize the complex web that connects stress, diet, exercise, and personality.

- Stress management ideas for reducing stress on the job are only one piece of the puzzle.
- Diet and exercise programs are not enough to develop a healthy attitude and lifestyle.
- Exercising and relaxation will not, by themselves, reduce the chances of coronary heart disease.
- Personality and a wellness perspective are important for maintaining health and reducing stress-related diseases.

If there is one finding that is most consistent throughout all the varied information about health and stress, it is that an effective method of stress management requires an integrative approach. A stress-free lifestyle and job flows from a healthy mind and stress management style, just as much as it does from caring managers and supervisors.

The need for an integrated set of principles is illustrated when we recognize that relaxation and meditation programs complement diet and exercise practices. Exercise programs can improve HDL cholesterol levels and reduce anxiety. However, some exercises create more stress in many of the body's organs, just as certain foods are more helpful in preventing stress while others can cause it. Exercise programs must complement dietary changes and a person's body type.

Certain jobs and lifestyles require different stress management approaches. It is realistic to expect that each of us handles stress in a different way.

The Stress Management Sourcebook is not just another book about health and stress and what to do and not to do. The book articulates the many facets of how stress and lifestyle affect us, from personalities and job pressures to our diets, exercise, and ways we relax. The information and wellness practices emphasized in this book are those identified as most effective, based on well-recognized studies in Western medicine as well as traditional practices.

The book allows the reader to integrate these practices with his or her personal lifestyle and provides opportunities for self-diagnosis. It illustrates ways of reducing stress and developing a more satisfying and happier lifestyle. The book includes a number of scales and tests for measuring stress-related issues and problems. These are based on measures that I have used in over twenty-five years of research on personal and organizational stress. Information on these can be obtained by contacting me at:

C.O.R.E.—Centre for Organizational Research and Effectiveness
c/o School of Public Administration
Box 1700
University of Victoria,
Victoria, British Columbia, V8W 2Y2

PART ONE

STRESS:

The Dragon That Threatens Our Lives

STRESS: A Dragon in Disguise

Although the world is full of suffering,
it is full also of the overcoming of it.

—HELEN KELLER

STRESS IS AS LETHAL A KILLER AS THE DRAGONS OF MYTHICAL HISTORY.

Throughout history, we have grown to know dragons as large, ferocious beasts that look at humans as a nice light meal. We have learned to fear dragons and to do everything to fight and kill them.

Dragons do not exist today in the same way they did in mystical history. Today's dragons appear less threatening and hostile and are even sociable and acceptable to us. The modern dragons are not carnivores that seek to kill and eat us. However, they are just as lethal.

The modern dragons are our jobs, our societal conflicts, our fractious relationships, our stress-prone personalities, and our unhealthy diets. These modern dragons are as lethal as any in the past. They kill and injure in many ways. The most vivid form of the modern dragon is expressed in the increasing incidence of workplace murders, the most frequent cause of workplace deaths. Less violent, but certainly as lethal, are heart disease and the many cancers that can be directly and indirectly associated with workplace and societal stress.

THE DRAGONS OF WORK AND LIFE ARE GREATER THAN EVER BEFORE.

No previous generation of people in history has experienced the variety and intensity of pressures, conflicts, and demands as ours has. We are living in an age of anxiety. We often hear comments such as, "I'm disappointed and hurt," "I'm angry and frustrated," "I've got too much to do," or "They treat their people like slaves." Some people turn to escapist behaviors such as drinking alcohol or coffee, smoking, or overeating. Others suffer psychological problems such as depression, withdrawal, and anger.

Stress has been linked to high absenteeism, poor decision making, and low morale. It has been associated with many illnesses and is associated with depression, peptic ulcers, asthma, diabetes, cancer, and coronary heart disease.

Other types of stress are induced by our dietary habits—the mode of eating that has evolved as a result of urbanization and mass production. Highly refined, processed, canned foods, fast-food outlets, and restaurants have become the norm in our eating choices. Our diets include caffeine, sugar, salt, alcohol, processed foods, and other chemical stimulants.

Lack of fitness and an inability to relax may contribute to increased levels of stress. Because of the hectic pace of life, many people find they do not have time to exercise, and television has become a major source of relaxation.

No previous age in history has included the variety and intensity of psychological pressures, demands, and expectations from work and lifestyle. The stress of work is blamed for billions of dollars per year in costs associated with lost productivity, absenteeism, and alcoholism and its treatment. In addition, there are very vivid personal costs resulting from the great number of chronic illnesses caused by unhealthy lifestyles and the effects of poor diet and lack of exercise.

The stresses of work and life are very different than they were even thirty years ago. They are likely to undergo even more changes in the next few decades. The amount of time and effort that is spent writing, reading, or discussing this topic is one indicator of its importance.

In responding to this situation, this book articulates the many facets of how work stress and lifestyles are affected by personalities, a job's design, our diets, exercise habits, and ways we relax. Its purpose is to develop an agenda for managing stress and improving general health.

THE WORK AND LIFESTYLE DEATH TRAP

The demands of life and work are contributing factors to our age of anxiety just as much as a person's lifestyle, diet, personality, and heredity. Whenever work or nonwork demands exceed an individual's coping abilities, some form of stress occurs. Stress is any action or situation that upsets the body's normal equilibrium. A person's ability to handle stress is unique and, for this reason, it is not possible to offer easy cures through relaxation, exercise, or improved diets. Some people have lived to the age of a hundred and yet they have rarely exercised; they have smoked, drunk excessively, and have been frantic workalcoholics. Other people who live seemingly "model" lifestyles may die from heart attacks at a very young age, in spite of their healthy lifestyles.

THE STRESS OF WORK AND LIFESTYLE CAN KILL, EITHER SUDDENLY OR GRADUALLY.

The more dramatic incidents of the effects of stress at work are seen in workplace murders. Workplace murder is now the fastest-growing kind of homicide in America. In Canada, a disgruntled faculty member sought to kill his dean, but killed four others instead. Other statistics—on suicide, heart attacks, and other illnesses—may not be as dramatic nor easy to link to problems in the workplace. Less dramatic but still alarming are the large number of work days lost to industry through stress-related illnesses.

The stress generated from a person's lifestyle is more difficult to define. Is stress more likely for those who have certain personality profiles or who have certain dietary habits? When the overweight actor John Candy died of a heart attack in March 1994, many of us might not have been surprised. Stress has been associated with so many illnesses that the U.S. Surgeon General's report commonly indicates that two-thirds of all illnesses before the age of sixty-five are preventable. Compared to the costs of treating stress-related diseases, the costs of prevention are relatively small.

Stress is not solely an American phenomenon. We see evidence of it throughout the world. In Japan, for example, corporate stress is rising, and its effects may be exhibited in a different way. It is increasingly claiming the lives of top Japanese managers, according to a chilling report by the *Asahi Shimbun,* one of Japan's leading newspapers. To blame are pressures from Western protectionism, the high yen's devastating impact on Japanese exports, the specter of rising unemployment, and an extremely painful period of industrial restructuring for the nation, not to mention a few bona fide corporate scandals.

It is believed that more than 10,000 Japanese are dying each year from overwork or *karoshi*, a phrase coined from *karo* (overwork) and *shi* (death). Japan's Labour Ministry, which runs a system of worker's compensation, has been less than ready to recognize strokes or heart attacks—the most visible signs of karoshi—as work-related. In 1992, only thirty-three such cases were covered by worker's compensation, which represented 5 percent of the total applications.

More recently, the growing publicity surrounding karoshi cases has resulted in public appeals by families of the deceased. Slogans such as "Stop the Karoshi" have been adopted by one citizens' group. Contrary to expectations, karoshi is a problem for both older and younger workers. About 60 percent of those suspected of being killed by overwork are in their forties and fifties. Another 20 percent of those who died were in their twenties and thirties.

This section should illustrate one thing. Work and lifestyle can kill. Preventing this from happening depends on many considerations.

DEFINING STRESS

Most people have their own unique definitions of stress and its effects. A useful exercise in any stress workshop is to ask participants to define stress by completing the following sentences: Stress is _____? Without stress, life would be _____? Here are some typical responses:

Stress is:

- frustration
- not knowing where my job ends and where someone else's begins
- having to relate to customers
- being unable to complete the many tasks that are expected of me
- being overweight
- feeling guilty when I drink

Life without stress would be:

- wonderful
- peaceful and relaxing
- boring and unchallenging

There is no single definition of stress, as one can see from the above comments. What is characteristic of many of these definitions is that they focus on work and the life-related stressors of having to deal with difficult people and having too much to do. The definitions point to ambiguity and conflict, or to miscommunication or differing expectations. In addition, they indicate that stress may cause discomfort, but also illustrate that life without it would be dull and unchallenging.

Experts do not agree on the definition of stress or its essential properties. A challenging and rewarding task for one person may be flooded with stress and anxiety for others. One person's appraisal or perception may be very different from another's. Stress occurs when an event is perceived to challenge one's resources or capabilities to respond. In this sense, stress is largely perceptual and is a function of how important the situation is perceived to be in personal terms and the extent to which individuals are not bothered by situations unimportant to them.

Since there are so many different interpretations of stress, how can we define it? In responding to this question, it might first be appropriate to list certain assumptions, suggesting that stress is individual, variable, and cumulative.

STRESS IS OFTEN THOUGHT TO BE AN INDIVIDUALIZED RESPONSE.

Different people will respond differently to the same stressful event. Many people would feel very stressed on meeting a black bear in the woods, but it is alleged that Daniel Boone would say, "What luck, . . . I have not had a bear fight in a week." In the same way, flying, bungee jumping, and sky diving would be exhilarating to some, very stressful to others. If you observe another person and find yourself saying, "I don't know how you do all that work," you are really acknowledging that another person can handle stress better than you can.

STRESS ALSO VARIES FROM TIME TO TIME FOR EACH INDIVIDUAL.

Individuals may have experienced stress when they first drove a car, gave a speech, or had a relationship with a member of the opposite sex. However, with practice and development, many experiences become less stressful. In the same way, individuals may find it more stressful to drive certain cars at certain times, just as they would find some speeches more stressful than others. Indeed, the stress of a relationship varies from time to time, just as it varies from individual to individual.

Prolonged periods of stress can produce overloading and taxing effects. Individuals may find it relatively easy to respond to one or two stressful incidents during a week, but a long series of such events may cause overload. The stress felt after being fired from a job may be very large, but it may be even greater after the individual is fired from a second job. These cumulative effects may not always be overloading for some people; they might produce an increased capacity to resist and tolerate future stress of the same kind.

STRESS: STIMULUS OR RESPONSE?

Most of us can identify with the many stressful incidents that people talk about. Stress might be the force—the supervisor, the person in the conflict, or the workload—that creates discomfort or strain. This stimulus definition of stress suggests that some stimuli or force acts on us and causes us to react positively or negatively. This definition is similar to the one borrowed from the physical sciences, where stress includes the number of external forces (stressors) that cause tension. For example, the forces of tons of logs and debris in a flooding river may be too much for the piles of a bridge to withstand. Similarly, the stress and strain of too much work may overly tax the coping powers of certain individuals. Using this definition, the stressors faced by individuals are no different from those faced by a bridge. When the stress exceeds the capacity to resist or cope, there is likely to be a collapse. This definition of stress suggests that we should: (1) reduce the forces of the stressors we face; (2) improve our capacity to resist or strengthen ourselves so damage is not caused; and (3) be aware of early warning signs so that we can take action to prevent severe damage.

Upsetting stimuli might be called stressors, and the manifestation of stress might be called strain. This definition of stress is associated with the late Dr. Hans Selye, an endocrinologist at the University of Montreal who is frequently referred to as the "father of stress." He introduced the term *stress* in his writings in referring to the body's nonspecific response to any demand placed on it, pleasant or not. These are outside forces or agents acting on the organism, or the general wear and tear of life on the body. These agents might be called stressors. Selye identified three phases of reaction to stress as a "general adaptation syndrome." Stress has consequences for several areas of the body, and the body adjusts or deals with these stressors through a series of defenses designed to help the body adjust. The reactions occur more or less together and are partially interdependent.

Stress is a universal human (and animal) response resulting from the perception of an intense or distressing experience (boss, death, an airplane flight, too much work). Stress has tremendous influence on our behavior (makes us fearful, nervous, edgy). Stress challenges our ability to endure, cope, or defend ourselves (wears us down, erodes our energy, attacks our immune systems, makes us less capable of fighting diseases, makes us less confident). Stress might be referred to as anxiety (which in fact is a consequence of stress), conflict, frustration, pressure, and emotional trauma.

This definition illustrates how work stress may affect our general health or capability of fighting diseases. Obviously, the stress response will differ from person to person. That is, it might be expected that people who have healthy lifestyles are more capable of managing their stress. They have a healthier immune system resulting from good diet, proper exercise, and general wellness.

In a stimulus definition, stress is an external agent or stressor. In the response definition, stress involves the consequences. Both definitions have their proponents. When we seek to understand work and organizational stressors in Part II of this book, we are using a stimulus definition of stress. However, we are also interested in understanding what happens when people experience stress. The response definition illustrates consequences and devises strategies for answering.

WHAT HAPPENS WHEN PEOPLE PERCEIVE A STRESSFUL EVENT?

When a threat or stressor is encountered, the body's entire stress-response system can be activated. This mobilization draws on the body's energy reserves, and digestive processes decrease while blood is diverted to the needed areas.

When a situation is appraised as potentially harmful or threatening, internal and external responses immediately occur, some of which are clearly visible (for example, blushing and perspiring). When a threat or stressor is encountered, an individual's perception of it can activate the body's energy defense mechanisms. The body mobilizes its various systems, especially the brain, nervous system, and endocrine system, in response to stress. When we perceive a stressful situation, such as an angry customer, a message is placed in the cortex area of the brain. The hypothalamus responds to the messages from the cortex by registering emotions such as fear or anger, and it is involved in raising the body's temperature and controlling appetite and sexual behavior. In the stress response, the hypothalamus triggers the nervous and endocrine systems.

The autonomic nervous system controls gastrointestinal, cardiovascular, and reproductive activities. When we experience stress, the hypothalamus stimulates the autonomic nervous system to respond. A person's heart rate may increase, and he or she may sweat or feel tense in his or her stomach.

In response, the endocrine system allows the release of various hormones into the blood. The pituitary gland discharges hormones into the bloodstream that activate other parts of the endocrine system and prepare the body to deal with the stressors. As a result, blood flow and respiration may increase. The adrenal glands produce the hormone adrenaline and other hormones called corticoids that increase a person's stamina and muscular tension. For example, after President Reagan was shot and wounded, the news reports indicated that he walked into the hospital like nothing had happened. In this time period after the shooting, the president seemed to possess superhuman abilities as the adrenaline helped prepare his body to fight the injury it had just received. Later, hours after this adrenaline surge disappeared, the president felt the true pain of his injury. The length of time that the body can continue to supply adrenaline and other hormones is limited—these hormones become depleted.

As stated above, muscles tense in anticipation of the stressors, and a person's endocrine system produces hormones like adrenaline. The adrenaline acts on muscles and fat tissues, causing them to release various chemicals they store. The liver subsequently converts these chemicals into glucose, which is usually directed by the heart and the other organs as an energy source. The digestive processes cease, and blood is diverted to assist the muscles and the brain. Effects include increases in respiration, heart rate, blood pressure, blood cholesterol, and decreases in digestive processes while blood is diverted to the needed areas. There is also some activation of blood-clotting mechanisms, a safety device in case of injury, and pupil dilation. These responses are necessary for defense. In addition, energy is mustered from the release of such products as glycogen and lipoproteins.

The body produces 80 to 90 percent of its total cholesterol content, with the remainder coming from ingested foods. One early study investigating the relationship between stress and cholesterol was carried out by Friedman, Roseman, and Carroll. Subjects were accountants who, because of their work, were required to meet specific deadlines during a year. Throughout the six-month observation period, the more strenuous work times coincided with the highest levels of cholesterol. Such studies do not establish a causal link between stress and cholesterol levels, but they do pinpoint its importance.

We need to better understand the relationship between stress and lifestyle and general health. For a number of years, many people believed that the more frequent and serious the stress in one's life, the greater the chance of getting sick.

Certain relationships seem more central:

1. The stress that a person perceives may be related to increases in cholesterol and ill health.

2. People with certain personality profiles are more likely to suffer stress-related illnesses. For example, those who are anxious, aggressive, hostile, and compulsive may be more likely to experience stress.

3. Certain diets can help improve health and reduce stress-related illnesses.

4. Those who have a proper exercise program may be more capable of handling stressful experiences.

5. Certain relaxation practices—meditation, yoga, hypnosis, and biofeedback—may increase a person's ability to handle stress.

PERSPECTIVE 1. STRESS AND DISEASE

Is stress associated with disease? The following formula has been used to illustrate the relationship between chronic stress and disease.

$$Disease = S \times C \times F$$

S = emotional stressor(s)

C = your personal stress, managerial style, and general state of health

F = other factors such as environment, medical history, genetics, and so on.

The formula, developed by H. Lagerlof in 1967, illustrates the complex interrelationship between stress and lifestyle and lifestyle and a range of environmental and individual factors. It illustrates why one person might succumb to stress-related diseases and another might not.

No magical solutions exist for dealing with stress and improving health. There are several popular reports and studies on stress, health, and longevity. For example, in one such study of twenty-seven people in the mountains of Thailand, certain characteristics were associated with longevity. These people were all over 100 years of age, one was 124 years old. They ate a great deal of fish, walked a lot, and lived near mountains. They were also poor, and drinking and smoking did not seem to have any effect on their longevity.

Despite such popular reports and several research studies, we are not able to discover the "sure-fire," or complete approach to handling stress and improving lifestyle. Hypnosis, meditation, exercise, and diet are not, in themselves, sure solutions. Individuals and companies may offer cure-alls, magical potions, and unique discoveries. Many such approaches offer little more than what one would find in a "witch's brew" or astrology chart. Stress management is probably best described as a combination of various strategies for:

1. Building up general health through proper nutrition, diet, rest, exercise, and other positive health practices.

2. Reducing the sources of stress.

3. Altering one's beliefs and perceptions of life and work.

Out of clutter, find simplicity
From discord, make harmony,
In the middle of difficulty lies opportunity.
—ALBERT EINSTEIN

This book's principles are both scientific and personal. It is most important for people to design their own programs to respond to their unique needs. The purpose of this book is to provide the reader with ways of managing stress and developing a healthier and more satisfying life. These principles will be developed in the following chapters. The first part of this book describes many of the common myths about stress, provides some new information, and illustrates how stress kills. You will learn about the long list of chronic diseases and the most well-known risk factors. You should develop an understanding of the complex relationships that affect your general health and well-being.

Your personal style for managing stress is actually important for preventing stress and improving health. This book is based on the assumption that your personality—which is made up of your beliefs, values, personal habits, and conventions—governs the way you manage your stress and health. Your personality and style is articulated through the principles you value. These principles are like your natural laws and are as fundamental as laws in the universe. If you want to be effective in changing the way you manage stress and health, you must work within your unique style or paradigm.

Part II of this book focuses on methods for coping with personal, work, and life stressors. It describes what is known as the stress-promoting personality, the stress-promoting organization, and a range of stressful work and organizational environments. It provides a number of instruments for you to diagnose your personal style and to understand the stress potential in your work and organizational environment. Part II also describes the characteristics of a stress-promoting diet and then illustrates methods for controlling cholesterol. It will help you recognize your potential stressors and then suggest ways to respond to them. Part II outlines how work and organizations might be more effectively designed so that they are less stressful.

The purpose of Part III is to illustrate ways of fighting back and taking control. Instead of being besieged, you can build up your immunity and strength to conquer the stress you face. This part of the book outlines specific principles for improving our capabilities to withstand the stressors around us. It highlights many Eastern ideas for improving relaxation, exercise, and diet. It also blends these ideas with supporting Western research.

Part IV illustrates how you might enrich your life and begin the change process. Much has been written about stress and lifestyle. However, there is a vivid need for some integration to pull together these many different points of view and relate them to one another. This book treats stress as an issue that is affected by one's personality, work, lifestyle, diet, exercise routine, and ability to relax.

2 Myths Associated with Stress

SOME NEW INFORMATION

*There is a moment of difficulty and danger
at which flattery and falsehood can no
longer deceive, and simplicity itself
can no longer be misled.*

—*THE LETTERS OF JUNIUS:* AUTHOR UNKNOWN

Academic and popular writings have played a key role in drawing our attention to the stress of our lives, both during and after work. Self-improvement books encourage everything from positive thinking, diets with oat bran and fish oil, vitamin therapy, and aerobic exercises. Personal stories of how people improved their lives are displayed in Jane Fonda's exercise videos, the Pritikin Diet Plan, and Anthony Robbins's "Awaken the Power Within."

Such portrayals—whether through medical or psychological journals or popular books or articles—have had an interesting and varied impact on the consciousness of many of us. Some stories suggest that stress-related problems and illnesses are preventable and can be managed if people take charge of their diets, lifestyles, and work and nonwork lives. The fact that there are so many popular books and articles on the subject merely underscores the reality that stress and health are very important issues about which people are searching for information.

Thirty years ago, the leading causes of death among humans were acute (sudden) and infectious diseases caused by germs or other external agents.

Disease conditions such as tuberculosis and poliomyelitis were frequent killers. Advancements in hygiene, sanitation, diet, and antibiotics, however, have reduced the incidence of many diseases in most developed countries.

The American Medical Association has indicated that the leading causes of death today are lifestyle induced—stress, diet, smoking, drinking, and inactivity. Cancer, coronary heart disease, and strokes are now prominent.

PERSPECTIVE 2.   STRESS QUIZ

How much do you know about stress? Test your knowledge by answering the following statements as true or false.

- The greatest stress comes from overwork.
- If I really enjoy my work, I can work as long and hard as I want with out suffering.
- Stress is a personal issue, not an organizational one.
- If I exercise vigorously, I will be less likely to feel stress and be less prone to heart attacks.
- Stress is associated more with overwork than underwork.
- As the person goes up in the hierarchy, he or she is likely to experience more stress.
- Certain jobs are, by definition, more stressful, including police work, air traffic control, and so forth.

The correct answer to all the questions is False. If you answered True to any of them, you may be a victim of the wide range of misinformation about stress.

QUESTIONING SOME POPULAR IMPRESSIONS

Who is the person most prone to stress? We all have firmly held beliefs about those people who are more prone to stress. My interviews and studies with people who experienced stress, my conversations with academic colleagues, and my review of the literature suggest that seven beliefs about stress are common. However, each belief has some possible misinterpretations.

Popular Impression 1:
The greatest stress comes from overwork

Possible Reinterpretation: The stress of too much work is something that many of us complain about. We feel overworked or harassed by the many tasks we have to undertake. However, work overload may be less dramatic than other sources of stress, such as interpersonal conflict and not doing fulfilling work.

The greatest source of stress in the workplace results from poor interpersonal relations and conflicts. At its most serious level, stress in the workplace is vividly illustrated by the increasing number of workplace homicides. The effects are also shown by feelings of frustration and discouragement, lost sleep, or endless hours of wasted time that people spend thinking and discussing the horrors of stressful interpersonal relationships. When asked to describe these difficulties, people most often mentioned a breakage of trust or breach in honesty.

People are sometimes hard-pressed to define the details underlying their feelings of mistrust of others. A lawyer or empirical researcher would be unable to identify the facts that cause these feelings. Some people would use terms such as *dishonest, self-serving, back-stabbing, political,* and *selfish* to describe others. The facts behind these labels may be hard to determine, although the words used are rather uniform.

Trust develops only marginally through logical processes; it is more of an emotional response. It evolves from experiences and interactions. Commitment and fairness are the basis of trust. Trust implies accountability, predictability, and reliability. It is the glue that maintains organizational integrity. When trust is absent, organizational members can still feel committed and willing to work, perhaps because of feelings toward other workers or a general commitment to professionalism. However, there is no impetus to go the "extra mile," especially when the organization truly needs it.

A second factor producing workplace stress is not doing fulfilling work. People experience stress when they believe that their jobs are meaningless or have little significance. Such is the case when someone says, "I feel my work is trivial and meaningless."

Workload is also a major stressor. The stress of too much work, or overload, may cause emotional and/or mental paralysis, or an inability to carry out the work. There are two different types of overload: quantitative and qualitative. Quantitative overload exists when people perceive that they have too much work to do, too many different things to do, or insufficient time to complete assigned tasks. Qualitative overload, on the other hand, occurs when people feel they lack the ability, training, or education to complete their jobs or that performance standards are too high, regardless of how well they perform or how much time they have. A person may also experience stress from being improperly trained or feeling incapable of carrying out work assignments. A person might experience conflicting job demands, lack of job security, or lack of authority to carry out the work assigned to him or her.

An engineer who has to design a containment system for a new nuclear power plant within three months may feel that, given the other jobs that he or she is responsible for, this is insufficient time. This is quantitative overload. The same assignment, given to a nonengineer, may cause qualitative overload, since the individual may lack the necessary skills to complete the project. Quantitative overload—such as working more than sixty hours a week, working two jobs, and foregoing vacations—may cause biochemical changes; specifically, elevations in blood cholesterol levels.

Popular Impression 2:

If I really enjoy my work, I can work as long and hard as I want without suffering.

Possible Reinterpretation: This may be analogous to saying that as long as I enjoy excessive eating and drinking, I will not suffer any harm. Although it may be more enjoyable to perform activities that are challenging and interesting, it can still produce several negative consequences on one's health and well-being. It is true that work or activity that includes conflict and pressure is likely to produce stress. However, athletes enjoy their work, but they also suffer much stress, as do doctors, managers, police officers, and lawyers. Enjoying one's work may blind people to the fact that it can cause tremendous stress, just like punishing the body through physical exertion and forcing it to work beyond its limits. Many people who enjoy their work ignore and underestimate the importance of keeping an even balance between work and nonwork activities.

Popular Impression 3:

Stress is a personal issue, not an organizational one.

Possible Reinterpretation: The personal costs of stress are reason enough to be concerned. Individuals can experience a range of stress-related illnesses such as hypertension, headaches, and heart attacks. Added to this are the frustrations and intense emotions caused by stressful experiences.

Stress is much more than a personal issue, however. Stress costs the U.S. economy from $50 to $90 billion annually. Some experts put the total costs to the economy as high as $150 billion a year. These include not only the direct costs of treatment and medical benefits companies pay to employees, but also the costs of absenteeism and low productivity. Costs include a record number of stress-related claims, citing everything from surly supervisors to unsafe offices. These claims account for over 10 percent of the total workers' compensation claims in recent years.

Claims of mental stress from the cumulative effects of exposure to the psychosocial demands of the workplace are also increasing. In California, the number of cases has increased fivefold since 1980. These complaints are both tragic and bizarre. A female deputy sheriff recently claimed chronic psychiatric disability on the ground that her personality wasn't suited for police work. An assistant probation officer said he suffered acute tension because he could not adjust to interviewing angry and emotionally disturbed clients.

Many upset and aggrieved employees are taking action that hurts employers, by taking time off work and claiming stress leave. Take the case of Terri Landon, a trainer in a government office. As she described it, her stress was induced by a "chilly climate," where she felt unwanted in the office. She was on stress leave and reduced time at work for over a year with full pay. Tom Whitehall, a manager of a furniture store, is another example.

As Tom describes it, his stress was induced by a hostile supervisor intent on blocking his rise in the company. While auditing the showroom for the first time in several years, the supervisor gave him bad marks for a dead cricket she found on the floor and blamed him for another store's long-distance phone bills. After suffering a mild stroke while on the job, Tom filed a workers' compensation claim charging that stress contributed to his illness. After more than a year of hearings, Tom Whitehall settled out of court for roughly $50,000.

Other frazzled workers take the law into their own hands. One employee in a telephone company recently became so distressed over the loss of his retirement benefits that he took hostages and destroyed millions of dollars worth of the company's telephone system. An editor for a publishing company sought revenge for his dismissal by sabotaging the company's computer system and trying to rewrite history. Before he was caught, the man had changed the names of historical figures in books and substituted Allah for Jesus in numerous passages in the Bible. The costs of stress are much more than personal. They affect our society at large and are seen in increased health costs and lower productivity.

Popular Impression 4:
If I exercise vigorously, I will be less likely to feel stress and be less prone to heart attacks.

Possible Reinterpretation: Exercise can be a break from stressful routines and a catharsis to let off steam and is helpful in reducing physical and muscular tension. However, some activities are actually extremely stressful. Competitive sports such as squash, wrestling, and boxing increase rather than reduce stress. In fact, even solitary exercises and television programs can be stressful if individuals pursue them in an aggressive, winner-take-all fashion. Several people have died participating in rigorous competitive exercise such as squash.

Nathan Pritikin's book, *The Pritikin Promise,* provides a very convincing description of heart-related problems among marathon runners. The runners in the study showed no evidence of heart disease before they started running, and all died while running. All had coronary arteries severely narrowed or closed with cholesterol deposits. The study challenged a conception that marathon runners were immune to heart disease. It concluded that coronary heart disease appears to be a major killer of conditioned runners who are forty years old and over, but that the possibility of damage is reduced when exercise is combined with proper diet.

Keeping in physical shape is an important antidote to stress-related problems, but it is no cure. Exercise can increase a person's capacity to handle stress, as it increases the flow of oxygen throughout the body and increases a person's stamina. While moderate exercise makes it easier for people to do much more work, excessive exercise may actually cause serious damage. The capacity or stamina to do more does not mean the person will go uninjured. It is like the analogy of a drinker who can handle alcohol better than others can. This does not mean that the alcohol is not causing damage. People who have the stamina for more stress can suffer the same fate as the problem drinker. The stronger and more competent they are, the more they are likely to take on difficult assignments.

Popular Impression 5:

Stress is more associated with overwork than underwork.

Possible Reinterpretation: Stress is not always a bad word. A world without stress might be very boring. Imagine getting up in the morning, not sure where you are and not at all concerned about the present or future. This is that lazy, hazy feeling where there is nothing to do and a low interest in anything. We all experience some feeling of stress as we perform our tasks. Without some degree of stress or pressure to perform (whether external or internal), there is little desire or motivation. A certain amount of stress, stimulation, or arousal is necessary for human functioning or activity. A moderate amount of job stress or arousal is associated with higher performance in work, on exams, or in life in general.

People increase their performance when they are aroused by certain stressors. The phone might ring, a spouse yells, "You are going to be late for work," or you suddenly realize that you are tardy for an important appointment. In fact, people can increase their performance substantially because of the arousal of certain stimuli. Low performance, however, can also be associated with stress. There may be an optimum level of stress that we need to be satisfied and perform well.

The inverted U-shaped curve, in Figure 2.1, is one way to picture the relationship between stress and performance. When there is little stress or desire, performance might be very low (underload). Most of us realize that at very low levels of stress, a little challenge can improve performance and help people develop their abilities. Challenge is another word for a positive kind of stress. With greater stress, performance will increase in the same way that a student might be motivated to study for an examination.

FIGURE 2.1 STRESS AND PERFORMANCE: THE INVERTED "U" SHAPED CURVE

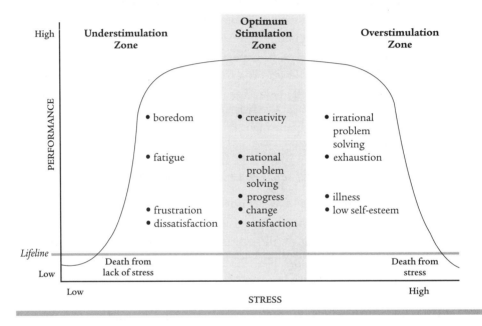

However, too much stress can be dysfunctional, and a person might be incapable of performing because of feeling overloaded. The idea of a curvilinear relationship between stress and performance is not really surprising. Everyone has seen someone perform extremely well during a stressful situation, such as giving a speech, playing a game, averting a dangerous accident, studying for an exam, or doing an assignment. When a person experiences stress, the body's energy is focused to fight potential dangers or competition. There are also several reports of people performing poorly during stress. Some people have "frozen" in front of an audience or completely broken down in situations of adversity or conflict. Thus, there does not seem to be any strong positive or negative relationship between stress and performance. This suggests that stress is truly individual and variable. The same events may be stressful for some people but not for others.

The size of the inverted U-shaped curve may be different from individual to individual, from time to time for each individual, or as a result of the cumulative effects of stress. We might have a wide-ranging curve for people like Winston Churchill and Lee Iacocca, who are able to withstand a number of stressors of almost impossible odds. Most of us would expect to have much narrower inverted U-shaped curves.

The human organism needs a certain level of stimulation from the environment, which is not too high but not too low. At each end of the inverted U-shaped curve, different types of stress are associated with low performance. "Rustout" is lack of stress or stimulation. It might take place if an individual worked in the same job and had the same life experiences for a long period of time. One example would be the person who worked for fifteen years in a dark kitchen cooking hamburgers and who had little other life experience.

In the case of understimulation, we become mentally impoverished, bored, and alienated. Our tension level goes down, we become easily distracted and lose initiative and the capacity for involvement. Monotonous, primitive, simple uncomplicated acts tend to produce boredom and feelings of sleepiness. In this situation, workers are forced to keep themselves under tension all the time, fighting against drowsiness. This is rustout or understimulation, characterized by boredom, fatigue, frustration, and dissatisfaction. It is "rusting out" from lack of activity with no variety, change, conflict, or stimulation. Skills, attitudes, and ideas are not fully utilized, and they become obsolete or routine, leaving people with little or nothing to do.

"Burnout," or overstimulation, is caused by the long-lasting effects of prolonged stress and feeling overloaded and unable to cope. The person cannot carry out his or her activities and feels exhausted and without energy. In cases of prolonged overstimulation, the effects may be fragmentation of thought, loss of integrating ability, and what is called tunnel vision, meaning that we perceive only small parts of the processes going on around us and miss essential information.

Rustout and burnout have rather negative implications. Negative stress is associated with overload and underload and is characterized by anxiety, frustration, worry, tension, and frustration, as well as inability to handle conflict, change, or challenges.

Stress can also be positive. Positive stress (eustress) results from situations of progress and opportunity provoked by challenge, conquest, control, collaboration, and communication. It is the stress associated with good news and stimulation, such as working hard and performing well.

A popular suggestion is to reduce the stress we are facing. However, in some situations, people may suffer from lack of stimulation or challenge. Thus, we need to maintain some level of moderation, some balance or equilibrium.

Popular Impression 6:

As a person goes up in the hierarchy of an organization, he or she is likely to experience more stress.

Possible Reinterpretation: People at the top of an organization's hierarchy may not experience more stress than those at lower levels. Stress may be just as high for those who are at the lower ends of the organization.

In fact, there does not appear to be any positive correlation between the level of the job and the stress that a person experiences. If anything, the relationship is negative. Stress is highest at the lower levels of an organization, increases as the person moves up to middle management, and then decreases at the senior or top levels. What explains this? Every person likes to feel, "I did that all myself." Control or the inability to control your work may be one variable that explains why one may experience more stress. People at top or senior levels have more command over what they are doing and can decide on what is important to do. They can control the volume of work they generate and the time when they do it. People at the bottom of the hierarchy are assigned tasks by others. They usually have less control over what the tasks are and when they must be done. These workers' objectives are often determined by others.

Middle managers may be more stressed because they play a buffer role in the relationship between top managers and lower-level supervisors. They are often asked to interface, coordinate, deal with problems, or anticipate events. They are often in ambiguous situations and have little responsibility or control.

All positions in an organization have a higher potential for stress if they are designed so that people have little control over their work or if their tasks are ambiguous and poorly defined. Thus, job redesign may be an effective tool in reducing stress.

Popular Impression 7:

Certain jobs are, by definition, more stressful, including police work, air traffic control, and so forth.

Possible Reinterpretation: There is a widespread belief that certain occupations are more stressful than others and will adversely affect one's health and well-being. However, a more comprehensive examination of a range of occupations indicates that many other jobs are just as stressful.

Using coronary heart disease as an indicator, high-stress groups include air traffic controllers, physicians, dentists, assembly-line workers, and police officers, as well as lawyers, judges, pharmacists, insurance agents, and real estate agents. A few occupations have traditionally been considered so stressful that they have been subject to intense individual study. One of the most frequently studied is police work. Interestingly, contrary to the TV-produced impression many people have of police work, the primary stressors are not life-threatening situations. Very seldom, in fact, is this aspect of police work cited as a source of stress. Rather, major stress stems from administrative issues and contacts with the court system. Air traffic controllers have also been the subjects of a number of stress studies. In spite of ideal physical working conditions, air traffic controllers experience considerable stress, presumably because of the long periods of intense concentration required and because of the life-and-death impact of their decisions. They are said to suffer from an incidence of ulcers, hypertension, alcoholism, divorce, and suicide many times the rates for the general population. The toll is so great that it is most unusual to find a controller who has been on the job for as long as fifteen years.

The stressfulness of difficult occupations has been debated for many years, leading to more comprehensive studies of a wider range of jobs. When a wider range of occupations is studied using similar criteria, we find that stress is just as high for general and construction laborers, administrative assistants, secretaries, inspectors, clinical laboratory technicians, office managers, food servers, mine operatives, farm workers, and painters.

The nature of the occupation also does not appear to show any relationship to stress. Middle managers and supervisors as well as white- and blue-collar workers all exhibit high levels of stress-related diseases. These results lead to the conclusion that many so-called stressful occupations are thought of that way from the public attention we gave to them. We spend more time and interest on high-profile occupations like police work and air traffic control.

This is also consistent with other studies showing that the highest incidence of stress-related diseases may be associated with the lower end of the socioeconomic continuum. Administrative assistants and food servers are as prone or more prone to stress reactions as those in the middle or upper class such as physicians and top managers. What might explain these findings?

Some jobs are designed so that people have little control of what, when, and how they are done. These jobs cause higher levels of distress—exhibited in ulcers, heart disease, absenteeism, and hypertension—than those that allow people to exercise control. The challenge is to rethink the way certain jobs are designed. Food servers, administrative assistants, assembly-line workers, and file clerks will perceive less stress if their jobs are redesigned to give them more control of how and when they do their work.

Job stress is a complicated interaction between people and their work environments. By saying that certain occupations are more stressful than others, we imply that they contain more stressors and/or they intensify the stressor-stress relationship by virtue of what is involved in the occupation. This is generally true. There are, however, a number of problems in rating specific occupations as stressful or not stressful, not the least of which is the possibility that stress-prone individuals are drawn to certain occupations.

CONCLUSION

Our popular impressions about stress may need to be changed. We should not have any fixed ideas about what it takes to improve our ability to respond to the stress we face, just as there are no fixed characteristics for people in general. A program for reducing stress is best described as a desire for independence and control of one's own destiny and a willingness to change one's habits and beliefs.

3 How Stress Kills

Better put a strong fence 'round the top of the cliff
Than an ambulance down in the valley

—JOSEPH MALINS

TODAY, WE FACE MANY MORE STRESSES THAN OUR ANCESTORS DID, AND WE HAVE A MUCH DIFFERENT LIFESTYLE, FOR ALL OF WHICH WE ARE NOT WELL PROGRAMMED.

Everyone knows someone who seems out of control of his or life. The person I know is John Graham. He is forty-nine years old and is an energetic manager in the Department of Defense. He works hard, is eager to get ahead, and is very meticulous and careful in completing his work. He is sometimes involved in some of the office conflicts, and there are occasions when informal office politics takes more time than the work at hand.

John grew up as a child who loved food, especially bacon and eggs, and he even put salt on the bacon. He coated his bread with peanut butter and loved steaks and french fried potatoes with gravy. He smoked when he was younger. As he grew older, he developed a fondness for a few beers and welcomed the opportunity to drink wine. At one time, he carried 230 pounds on his six-foot frame.

John Graham went to his doctor in 1985 and was warned that his cholesterol level was dangerously high. Five months later, he required a quadruple coronary bypass operation.

Today, he does not smoke and he swims 2 kilometers three times a week. He sticks to a high-fiber diet. He has not eaten bacon or butter (or margarine) in five years. He took up self-hypnosis and meditation and became involved with yoga. He is proud and relieved that his cholesterol level is normal and that his exercise program keeps him fit. Heart disease was the dramatic event that forced John Graham to change his perspective on life. John Graham and many other people have changed their lifestyles as a result of a traumatic experience or a close call. Fortunately, this is not always necessary. Stress-related illnesses can be prevented.

Physical health reactions to stress include:

- asthma
- chest and back pains
- coronary heart disease
- diarrhea
- fainting and dizziness
- frequent urination
- headaches and migraines
- nightmares and insomnia
- psychosis
- psycho-somatic disorders
- diabetes
- skin rash
- ulcers
- loss of sexual interest
- weakness

Stress and lifestyle affect health. Acute problems such as accidents and poor performance are evident and their costs are tremendous. Chronic problems, such as alcoholism, anxiety, and high blood pressure are less noticeable, but may have more detrimental effects. At the very least, stress and lifestyle may affect the capacity to resist diseases, both infectious and acute and those that are chronic and stem from maladaptation of the body's systems.

THE MOST SIGNIFICANT OF THE POTENTIAL STRESS-RELATED PHYSICAL ILLNESSES IS CORONARY HEART DISEASE.

In trying to reduce heart disease and improve general health, some researchers have focused on Western dietary habits as major villains. We are learning that diet is, however only one piece of the picture. The total puzzle may include a range of factors such as obesity, high blood pressure, smoking, stress, and lack of exercise. It is even more complicated when we take into account an individual's susceptibility and inherited traits. Thus, while a fatty diet and smoking may mean a heart attack for one person, another might be able to puff away until the age of 100.

Stress is a multifaceted problem affected by diet, personality, working conditions, and lifestyle. Better management of these factors will reduce chances of heart disease. In the same way, they reduce the possibility of other lifestyle diseases, such as some types of cancer.

In this chapter, the goal is to outline the most obvious changes that have occurred in today's industrialized countries. We face many more stresses than our ancestors did, and we have a much different lifestyle, for all of which our bodies were not designed.

HOW STRESS KILLS

Exposure to life's stresses can lead to a variety of pathological outcomes and may eventually use up a great deal of the body's energy. The organs that normally fight the reactions to stress become exhausted, and other organs in the system are taxed. Relatively permanent injury or deformation might include coronary heart disease, ulcers, hypertension, and even certain types of cancer. Most people mention sleep difficulties, anger, loss of control, or difficulty coping when asked about the effects of stress.

> *Darwinian Man, though well behaved*
> *At best is only a monkey shaved!*
>
> —W.S. GILBERT

Our mechanisms for responding to stressful incidents have been conditioned on the basis of the way we lived thousands of years ago as a Stone Age and tribal society. The foods that we ate were fresh, raw, and in season, and our digestive systems evolved to respond to them. Survival entailed gathering food and protecting ourselves from wild animals. The jobs of planting, hunting, and building all required activity and exercise. The stresses were tangible and produced concrete "flight or fight" responses. When we were hungry, we searched and hunted for food; when we faced danger from an animal or foe, we ran or fought. When we knew winter was approaching, we built shelter. These responses were mostly physical, involving exercise.

The struggles for survival through hunting, planting, and building do not exist in most developed societies, and are replaced by dangers such as unfriendly co-workers, fears of losing a job, loss of data on a computer, or needing to complete a task in a hurry. The "flight or fight" response we used in the past is no longer appropriate. We cannot attack or run away because social conventions do not encourage it. We accept the stress and internalize it.

The same biochemical process occurs when we face stresses today that occured during Stone Age and tribal life. The problem is that our bodies are programmed to respond to stressors in a physical way. Instead of responding and dealing with the stress as our ancestors did, we now have to internalize the response. It is likely that the stressors in our modern society are more frequent, intense, and severe than they were in times past.

LIFE IN MODERN SOCIETY

Kenneth Blanchard's popular book, *The One Minute Manager,* captures the society that seems to be evolving. In the book, Blanchard suggests that people are so busy that they have to learn to do things very quickly; they do not have hours to contemplate, discuss, or plan their futures. Thus, a manager must learn to find "one-minute solutions," in assessing a problem, stating objectives, reprimanding an employee, or laying out a plan. We may all be searching for the instant, one-minute solutions or programs that are "quick fixes"—to keep as fit as we can with minimum effort, to resolve our anger, to lose weight, to become successful, or to continue a relationship.

In our homes, many of us have found ourselves trying to read the morning newspaper while finishing a last cup of coffee before going to work. The television may be on, one of the children may be asking for clean underwear, and another may be refusing to get out of bed. Everyone is eating a different breakfast because no one likes the same foods, and each family member has a special request for his or her packed lunch. After the children are out of the house and on their way to school, if you are fortunate enough not to have to drive them, you might be able to begin your travels to work, either by bus, commuter train, or car. A traffic jam, a push from an overanxious commuter, and the horn of an irritated driver are to be expected on most journeys.

At work, many of us face ambiguous tasks and assignments, and most of them require someone else's assistance or agreement. Much of the day is characterized by interruptions from phone calls, scheduled meetings, or informal gatherings. You begin to attack the mound of work before you. A colleague stops in front of your desk to talk. This chat sometimes continues for more than thirty minutes, and it is often about the frustrations of work or some other colleague. Luckily, your phone rings again and your colleague moves on.

> **THE TASKS AT WORK CONSUME YOU AND YOU SEEM TO TAKE ON MORE AND MORE OF THEM.**

During lunch hour, you sometimes eat a quick lunch and then run around doing maintenance chores like paying a bill at the bank, mailing a letter, or going to the cleaners. You often buy fast foods for lunch because you did not have time to make your own. You eat quickly so that you can do some other chores. There is little time for relationships, other than a few special ones, but you may not even have the time to give them the attention they deserve. If people move away, you rarely write to them, because you are busy. You do not even have enough time to take a walk or relax because the day is so full of the priorities of your job and domestic responsibilities.

The pace of change and pressures of life are not decreasing. More and more of us are living and working in large, crowded cities. Population density is increasing very quickly. As density increases, so does crime, mental illness, suicide rates, and a host of other stress and lifestyle-related factors.

PERSPECTIVE 3. THE EFFECT OF CROWDING

Four Sitka deer were released on James Island in Chesapeake Bay in 1916. The Naval Research Institute in Bethesda, Maryland, noted that the deer population had grown to 300 by 1956, some forty years after that. Just two years later, over half the deer had died. The population leveled off at 80. The island had a very adequate food supply although it had only one-half square mile of area. Autopsies revealed that 81 percent of the deer that had died during the population crash had significantly enlarged adrenal glands. Prolonged stress is thought to be a major cause of enlarged adrenal glands. This condition has been noted in other animal studies.

Would overcrowding affect humans in the same way? Such a mortality link is found in studies of hospitals and prisons with overcrowded conditions. An increase in population of less than 100 percent is associated with death rates that are ten times as high as before. Control factors, such as diet, environment, health care, and personal schedules and habits, do not account for a significant change in the results.

Does overcrowding affect stress?

Matteson and Ivancevich, in their book *Managing Job Stress and Health,* suggest that we encounter a range of stressful situations on a daily basis. Some are of short duration—these include minor encounters like sitting next to a smoker and listening to a noisy radio. Others are more severe and last from several hours to a number of days; these might include a continuing grievance with a supervisor or fear of having to give a speech. Chronic stress situations are those that last for weeks, months, or even years. These may be the death of a loved one, a divorce, a prolonged physical illness, years of an unhealthy diet or no exercise, and the long-term demands of an extraordinary work schedule. It is these chronic stress reactions that are most damaging to our health.

THE MANY EFFECTS OF STRESS

Look at Perspective 4 and ask yourself which of the stress warning signs affect you. Then, read the following section.

Health is a rather nebulous term. The World Health Organization defines it as a state of complete physical, mental, and social well-being, not merely the absence of disease and infirmity. A disease is rather easily identified because it is tangible and recognized. Hans Selye identified a variety of health impairments as diseases developed in the process of the human organism's adaptation to the specific conditions in its environment. The term *diseases of adaptation* has been used to refer to these. Physical diseases of adaptation can be divided into cardiovascular, digestive, immunological, and skeletal-muscular diseases. In addition, there are several emotional reactions.

PERSPECTIVE 4. STRESS WARNING SIGNS

Which of the following warning signs affect you?

Cardiovascular Warnings
- ☐ Faintness
- ☐ Out of breath
- ☐ Tiredness
- ☐ Racing heart
- ☐ High blood pressure

Digestive System Warnings
- ☐ Indigestion
- ☐ Compulsive eating
- ☐ Stomachaches
- ☐ Diarrhea or uneven stools
- ☐ Nervous stomach
- ☐ Excessive gas
- ☐ Constipation

Immunological System Warnings
- ☐ Feeling overworked
- ☐ Tired
- ☐ Trouble thinking clearly
- ☐ Forgetfulness
- ☐ Memory loss
- ☐ Inability to make decisions
- ☐ Constant worry
- ☐ Loss of sense of humor

Muscular-Skeletal Warnings
- ☐ Backaches
- ☐ Muscle tightness
- ☐ Tight neck, shoulders
- ☐ Headaches

Emotional and Psychological Warnings
- ☐ Anger
- ☐ Sweaty palms
- ☐ Sleep difficulties
- ☐ Loneliness
- ☐ Crying
- ☐ Anxiety, nervousness
- ☐ Easily upset
- ☐ Feeling powerless
- ☐ Edginess—ready to explode

Cardiovascular System Diseases

Although virtually unknown in most countries sixty years ago, diseases of the heart account now for over 50 percent of the deaths in Canada and the United States. These diseases were relatively uncommon in North America as late as 1920, but are now so commonplace that one heart attack occurs somewhere in the United States every thirty-two seconds. They are so pervasive that American males who are now between the ages of forty-five and fifty-five have one chance in four of dying from a heart attack in the next ten years. Traditional risk factors, such as poor diet and smoking, can account for no more than about 25 percent of the variance in the association with coronary heart disease. There is evidence that stress may be important in explaining the remaining 75 percent of the variance.

Among the conditions known to precipitate coronary heart disease (CHD) risk are working hard and being dissatisfied with work, not being appreciated by superiors, having more or less than the desired amount of responsibility, serious and enduring interpersonal difficulties with supervisors and/or colleagues, threat of unemployment, and similar other threats. Prolonged or habitual exposure to stressful conditions gives rise to a number of cardiovascular diseases including cardiac arrhythmia (eccentric or neurotic heartbeat), angina pectoris (sharp, stabbing pain in the chest due to insufficient supply of blood to the heart), myocardial infarction (death of heart tissue), and arteriosclerosis.

Women have not experienced the stress levels encountered by men, nor, it seems, have they shown the negative effects. Women started this century with a longer life expectancy than males and have increased that lead through today. According to predictions by the National Center for Health Statistics, they may increase the lead even further in the next century.

Arteriosclerosis literally means "mush in the arteries" and is caused by fat in the blood adhering to the arterial walls in globs, which in time makes the arteries narrow and hard. The effect is to increase the pressure of the blood pumped from the heart.

About one in five North Americans have high blood pressure, and about 50 percent of the group are doing nothing about it. Normal blood pressure is 120/80 but varies with age and weight, and therefore can range from 90/60 to 140/90. Even mild hypertension, such as blood pressure above 140/90, can double cardiovascular risk. Nearly 20 percent of Americans and Canadians have blood pressure measurements of 140/90 or higher. This percentage is even greater if we do not include younger people in this sample.

Finally, a relatively common cardiovascular system ailment is the migraine headache caused by the dilation of blood vessels in the head. Approximately 50 million Americans spend something like half a billion dollars per year to ease their aching heads. Somewhere between 12 and 25 million have frequent migraine headaches.

Digestive System Diseases

Typical diseases of the digestive system include ulcers, gastritis (inflammation of the stomach), colitis (inflammation of the colon), diarrhea, appendicitis, constipation, and diabetes. The most common digestive system disease among workers is ulcers, possibly affecting more than 10 percent of the population. Ulcers are sores on the walls of the stomach or intestines caused by excessive secretion of gastric juices (for example, hydrochloric acid), glucocorticoids, and enzymes.

> How has he the leisure to be sick,
> In such a justling time?
>
> —WILLIAM SHAKESPEARE

The incidence of gastrointestinal or duodenal ulcers is highest among blue-collar workers, first-line foremen and supervisors, middle managers, and female office workers. An examination of the health records of members of 130 different occupations enabled a researcher to conclude that the most stressed groups (defined as incidences of hypertension, CHD, and ulcers) were unskilled laborers, assembly-line inspectors, clinical laboratory technicians, middle-level office managers, foremen, manager administrators, food servers, and machine operators.

Immunological System Diseases

> Health that mocks the doctor's rules,
> Knowledge never learned of schools.
>
> —A.D.T. WHITNEY

The body's defense system, or immune system, protects it from infection. We are only beginning to understand it. Run-down, overworked, tired people tend to have immune systems that are more vulnerable to viral infections. These people have higher levels of hydrocorticoids in their systems. Their bodies are left open to viruses. Viral-caused cancers are being attributed to a reduction in the body's immunological efficiency.

North America has one of the highest incidence of cancer in the world. Over 300,000 Americans die every year from cancer, which is diagnosed in over 650,000 people a year. Cancer is associated with a range of factors related to stress, diet, and lifestyle.

Muscular-Skeletal System Diseases

THE MOST COMMON PROBLEM IN THE MUSCULAR-SKELETAL SYSTEM RELATED TO STRESS IS PAIN IN THE LOWER BACK OR IN THE MUSCLES.

Muscular tension is a stress reaction. The body's initial defenses in the face of stress are in preparation for a "flight or fight" response.

Rheumatoid arthritis, gout, and bursitis are diseases reflecting stress-induced disturbance in the adrenal gland's production of cortisone. Some 24 million Americans are said to suffer from rheumatoid arthritis, accounting for some 200 million days of absence in the work force each year.

Emotional and Psychological Costs

In addition to physical illnesses, individuals experience significant pain, discomfort, and cost due to disturbances of the psychological and emotional systems. An angry, frustrated, emotionally unstable person is not capable of rational responses and good judgment. Such stress repercussions hinder a person's effectiveness in relating to others. They result in emotional disturbances, alcohol or drug use, impaired relationships, sleeping difficulties, disturbances in one's thought processes and concentration, behavioral disruptions, and occupational burnout.

> In every new and smart disease, from housemaid's knees
> to heart disease, she recognizes the symptoms as her own.
>
> —GUY WETMORE CARRYL

Emotional disturbances are particularly reflected in anxiety or depression. Anxiety is indicated by an inability to sleep, arm and neck pains, fast breathing and heartbeat, depressed feelings, headaches, trembling, nausea, heavy perspiration, diarrhea, and other symptoms. Depression is characterized by passivity, loss of interest, decrease in energy, lack of motivation and ambition, inability to accomplish tasks, difficulty with concentration, and the inability to cope with responsibilities. Many of these symptoms are interpreted as a lack of motivation. Burnout is an advanced state of impaired relationships. It starts with a feeling of frustration, powerlessness, and overwork.

A common response to anxiety, depression, and frustration is withdrawal. We withdraw psychologically (alienation), physically (absenteeism), and into other worlds (via alcohol and mood-modifying drugs). This withdrawal affects our relationships with spouses, children, and colleagues. Many of these effects can be witnessed by statistics indicating that nearly one of every two American marriages will end in divorce. Increased violence in the home is evident, and a large number of children are being brought up by single parents.

STRESS AND CANCER

The first law of ecology is that everything is related to everything else.

—BARRY COMMONER

Our understanding of cancer and how it might be cured or prevented has improved dramatically. In particular, mortality in persons younger than fifty-five years of age has declined significantly. However, the disease is still widespread. Lifestyles and dietary habits may be part of the problem. Recent studies indicate that the generation of people who are now aged twenty and over stand a much higher chance of developing cancer compared to those born at the turn of the century. White men born during the middle of the baby boom in the United States (1948–1957) are three times as likely to get cancers unrelated to smoking as their grandfathers were. White women born during this same period of time are 30 percent more likely to develop cancers unrelated to smoking. Smoking-related cancers are up 10 percent in males and 500 percent in females. While smoking is still a primary risk factor, environmental exposure to cancer-causing substances other than cigarettes is partly to blame.

In many forms of cancer, cigarette smoking is said to be a main factor, and the American Cancer Society estimates that it contributes to 30 percent of all cancers. Colorectal cancer is linked to a high-fat diet.

While there has been a great deal of research linking stress and heart disease, the research linking stress and cancer is just beginning. Various life events, personality dispositions, and work environments may affect our immunological and central nervous systems and may accelerate the development of various types of cancer.

Written work on the relationship between stress and cancer was present in the medical literature as early as 1701, when Gendron, an English physician, indicated that cancer may be linked to the emotional experiences a person might have. Life disasters such as the loss of a relative were important traumatic events associated with the development of certain types of cancer.

> *Air pollution is turning Mother Nature*
> *prematurely grey.*
>
> —IRV KUPCINET

In the twentieth century, the lion's share of cancer research is focused on external agents. According to this body of inquiry, the major culprits might be a host of carcinogens in the air we breathe or the foods we eat and smoking. This approach has ushered in a series of vaccines, antibiotics, vitamins, and so forth.

Others, interested in the relationship between stress and cancer, point out that many cancer patients have lost a close emotional relationship before the illness. Cancer patients might have a greater inability to express true emotions or get things "off their chests." One study of the life histories of twins indicated that a biological twin who contracted and died of leukemia had experienced a catastrophic emotional experience, while the healthy twin did not have a similar trauma.

STRESS HAS BEEN IMPLICATED IN THE RATE A MALIGNANCY SPREADS AND ITS POTENTIAL CURE.

The rate of tumor growth may be associated with personality traits and attitudes toward life. In one recognized study, two groups of cancer patients were matched by age, intelligence, and stage of their cancer. Those dying in less than two years were compared to those who had lived for more than six years and were found to have significantly fewer outlets for emotional release. Several recent studies illustrate the effects of stress on cancer growth in laboratory animals.

Testimonials exist about many people who have been diagnosed as having cancer, yet resisted the odds and, in some cases, were cured. In particular, Norman Cousins's book, *The Anatomy of an Illness,* illustrates a number of cases where patients' deep beliefs were a powerful factor in their recovery. Certain religious groups such as Mormons and Christian Scientists appear to be more resistant to malignancy, and much of this is attributed to lifestyle, positive emotions, and a sense of control. Reports exist of cancer cures from shrines, faith healing, various nontraditional medicines such as laetrile and krebiozen, acupuncture, and macrobiotic diets. These cures suggest that the benefits derived may have much to do with emotional attitudes and beliefs.

Cancer is more prevalent in industrial societies with Western-style habits and foods. Cancer is a disease from which many primitive peoples seem immune. It was not present among Eskimos until close contact with Western civilization was established, and it is more prevalent in areas where poverty, crowded housing, divorce, and fragmented families are common. The medical missionary Dr. Albert Schweitzer said that on his arrival in Gabon in 1913, he was astonished to encounter no cases of cancer.

RISK FACTORS ASSOCIATED WITH HEART DISEASE AND CANCER

Heart disease and cancer are associated with a number of risk factors, including stress, age and gender, hypertension, diet, and exercise.

Stress

Both negative and positive stress affects the cardiovascular system. When faced with stress, a person's heart rate and blood pressure will increase significantly. Stress causes an outpouring of adrenaline-like products and other changes in body chemistry. These products can accumulate in the body and result in a continued fast heartbeat.

Depressed people are five times as likely to die within six months of leaving a hospital. Generally, about one in five individuals are significantly depressed after a heart attack, but depression can play a key role in rehabilitation. In one study involving 222 patients who had just suffered heart attacks, researchers interviewed people who were hospitalized. Thirty-five could be classified as depressed (low mood, prolonged periods of sleep disturbance, and problems in concentrating). Within six months of being discharged from the hospital, 12 of the 222 patients died. Seven had succumbed because their hearts had slipped into an ineffective beat in rhythm, four died from another heart attack, and one died from congestive heart failure. Seventeen percent of the depressed patients died compared with 3 percent of patients without depression. The results were significant even after other risk factors were taken into account (being a smoker, having a prior heart attack, and having impaired function). The results indicate that treating depression may be very important to recovery.

Age, Gender, and Heredity

Age, gender, and heredity are associated with heart disease. The dietary habits and personality traits of fathers and mothers may become those of their offspring. A person's age is also associated with heart disease. As a person gets older, there is a greater likelihood that the effects of diet and lifestyle will show up. That is, a person in her fifties has four times the risk of a person in her thirties.

During the 1960s and 1970s, males were thought to be more prone to heart disease. While women are less susceptible to heart disease because of the estrogen they produce, large doses of estrogen seem to increase cardiovascular mortality in men.

Women and their physicians have long labored under the myth that heart disease is an affliction mainly of men. These notions grew because women under the age of fifty rarely have heart attacks. As a result, researchers focused on men, especially middle-aged men. A different picture is emerging, one which indicates that heart disease kills almost as many women as it does men. Once it strikes, the prospects for a lasting return to health are much gloomier for women than for men.

Women are not spared the underlying damage to coronary arteries resulting from decades of unhealthy living, although heart attacks do not seem as predominent in premenopausal women. Women have a mysterious protection from heart attacks, associated with estrogen and the cycling sex hormones. However, once menopause is reached, the effects of the damage become quite obvious.

WE ARE NOW AWARE OF SOME SOBERING FACTS ABOUT HEART DISEASE AMONG WOMEN.

- Fully half of North American women die of blood vessel diseases, primarily heart attacks and strokes. As the leading overall cause of death in women, heart attacks account for twice as many deaths as cancer.

- After menopause, heart attack rates in women rise sharply and reach the rate found in men. While heart attacks become the leading cause of death in men at age thirty-nine, in women they remain second to cancer until the age of sixty-six.

- High blood pressure and raised levels of fat in the blood are as serious a risk factor for women as for men. For every 1 percent rise in blood cholesterol, there is a corresponding 2 percent increase in the risk of heart attack. This is true for both women and men. Raised levels of blood fats (triglycerides) are linked to increased coronary risk.

- Men and women with diabetes face a much greater risk of heart disease.

- Obesity is as damaging to women's hearts as it is to men's.

- Women, like men, are affected by certain kinds of behavior. Women classified as Type A are twice as likely to suffer heart attacks as those that are not.

- The percentage of women in the workforce has grown over the last thirty years. The five-year advantage that women have over men in life expectancy in most developed countries may change as the full toll of work stress has its effects. Rates of alcoholism, smoking, and suicide are increasing in women.

What keeps women more immune to heart disease? The female hormone estrogen, which allows women to bear children, may be the important element in keeping females healthier during the premenopausal period. It makes female tissues more elastic, so that blood vessels can expand to accommodate extra blood volume during pregnancy. This allows the female body to feed the fetus, and in the process increases the production of artery-clearing high-density lipoproteins (HDLs). It builds an immune system that supports pregnancy, and the increased sophistication of the system scavenges more effectively for waste products called "free radicals," which may be responsible for some of the physiological changes and illnesses that result from stress and poor lifestyle choices..

Hypertension

HYPERTENSION IS ONE OF THE MOST UNEQUIVOCAL RISK FACTORS ASSOCIATED WITH ATHEROSCLEROSIS.

Individuals with elevated blood pressures show accelerated atherosclerosis, an increased incidence of coronary heart disease, and an increased incidence of cerebrovascular disease. (See Table 3.1.)

The World Health Organization indicates that over 50 percent of the adult population might be classified as having high blood pressure. A person whose systolic blood pressure is over 150 has more than twice the risk of heart attack and nearly four times the risk of stroke of a person whose systolic blood pressure is under 120. (See Table 3.2.)

Diet

Dietary lipids (fats) are considered to be one of most important environmental agents associated with atherosclerosis.

THE INTAKE OF SATURATED FATS SEEMS TO BE RELATED TO ELEVATED CONCENTRATIONS OF PLASMA CHOLESTEROL AND TO ATHEROSCLEROSIS.

A person with a serum cholesterol measurement of 250 or above has about three times the risk of a heart attack and stroke of a person with cholesterol below 194. It is not possible to demonstrate an unequivocal association between the ingestion of dietary cholesterol and plasma cholesterol levels on a daily basis. Indeed, individuals respond differently to the same diet.

One study of nonsmoking women suggests that eating saturated fats may increase a woman's risk of lung cancer fivefold. Researchers divided the

TABLE 3.1 RISK FACTORS AND MAJOR DISEASES

	Improper diet	Excess drinking	Tobacco	Lack of exercise	Stress	Pollution
CARDIOVASCULAR DISEASES:						
Heart disease	**	*	**	**	**	
Stroke	**	**	*	**	**	
Hypertension	**	**	*	**	**	
DIGESTIVE SYSTEM:						
Ulcers, gastritis						
Colitis	*				**	
Diabetes	**	**		**	**	
Nutrition[1]	**	*	*	**		
IMMUNOLOGICAL	*	*	*	*	**	
SKELETAL-MUSCULAR:						
Lower Back Pain				**	**	
Osteoporosis[2]	**	**	*	**		
EMOTIONAL		**		*	**	
CANCER:						
Colorectal	**					
Lung			**			*
RESPIRATORY DISEASES			**		**	

1. Includes malnutrition, obesity, nutrient deficiencies

2. Brittle bones

Key: High risk **
        Some Risk *

Source: World Health Organization

TABLE 3.2 INTERPRETING BLOOD PRESURE

Congratulate yourself if your blood pressure is in the safe range below 140/90. The higher number is the systolic blood pressure (highest pressure), representing the contraction of the heart. It should be below 140 when the diastolic pressure (the lowest pressure) is below 90. This is the state of rest of the heart, when it is dilated and filling with blood, in preparation for the next contraction.

Range (mmHg)	Category
Systolic blood pressure (when diastolic pressure is below 90)	
Below 140	Normal pressure
141 to 159	Borderline isolated systolic hypertension
Above 159	Isolated systolic hypertension
Diastolic blood pressure (the lowest pressure and the bottom number in your reading)	
Below 85	Normal blood pressure
86 to 90	High normal
91 to 104	Mild hypertension
105 to 114	Moderate hypertension
Above 114	Severe hypertension

These categories are from the Joint National Committee on Detection, Evaluation and Treatment of High Blood Pressure, 1988.

women into five groups based on fat in their diet. The conclusions indicated that: (1) women in the top fifth of fat consumption—more than 40 percent of daily calories from fat—had a five-times higher risk than women in the bottom fifth (who got less than 30 percent of calories from fat) and (2) the cancer-fat link appeared strongest for common adenocarcinoma. This type of cancer forms solid tumors in tissue linings such as the breast, colon, and prostate glands. Several other studies in this book will illustrate the importance of diet.

Exercise

Sensible exercise can help a person maintain a more ideal weight and reduce the chance of obesity. Aerobic exercise, or exercise that raises the immediate heart rate and level of breathing without overtaxing the lungs, strengthens the respiratory system and the heart. With consistent exercise, a person's overall heart rate will drop, because the strong heart can pump a greater volume of blood per beat. Regular exercise can also alleviate muscle tension and stress.

> *A vigorous five-mile walk will do more good for*
> *an unhappy but otherwise healthy adult than*
> *all the medicine and psychology in the world.*
>
> —P.D. WHITE

Physical activity offers benefits to physically capable adults, primarily in reducing the risk of functional decline and mortality. Lack of physical fitness is also a long-term predictor of mortality from cardiovascular causes in middle-aged men and is generally associated with lower mortality for most people.

MALADAPTIVE COPING MECHANISMS

A partial indicator of the effects of stress is the increased use of alcohol, tobacco, and drugs. Abuse of alcohol, tobacco, and drugs is killing more than 500,000 Americans a year and placing a tremendous burden on the health-care system. Substance abuse and addictions are destroying many families. The social costs are violence in the home, lower educational attainment, higher crime rates, lowering of social values, and the direct financial costs of treating the health effects.

Alcohol

> *Drunkenness is nothing but voluntary madness.*
>
> —SENECA

The ingestion of alcohol is one fairly common maladaptive coping mechanism widely used in our culture to deal with the anxiety and tension caused by our lifestyles. Alcohol plays a role in one-third of all failed marriages and one of every four family problems. As many as two-thirds of homicides and serious assaults involve alcohol. One report suggested that many of the estimated 520,000 deaths each year linked to substance abuse could be reduced if not eliminated by changing people's drug habits. The costs include $99 billion in alcohol-related costs, $72 billion for smoking, and $67 billion for drug abuse.

A statistical relationship between drinking alcohol and cancer has long existed, and the more a person drinks the greater the risk of cancer. Some people speculate that alcohol bathes the body's cells to such a degree that they become vulnerable to known carcinogens like tobacco. Researchers are not sure whether alcohol is the carcinogen. Others suggest that the relationship between alcohol and cancer may be based on a chemical interaction. Alcohol and acetaldehyde—to which alcohol converts in mammalian cells—combine to change DNA in a manner similar to changes produced by other cancer-causing chemicals. These reactions could play a role in the recently documented association between moderate use of alcohol and increased incidence of breast cancer.

How much is heavy drinking? Although there is no universal agreement, the consensus is that risks appear to rise after the consumption of the equivalent of 28 grams of absolute alcohol, or ethanol, a day. This is approximately the same amount found in a two 1.5-ounce martinis made with 80-proof gin, two 5-ounce glasses of 12 percent wine, or two 16-ounce cans of 4.5 percent beer. The alcoholic beverage industry disputes such calculations and indicates that physical, genetic, and cultural factors must be taken into account. It contends that most Americans are moderate and social drinkers. Americans drink much less than the Portuguese and French (about half as much) and much less than the Germans, Italians, and Swiss. While the industry can logically resist any categorization of drinkers by the absolute amount they drink (physical and genetic characteristics *are* important), American consumption of alcohol may be heavy, not moderate. During the 1950s, American consumption held steady at 2 gallons per year per person. In the 1960s, it rose steadily and reached a high of 2.7 gallons in the early 1980s, before tapering off to 2.62 in 1985. Canadian figures are similar.

Heavy drinkers—people who drink more than six drinks per session—risk serious damage to their long-term memories. It is not known whether this memory loss is reversible, or whether it is aggravated by continued heavy drinking. The typical alcoholic is discontented with his or her life and is unable and unwilling to tolerate tension and stress. Alcoholism is often a conditioned response, as an individual finds a means of relieving anxiety, resentment, depression, or other unpleasant feelings resulting from the stressful aspects of life. One out of six professional men is a heavy drinker. Several hundred thousand people in the workforce in most countries have severe alcohol-related problems.

Some groups of drinkers—women and some Asians—appear to be twice as vulnerable as men to biomedical problems associated with alcohol. As a health problem in some countries and regions, alcoholism ranks third in importance after heart disease and cancer. Of every $1 billion that alcoholism costs, about 36 percent is spent on lost production and absenteeism, 33 percent on health and medical costs, 25 percent on motor vehicle accidents, 2.5 percent on alcohol programs and research, 2 percent on the criminal justice system, and 1 percent in the social welfare system. Problem drinkers have twice as many accidents at work as other employees. The accident rate away from the job also is very high.

Drug Use

In many Western countries, by the eighth grade, 70 percent of youths have tried alcohol, 44 percent have smoked cigarettes, 10 percent have tried marijuana, and 2 percent have used cocaine. Drug use, drinking, and smoking among teens in the United States is on the rise. In a yearly survey by the University of Michigan, there are indications of a relaxing of attitudes toward drugs. According to the 1994 survey, of 17,000 students in 139 schools, nearly 43 percent of high school seniors indicated that they had used illicit drugs at least once. This is up more than 2 percent from the previous year. Nine percent of the eighth-grade students and 19 percent of tenth-graders reported smoking marijuana or hashish within the last year. Among senior students, the rate was 35 percent.

Almost 8 percent of senior students indicated that they smoked tobacco during the past thirty days and 3 percent had tried a hallucinogenic drug. Many had five or more drinks in a row on at least one occasion in the prior two weeks (14 percent of eighth-graders, 23 percent of tenth-graders, and 28 percent of seniors).

Smoking

A person who smokes more than a pack of cigarettes a day has nearly twice the risk of heart disease and nearly five times the risk of a nonsmoker. Smoking increases the pulse rate and restricts the amount of blood the heart can pump, in addition to increasing blood carbon monoxide levels and blocking the red blood cells' capacity to carry oxygen. Nicotine also raises the blood platelets adhesion index, leading to atherosclerosis.

Smoking may increase the risk of developing a common form of leukemia. This is based on a study of the smoking habits of 175,000 men and women who received medical checkups from 1964 to 1972 and who were then followed until 1988 to determine whether any of them developed cancer. The study found that current male smokers had a 2.8-fold increased risk of developing acute nonlymphocytic leukemia, a common form of adult leukemia. Former smokers had a 2.3-fold increased risk. For some reason, the link was only present in men, and seemed to increase with the number of cigarettes smoked per day.

Smoke from cigarettes contains benzene, radioactive substances, and cancer-causing compounds. Increased mutations in white blood cells have been observed in smokers. Leukemia, a cancer of the blood-forming organs, is marked by abnormal white blood cells circulating in the body.

People who work or live in the presence of smokers or other forms of air pollution may also be at risk. The United States Environmental Protection Agency (EPA) has classified tobacco smoke as a "Group A carcinogen," putting it in the same deadly category of cancer-causing substances as benzene and asbestos. Cigarette smoke is said to contain forty-three chemicals that cause cancer in humans or animals.

This EPA report had certain key findings:

- Secondhand cigarette smoke causes lung cancer and kills 3,000 nonsmokers annually.

- Cigarette smoke is responsible for 150,000 to 300,000 cases of bronchitis and pneumonia and other lower respiratory infections in children up to eighteen months of age each year.

- Cigarette smoke increases the frequency and severity of symptoms in 200,000 to 1 million children with asthma, and increases the risk of new cases of asthma.
- Tobacco smoke also causes buildup of fluid in the middle ear, a condition that can lead to ear infection.

The tobacco industry, however, suggested that the scientific evidence did not support the EPA's conclusions.

TWO MILLION DEATHS ANNUALLY ARE CONNECTED TO SMOKING.

A report by the World Health Organization to mark No-Tobacco Day indicated that tobacco use accounted for 2 million deaths annually in industrialized countries and 1 million in developing countries.

Cigarette consumption has risen some 70 percent over the past twenty-five years in developing countries. Using present trends, 7 million people will die from smoking each year in the Third World within the next two or three decades; about 2 to 3 million of these deaths will be in China. The report estimated that tobacco use is associated with 90 percent of deaths from lung cancer, 30 percent from other cancers, 80 percent from chronic bronchitis, and 20 to 25 percent from heart disease and strokes. Smokers are three times as likely to die before the age of seventy than nonsmokers. The gap is much wider than it was twenty years ago, partially because non-smokers have a longer life expectancy and they are more likely to have healthier lifestyles.

Prescription Drugs

There are remedies worse than the disease.

—PUBLILIUS SYRUS

In response to emotional and lifestyle problems, Americans and Canadians spend over $3 billion per year on over-the counter drugs, with almost $1 billion going for analgesics such as aspirin and for cold and cough remedies. In addition, over $4 billion per year are spent on prescription drugs. According to one estimate, two of three North Americans resort to a medically prescribed chemical each day. They consume over 8,000 tons of sedatives and tranquilizers bought with over 100 million prescriptions per year. This is equivalent to 1,000 dump trucks lined up bumper to bumper. Commonly used drugs are Valium and Librium. Women constitute the largest single block of prescription drug users in the United States, and the second largest group are people over age sixty-five (also mostly female).

The prescription drug industry is a lucrative business. Drug companies indicate that they need high incomes to support innovative research, although a great percentage of their costs goes into advertising and promotion. What make this a concern is that society is spending a great deal of money to promote and use prescription drugs, rather than preventing the problems that create a need for their use.

A STRESS FRAMEWORK

We have already learned a great deal about how individual variables may affect stress. Perception may be a key factor in understanding how people respond to stress-related situations such as an angry customer or an harassing colleague. We also know that people may experience more stress in jobs that are poorly designed or when they face the difficult challenges of supervising others.

We have a growing understanding that lifestyle can provoke or inhibit many of the stressors people experience. That is, when people are physically fit and in good health, they are much more capable of responding to the difficulties around them. Three important and definable aspects of lifestyle are diet, exercise routines, and relaxation. Certain types of foods are more stressful to the body and create stresses for the body's digestive system. Some food combinations are difficult to digest. The most obvious examples of stress-provoking substances are alcohol, drugs, and caffeine. Caffeine is a xanthine drug, an amphetamine-like stimulant that parallels adrenaline's role in activating the central nervous system's stress response. When we drink excessive amounts of alcohol, the digestive system has to respond by using energy to dissolve toxins, instead of constructing and maintaining cell growth. Certain foods are known to be associated with elevated bad (LDL) cholesterol levels and gastrointestinal problems.

Exercise may be an important factor in increasing longevity, both through metabolizing LDL and in producing good (HDL) cholesterol levels, and some relaxation programs may assist in changing people's attitudes toward stress and health. Exercise and relaxation methods will not automatically enhance a person's ability to respond to stressful events—much of this depends on the programs used. Indeed, some people who are very healthy in this regard have no recognized program, but they have naturally evolved a work- and lifestyle in which they are physically active.

Some people do not have to set aside times for meditation or relaxation, because they do this as a regular part of their lives. One couple I know spent years building a log house and constructing paths and rock walls around it. Joe and his wife Sue scaled and sawed every log that they used in constructing their house. They did it as a form of relaxation and fulfillment. Joe spent one entire summer constructing a rock wall that we called "The Great Wall of Joe." Joe's wall got washed away the following winter and again the winter after that. But, he rebuilt it again and again until it did its job of holding the foot of the mountain in place. What I learned from Joe is that some people do not have to take time to meditate. Joe did this naturally. He was in a trancelike state as he moved each rock from his truck to its place on the mountain. Some people reach this meditative state in prayer or when walking, swimming, or running. Others do it by listening to music. What is characteristic of these people is that they are allowing their minds and bodies to rest and regenerate.

To study and understand stress, we can think about our jobs and lifestyles as important starting points. However, we can become more focused in our study of stress by recognizing the relationship between an individual's personality and other personal characteristics. People with certain personality traits—those who are hostile and anxious, for example—may be prone to involve themselves in many tasks and to be stressed from overwork. Age, gender, race, and other variables also affects how a person responds to stress.

The general framework illustrated in Figure 3.1 suggests that a person's interpretation of the events around him or her can affect the stress response. The Chinese suggest that some of us exhibit yin characteristics while others are more yang. These ideas correspond to Western notions that we all have different body chemistries, which partially explains why certain foods or toxins will affect people differently.

The final part of the framework illustrates a number of responses to stress. These are the obvious frustrations and angers, or first-order stress reactions. The second-order responses are an indication of ongoing strain;

the stresses experienced are chronic, resulting in permanent tissue damage. For example, we know that accountants experience great stress during tax time, and that this affects their levels of cholesterol. Similarly, excessive alcohol consumption or cigarette smoking will have effects on the body. Two primary indicators of cardiovascular system problems are cholesterol and blood pressure. A useful initial measure of possible digestive system problems might come from a better awareness of gastrointestinal symptoms.

The framework outlined in this chapter is general and will obviously leave out some important causes and effects. A comprehensive framework will never be possible, because direct relationships are impossible to prove. However, there are some very strong associations, or relationships, which we would be foolish to ignore. Recognizing these relationships will not positively guarantee good health but will provide us with ways of reducing the odds of problems associated with stress.

There is no need to study the framework in detail and to use it in diagnosing every life event that you face. Rather, it should be a general tool to illustrate that stress is a multifaceted phenomenon. It is never really possible to measure each and every aspect of the framework. The framework is a broad overview of what many good researchers have done in their specific studies.

Finally, the framework illustrates that stressors can have positive or negative effects on health. When a job is poorly designed and a person is angry and frustrated with it, stress might be exhibited in unhealthy responses such as greater alcohol consumption. These effects are negative and costly. However, jobs can be designed so that people are challenged and willing to take on more responsibility. These effects are positive for the individual as well as providing the organization with an opportunity to increase productivity.

CONCLUSION

This chapter illustrates the many relationships that exist between stress and health. Many organizational and life stresses affect our personal health and our abilities to lead productive lives. What are these and how can we design our work and lives to have a positive influence? There are many lifestyle issues we have to resolve for health, relating to our diets, the exercise we do, and the ways we relax. Thinking about these issues should encourage us to question our lifestyles and to make a positive plan of action.

FIGURE 3.1 A FRAMEWORK FOR UNDERSTANDING THE EFFECTS OF STRESS AND LIFESTYLE

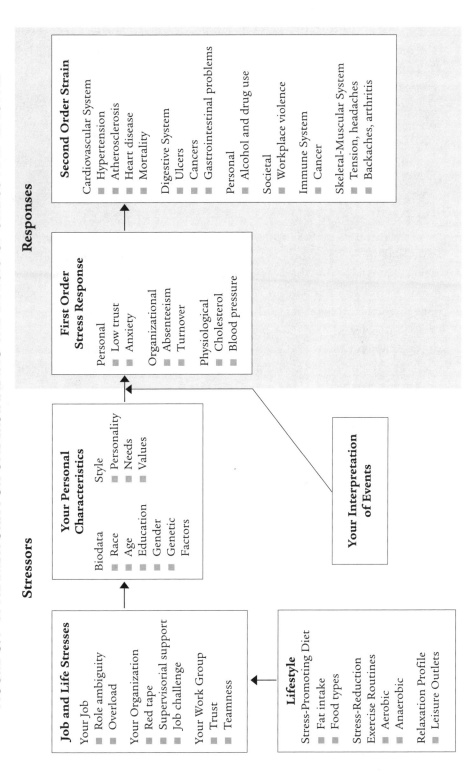

Our personalities and personal characteristics can increase stress. Certain individuals might be classified as having a stress-prone personality. What is your personality and how might you take steps to respond to stresses around you?

Your perception, or the way you interpret an event, may be key in giving you an understanding of why you may feel more stressed than other people. A stressful event will affect each of us differently.

Your biochemical structure is unique. What is it and how might it affect your health, the foods you eat, and your life profile?

There are certain indicators of serious stress, which include cholesterol levels, blood pressure, and gastrointestinal health. You should learn to use these measures as a guide to good health. This is important in using the framework underlying this book. Keep these indicators in mind as you read each chapter and use them as a guide to developing a general plan for responding to stress and improving health. This book does not suggest that poor physical and mental health are the only negative effects of stress and lifestyle problems. There are many organizational effects, such as absenteeism, high turnover, and the increased health costs faced by most societies. The major concern of this book, however, is to focus on personal health and well-being.

4 Principle-Centered Stress Management

Important principles may and must be flexible

—ABRAHAM LINCOLN

YOUR PERSONALITY OR STYLE, YOUR JOB STRESS, YOUR LIFE STRESS, YOUR NUTRITIONAL HABITS, THE WAY YOU EXERCISE, AND YOUR ABILITY TO RELAX ARE IMPORTANT ASPECTS OF YOUR OVERALL STRESS MANAGEMENT STRATEGY.

THE POWER OF A STRESS MANAGEMENT PARADIGM

Our actions normally result from the way we understand and interpret the world, based on our beliefs and expectations, values and cognitive styles. We behave based on our preferences and styles much more than on logic or anything else. This is usually thought of as a *paradigm*.

THE STRESS YOU EXPERIENCE DEPENDS ON YOUR CAPABILITY TO HANDLE THE MANY STRESSORS YOU WILL ENCOUNTER.

Each of us tends to think we see things objectively. You can test this by asking other people for their viewpoints on keeping in shape or dieting. I am often amazed at how easily people offer their viewpoints on health and diet—most of these are strongly held beliefs by people whom I would judge to be in poor health. I witnessed one colleague who was 25 pounds overweight lecturing another on a diet and exercise program that he highly recommended for losing weight and keeping fit. For me, there was something wrong with this picture. The other person might have been 5 pounds overweight and was physically active. He swam eighty lengths in a pool almost every weekday and had no trouble with going on a long hiking venture. This example illustrates that all people have strongly held beliefs, values, and behaviors which justify the way they act. Even those who are very overweight and underactive tend to think they "know it all."

> *Even when laws have been written down,*
> *they ought not always to remain unaltered.*
>
> —ARTISTOTLE

We see the world, not in objective terms, but in the way we condition ourselves to see it. When we open our mouths to describe what we see, we are really describing our beliefs, our perceptions, or our paradigms. When other people disagree with us, we immediately think something is wrong with them.

> *If you are out to describe the truth,*
> *leave elegance to the tailor.*
>
> —ALBERT EINSTEIN

Our paradigms are clusters of beliefs and values by which we select and filter the information we receive. It is illustrated by our style of relating to others, our self-interest, and our expectations. Effective paradigms, based on effective beliefs and expectations, insure the selection of important and relevant information. People with less effective paradigms often ignore, alter, or rationalize certain information. Beliefs and expectations provide commitment for many of the things people do. Without commitment, a person's tasks will be without value and purpose.

Suppose you are hiking in the North American Rockies and your compass is in error because of the magnetism of some rocks in the area. It says you are actually going east when you are going north. A second compass from a companion confirms this. Yet, you are aware that something was wrong. The rising and setting of the sun, the growth of the vegetation on the trees (different vegetation is found growing in different directions) and the location of a landmark mountain seem to affirm that your compass is giving you a false reading. Can you imagine your frustration?

No matter what your attitude, values, beliefs, or expectations, you could be lost. You have the wrong compass to guide you.

Each of us has many compasses or maps which guide us in our heads. We interpret our experiences through these maps or compasses and seldom question their accuracy because they are our personal mental guides to which we have grown accustomed. Each of us has a different compass or map to guide us.

MOST OF US KNOW PEOPLE WHO HAVE INEFFECTIVE PARADIGMS ON STRESS AND HEALTH.

No matter what their health problems, some people are quick to rationalize or offer reasons why they are not able to live up to their potential. Many alcohol abusers are quick to blame their spouses or managers, just as some people say that the diseases that plague them (in some cases, heart disease and liver cancer) are not associated with their diets and lifestyles. There are stories of smokers who adamantly rationalize how they have tried to quit smoking and just can't.

A fool sees not the same tree as the wise person sees.

—WILLIAM BLAKE

Equally impressive are a range of stories from people who have taken control of their health and stress management, in spite of the obstacles they faced. People have changed their health by reducing their stress and changing their lifestyles.

Our paradigms are a product of our conditioning, which teaches us to respect or value certain things, people, and ways of doing things. The powerful influence of beliefs and expectations has long been recognized by physicians, behavioral scientists, and teachers. It has been the subject of folk wisdom, from the teaching and writing of Zen masters to New Age health advocates. These teachings and others are showing that change requires a very intense focus and commitment. Without such a focus and commitment, it is unlikely that we will be able to muster the energy to change our attitudes and beliefs about diet, exercise, relaxation, and stress. Trying to change a person's beliefs and develop a stress management paradigm is like trying to encourage someone to quit smoking. While logic dictates the desire to change, old habits die hard.

THE TERM *PARADIGM SHIFT* IS OFTEN USED TO DESCRIBE WHAT HAS TO HAPPEN FOR PEOPLE TO COMMIT TO AN EFFECTIVE STRESS MANAGEMENT FRAMEWORK.

The term *paradigm shift* was introduced by Thomas S. Kuhn in his book, *The Structure of Scientific Revolutions,* to illustrate that almost every significant scientific endeavor had to break from traditional ways of thinking, or old paradigms.

Society's paradigms are the dominant and accepted ways of thinking. In science, we once believed that the world was flat. Everyone believed that. The discovery that the world was round introduced an entirely different way of thinking about navigation and ocean travel.

In 1976, a pharmaceutical breakthrough occurred that reversed the bleak record of transplant surgery. A new paradigm was established. It happened when Swiss researchers were examining soil samples in search of a new antibiotic. By chance, they found a fungus that produced a powerful immunosuppressant, a substance that blocks the body's defense mechanisms from rejecting foreign tissues. The new discovery, now known as cyclosporine, received its first clinical trials in 1980. A surge of transplants followed, increasing the chances of survival to better-than-even odds of success.

With cyclosporine, there is almost twice the chance that liver, kidney, and heart transplants will succeed. These advances signify dramatic improvements since South Africa's Dr. Barnard performed the first heart transplant in 1967 on a patient who died only eighteen days after receiving his new heart.

Logic alone will not allow people to shift their habits and beliefs. Nor will beliefs and values shift paradigms. Paradigm shifts are accompanied by "Aha" experiences, when someone finally sees the composite picture in a new way. The "light has been turned on."

A PARADIGM SHIFT RESULTS FROM ADJUSTING A PERSON'S SELF-INTEREST, BELIEFS, AND EXPECTATIONS IN A MORE RELEVANT DIRECTION.

A paradigm shift results from finding a more accurate compass or a more accurate and relevant road map to arrange the beliefs and expectations we use to select and filter the information we receive. Neuroscientists have long known that each hemisphere of the brain specializes in certain activities, with the left brain being actively involved in language and analytical skills and the right brain in spatial and pattern recognition. During peak performance, the mind seems to relax its analytical side while allowing the right side to control the body. The result is a focus that is directed and intense.

This intense focus and commitment might be developed through practice. Psychologists suggest that they can induce this commitment in athletes who go through certain mental routines. Similar practices can assist lawyers, who might make certain gestures before making a final argument. A speaker might walk briskly to the podium and tell a joke, and then use a visual image to provoke a new way of thinking about a crime.

What people do between moments of peak performance is also important. These include, for example in tennis, savoring a winning point or dismissing an error, relaxing, and psyching up for the next serve. The brain learns a new skill by fine-tuning the specific neural circuits that are involved in making the motion. When people are beginning to learn a new task, their brains become focused on the brain circuits directly involved in producing the movements. Before that time, they are "scatterbrained." This remarkable ability of the brain can falter if an athlete falls victim to the pressures of competition. Like muscles, the brain adapts itself through prolonged exercise. In studies of the brain activities of two groups of elderly people—one athletic and the other sedentary—the brain waves of the athletic group more closely resembles that of younger people.

In review, the paradigm-shifting experience might include the following steps:

■ **Readiness.** Achieving a state of readiness without going over the edge and panicking. This involves the development of routines to prepare oneself.

■ **Motivating.** Focusing on the right goals. This means having realistic goals and those that you can control. Rather than breaking an unachievable record, the goal might be to improve one's performance over previous ones.

■ **Concentrating.** This involves developing a state of concentration, a trancelike state. This might include using "focus" words to repeat in the midst of an event, for example, a swimmer might count 1, 2, 1, 2 breath, 1, 2, 1, 2 breath.

■ **Stress control.** Adjusting to setbacks and unexpected occurrences from a bad call or a mistake. This is a matter of "self-talk," the running commentary that people carry in their minds between events. Some people actually talk to themselves while team members talk to each other. What people believe about themselves is extremely important.

THE STRESS MANAGEMENT PARADIGM

Figure 4.1 offers a perspective on the relationship between stress and stress management, indicating that each of us must recognize our own personal chemistry and capability. The following are several health-related factors that individuals might consider:

■ personality and personal style

■ job stress

■ lifestyle

■ nutrition

■ exercise

■ relaxation

Individuals might involve themselves in programs where some people might be perceived to be uncommitted while others might be overly committed.

Figure 4.1 suggests that we can be overly involved and committed or overly uninvolved and uncommitted about our health.

Level 4 involvement can be exemplified by an overly committed and zealous athletic program, which can actually be harmful to health and longevity, physical endurance, and overall stress management. Zealotlike athletic exercises can be harmful to nutrition and cause bone wear and tear, as well as affecting our ability to relax and work productively. The programs are stressful and can harm long-term stress management.

Level 1 involvement might be exemplified by people who are uninterested and unaware of their stress levels and stress management. They find no meaning in life and are unfocused about health, exercise, and nutrition. Such people have no interest or commitment to stress management.

Level 2 involvement might characterize the majority of our population, who are aware of exercise and health programs. These people get involved in

FIGURE 4.1 TYPES OF STRESS MANAGEMENT PROGRAMS

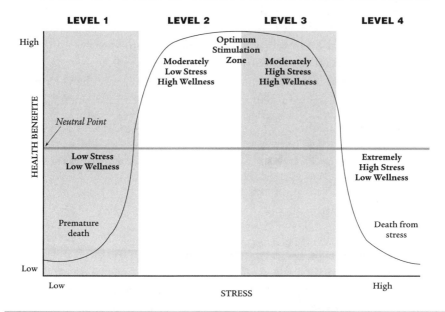

	LEVEL 1	LEVEL 2	LEVEL 3	LEVEL 4
LEVEL OF HEALTH INVOLVEMENT	**Unhealthy Stress** Unplanned Uncommitted	**Reactive Stress** Passive Involvement	**Proactive Stress** Focused Integrative	**Maladaptive Stress** Committed Zealous
Personality	Excessive Type B	Moderate Type B	Moderate Type A	Excessive Type A
Job Stress	Underload	Interesting Unfocused	Challenging Focused	Overloaded
Lifestyle	Underloaded	Interesting	Challenging	Overloaded
Nutrition	Fat, Unhealthy	Nutritionally Aware	Stress Management Nutritional Principles	Fad Diets
Exercise	Couch Potato	Active Western Exercises	Focused Stress Management Exercises	Zealot
Relaxation	T.V. meditator	Programmed	Focused Stress Management	Monk

programs because they are thought to improve health, a type of involvement which is motivated by others rather than oneself. These people might be relatively unstressed and healthy, but may not have fully integrated their stress management plans into their beliefs and habits.

Level 3 involvement might be characterized as ideal, because the person's involvement is motivated by a general pursuit of stress management. The stress management programs are integrated.

PRINCIPLE-CENTERED STRESS MANAGEMENT

Good health and good sense are two of life's greatest blessings.
—PUBLILIUS SYRUS

This book is based on the fundamental assumption that our personal paradigms—made up of our beliefs, values, and personal conventions—govern our stress and health. This paradigm is articulated through principles that each of us values. These principles are like each person's natural laws, and are as fundamental as the basic laws of gravity.

As we all recognize, these personal principles of life are hard to change. But they do change when we are faced with situations that offer a different perspective. The following transcript of an actual radio conversation between a U.S. naval ship and Canadian authorities off the coast of Newfoundland in October 1995 illustrates how a different perspective can offer a paradigm-shifting experience that adjusts one's principles of doing things.

Communication: Please divert your course 15 degrees to the north to avoid a collision.

Response: Recommend you divert YOUR course 15 degrees to the south to avoid a collision.

Communication: This is a Captain of a U.S. Navy ship. I say again, divert YOUR course.

Response: No, I say again, you divert YOUR course.

Communication: THIS IS THE AIRCRAFT CARRIER U.S.S. MISSOURI, WE ARE A LARGE WARSHIP OF THE U.S. NAVY. DIVERT YOUR COURSE NOW!

Response: This is a lighthouse. Your call.

This captain's paradigm-shifting experience illustrates how a new perspective can adjust one's way of looking at an issue.

A lighthouse has the same power as a principle. It offers a clear set of assumptions and beliefs that cannot normally be altered. It provides the beacon to guide you. All individuals have similar principles or laws that serve as the beacons to guide them. Such principles govern our values about religion, the role of government, the way we eat, and the way we handle stress.

We all have rather rigid principles about how to view stress and life, just like the captain of an aircraft carrier. However, most of the principles that individuals have are not as grounded as those that exist in nature. The lighthouse is grounded. Most of our principles are simply our mental maps of the way we view the world. They are interpretations, but they might not be the most accurate or the most effective ones.

In the same way, principles are not values. The principles described in this book are not complex or sophisticated. They suggest simple truths and commonsense rules of health and are grounded in scientific convention. For example, the principle of recognizing the values that are most important to one's life seems like a simple truth. It is described here as a convention, based on scientific evidence, that clarity of focus is one of the most important ingredients to guide you. Not being clear on one's focus is like trying see a lighthouse in a very dense fog. Lack of clarity brings confusion and ambiguity.

Other examples of principles are *enrichment* and *nutritional balance*. They create the foundation for effective stress management.

This book offers eight principles of stress management. These principles embody many of the fundamental rules of personal health. These principles are based on common sense and integrate science and personal well-being.

Principle 1: Recognizing the Dragon Within You.

In other words, know yourself and how your personality may affect the way you deal with stress.

Principle 2: Control Your Organization: Don't Let It Control You.

Your desire to fulfill yourself in your organization and career can provoke stress. This principle illustrates the importance of managing a stress-promoting organization.

Principle 3: Establish Winning Relationships.

Relationships, either at work or outside work, can cause the most stress. Conflictive relationships are an ever-increasing cause of stress. Healthy relationships can invigorate you and help you deal with other types of stress.

Principle 4: Enrich Your Job.

Jobs can be stressful because they are overloading or understimulating. Finding the balance is the key.

Principle 5: Control Life's Trials and Tribulations.

One of the keys to stress management is to develop a better understanding of your values. The goal is to focus your work and life on the values which are most important to you and your career.

Principle 6: Reduce Stress-Promoting Foods.

Certain foods can help you respond to stress. They can give you energy. In the same way, certain foods are more stressful for your body to handle. A nutritional plan allows you to understand how your diet can affect your ability to handle stress.

Principle 7: Kill Anxiety with Exercise.

Exercise is one of the most effective strategies for reducing stress. However, certain exercise programs can be counterproductive. An effective exercise program helps you deal with some of your anxiety. It also strengthens your ability to deal with the stress you encounter.

Principle 8: Use the Power Within You.

Meditation gives your mind a rest. It also helps you utilize your subconscious, and focus your mind in being proactive in handling stress.

These principles are not laws. They are rules of thumb that are based on scientific practice as well as commonsense experience. Principles go beyond science in that they encourage you to recognize your own style, body type, and genetic background.

I remember a mini-paradigm shift I experienced in my own stress management program. For years, I have tried to recognize the features of a Type A, stress-prone personality and have prided myself on the fact that I might be more Type B than A. But I still experienced certain levels of stress while others did not in similar situations. Clearly, certain aspects of my personality were making me more prone to stress than other people. What were they? I became disturbed one day when a colleague came to me and indicated that some of the material I had written had a few typing mistakes. She cautioned me that such memos give people a bad impression of me. As I reflected on this incident, I began to realize that many of my colleagues had the same type of orientation. They were perfectionists, and I wasn't one. I felt compelled to be like them.

This, to me, was a paradigm-shifting experience. It helped me explain why I was feeling so much stress in relating to my colleagues.

Taking Control

Lack of control may be one of the major reasons for feeling stressed. People who are overwhelmed by stress-related events often state that they feel that they cannot control the circumstances around them. They are overburdened with organizational changes, new procedures and policies, and challenges over pay and career.

PERSPECTIVE 5. THE EXECUTIVE MONKEY STUDIES

Joseph Brady reported on a study that illustrated how stress killed executive monkeys.

In one experiment, a monkey was subjected to a mild but uncomfortable electric shock every twenty seconds. If the monkey was to avoid the shock, he had to push a red button to reset the clock. The twenty-second period would begin again. Thus, the monkey could stop the electrical shocks if he could locate the button and press it before the twenty-second period had passed. If he pushed the button at the correct time, the monkey could avoid all the shocks. The experiment continued for six hours a day.

After a period of six weeks, the executive monkey died from a perforated ulcer. A second monkey also died, and he also had a perforated ulcer.

Brady set up a control where a second companion monkey sat alongside the executive monkey. The only difference was that his button did not allow him to stop the shock.

The companion monkey survived, and remained healthy and even happy, except for the shock. However, the executive monkey died.

For the companion monkey, there was no stress. No decision had to be made. It was as if the monkey thought, "I might as well accept it and get on with life." We spend so much time and energy in fighting things and people we cannot control.

The ultimate way of controlling stress is to leave the job or drop out. A happy medium may be someplace in between burning out and dropping out. People who are happier and less stressed are those who are not letting their environment torment them. They might experience the same stressors as others, but they have a mental map or paradigm that allows them to handle this stress. You might be able to reduce the stress you feel in your life, but you might find it just as effective to develop a different attitude or set of beliefs toward the stress around you. People who take greater control of their lives may have a lower incidence of ulcers, coronary heart disease, absenteeism, and hypertension. These include those in jobs such as food servers, administrative assistants, assembly-line workers, and office workers.

A range of strategies exists to help people control their stress by coping, managing, or conquering. Obviously, conquering stress is more beneficial than merely managing and coping with it.

Coping strategies are both physical and cognitive. Physical coping strategies include aerobic exercise and a range of relaxation activities (hobbies, hot tubs, vacations). What makes physical activity a preferred strategy is its potential to play an additional role as a retarder of the natural aging and hypokinetic (inactivity-induced) disease processes. However, physical activity, exercise, and stress reduction do not always go hand in hand. For example, physical activities such as bird watching do not provide exercise. In addition, some physical activities may actually increase stress if people dislike the activity or if it hurts the body.

Physical activity can reduce stress, promote personal fitness, and reduce the potential for hypokinetic disease. Such phrases as "keeping up a good sweat," "having a good puff," "keeping a brisk pace," and "feeling the effort" all describe physical states or conditions. Physical activity is a personal coping strategy to be enjoyed and nurtured for a better, more vibrant life.

Some people rely on having an afterwork drink or relaxing with a cigarette. While these breaks may help people get through the day, they become

TABLE 4.1 STRATEGIES FOR STRESS MANAGEMENT

Coping Strategies

- Physical Coping Strategies encourage exercise and ways to get away from the stress around us.

Four criteria might be used to judge the merit of a physical activity.

1. Is the physical activity personally enjoyable?

2. Is it of sufficient duration to provide a maintenance or training effect? Duration is the length of time an activity is to be performed on each occasion. A minimum of thirty minutes is suggested.

3. Is it of sufficient intensity to provide a maintenance or training effect? Intensity is the energy or physical effort expended. Several measures of intensity are appropriate.

4. Is it repeated at regularly scheduled intervals to produce a maintenance or training effect? Frequency is how often the activity occurs over a period of time. Three times a week is suggested.

- Emotional coping strategies assist in identifying support and emotional assistance.

Conquering Strategies

Conquering strategies encourage rethinking or restructuring potentially stressful work or lifestyles.

- **Diagnosis**

  Think about a recent event that was stressful to you.

  Write down three ways it could get better and three ways it could get worse.

  List ways to help it get better and ways to make sure it does not get worse.

- **Actions**

  Define more important objectives and responsibilities.

  Reduce people responsibilities.

  Redefine career objectives.

  Develop support structures in organizations.

  Enrich some tasks and give less time to others.

  Assess and recognize problems and values.

Change Strategies

- **Diagnosis**

  Think about recent events that were stressful to you.

  Write down why they were stressful or frustrating.

  List ways that stressors can be redirected as a challenge to be solved and enjoyed.

- **Actions**

  Reserve time each day for hobbies.

  Examine your values and priorities.

  Start saying "no" to activities that do not fit with your values
    and priorities.

---

part of who you are. You are not a normal person in that you are constantly on a high, either pumped up with caffeine or sedated with alcohol or nicotine. An individual who wants to quit these substances will suffer withdrawal, as he or she has to go through a transformation of habits and attitudes. In addition, the body has to adjust to no longer needing caffeine, alcohol, or nicotine.

Emotional coping strategies are those in which individuals find support and emotional assistance and involve opportunities for individuals to communicate with others by venting, crying, or other ways. During stressful incidents, individuals might talk to others and receive their counseling and support.

Conquering strategies, both cognitive and physical, encourage positive, proactive action. Cognitive strategies include identifying and resolving crises or problems, focusing decisions, communicating and gathering support, and redefining the situation through time management or focusing on more important priorities. Physical strategies include working harder or wiser to reduce the workload, delegating, changing to other work or nonwork activities, or redesigning the work. These strategies are intended to help the individual rethink or restructure potentially stressful work or life situations.

Changing strategies are those in which individuals shift their paradigms, so that their attitudes and values are less stress promoting. This might involve changing attitudes toward life, work, diet, and physical exercise. Changing strategies assist people in being more assertive, taking risks, learning from one's failures, controlling one's weight, and becoming more physically fit.

HOW TO USE THIS BOOK

I would like to recommend that you read this book in two stages. You might choose to begin by introducing yourself to the whole book and gaining a general impression of its content. You could scan certain sections and read others. Pay attention to the headings and the bullets as a guide to your reading.

The book is designed to be a companion in your continual process of managing stress and improving your health. It is organized to offer suggestions for developing a new stress and wellness paradigm. Before you begin, you might think of the principles that are most important to you. What is troubling you the most? Is it your job, your exercise, you inability to relax? In reading about each principle, you can gain some insights for your personal application. They should help you focus on individual needs or interests. You should seek to get involved in the material through completing the tests and exercises.

Go back and review some of your learning as you progress in your reading.

The final chapters of the book are intended to help you focus on long-term change and growth.

Your growth in reading this book will be evolutionary. Your paradigm shifts will come after an accumulation of reading, practice, discussion, and rereading. When you look back several weeks later, you will begin to recognize how you have changed.

You should come to see yourself in a new way. You should recognize your values, your personal style, and your stresses. The book offers coping and conquering strategies. Most importantly, it seeks to change you so that you live your values and recognize what stresses you.

Whatever your present situation, you can gain from the principles offered here. The principles have worked for me and many other people with whom I have come in contact. Be patient and persist. If you care, as I do, about stress and health, you will succeed.

I welcome you to this new paradigm of stress and health.

PART TWO

YOUR STRESS-PROMOTING WORLD:

Coping with the Dragon

PRINCIPLE 1:
Recognize the Dragon Within You

REFOCUS YOUR STRESS-PRONE PERSONALITY

*I have never seen a greater monster or miracle
in the world than myself.*

—MONTAIGNE

Personality is a key component in the stress response. The compulsive, time-pressured, aggressive, and hostile person may be a "walking time bomb" waiting to explode in almost any interaction.

The first principle is to recognize the dragon within you. Your personality is fundamental to understanding how you may react to stressful events and circumstances. Know your personality. You are responsible for understanding it. Doing this is key to how you effectively implement the other principles for managing stress that are outlined in this book. This chapter illustrates how you might implement principle 1—recognizing the dragon within you by knowing your personality—and make adjustments in your style to reduce the stress you face.

THE TYPE A STRESS-PRONE PERSONALITY

We learned a great deal about the relationship between personality and stress from the pioneering work of researchers Meyer Friedman and Ray Rosenman, the authors of *Type A Behavior and Your Heart*. Most of the medical journals at the time reported that heart attacks were most certainly linked to dietary indulgence, cigarette smoking, and lack of exercise. In their own medical practice, these researchers observed that many of their patients had personality characteristics in common. Many had a sense of time urgency and a excessive competitive drive. Often, the same patients showed some hostility.

FRIEDMAN AND ROSENMAN FOUND THAT ACCOUNTANTS' SERUM CHOLESTEROL LEVELS INCREASED IN THE MONTHS BEFORE THE TAX DEADLINE EACH YEAR WHEN THEY WERE FORCED TO WORK LONG HOURS TO MEET THEIR DEADLINES. IN MAY AND JUNE, AFTER THE SENSE OF TIME URGENCY DISAPPEARED, THE SERUM CHOLESTEROL FELL.

One of Friedman and Rosenman's studies compared eighty people who were characterized as Type A (competitive with free-floating hostility) with a control group of Type B people who felt no sense of time urgency and exhibited no excessive competitive drive or free-floating hostility. The Type B individuals had much lower serum cholesterol levels than the Type A individuals. Twenty-eight percent of the Type A sample already had coronary heart disease, which was seven times higher than those in the Type B group. Studies of Type A and B groups of North American white women had similar results. The occurence of coronary heart disease was more frequent in the Type A women, even though premenopausal women are not as likely as men to have heart attacks.

This experimental work sought to demonstrate that Type A behavior was a cause of coronary heart disease. Freidman and Rosenman observed:

> Following deliberate damage to a rat's hypothalamus, the emotional center of the brain, the affected animal almost instantaneously exhibited the rat equivalent of the human Type A behavior pattern. No longer did the brain-altered rat scamper timidly and gently with his fellow cage mates. Rather, he stared fixedly at us without fear, and were we to open the cage ever so slightly, he would lunge to attack us almost immediately. Nor would he tolerate a single cage mate without jumping upon its back, ready to sink his teeth into the flesh of the other animal. If the cage mate were a shy, gentle control rat (exactly similar to the Type A rat prior to his brain surgery), the Type A rat eventually sensed absence of competition, dismounted him, and ignored him. But if the second rat were also another Type A rat,

a vicious, no-holds-barred battle ensued, which if not interrupted would end only with the death of either or both of them.

The change in behavior of the rats in the above experiment was also associated with an elevation in serum cholesterol. An alteration in the brain resulting in a change in emotional state could change an animal's serum cholesterol level. Increasing serum cholesterol levels is one of the most definitive methods for inducing coronary heart disease.

Research in this area continues, and we are developing a better understanding of how one's personality affects the chances of succumbing to coronary heart disease. Investigations of personality and an individual's capability of dealing with stress have increased dramatically since this pioneering research began. In addition to Type A behavior, we have become concerned with personality traits such as anxiety, self-esteem, locus of control, and other traits.

TYPE A BEHAVIOR IS A BEHAVIORAL AND EMOTIONAL PATTERN THAT IS OBSERVED IN PEOPLE WHO ARE STRUGGLING TO ACHIEVE MORE IN LESS TIME.

Type A behavior is not a personality disorder, but might be called a socially acceptable obsession. Type A individuals are likely to experience a great deal of stress, compared to more relaxed and easygoing Type B individuals. However, Type B individuals can be just as goal oriented and just as desirous of success and achievement. The Type B individual works toward his or her goals in ways that do not create psychological and physical stress.

Type A behavior is an important correlate of coronary heart disease and a number of studies have identified it as a risk factor. Type A behavior has also been associated with increases in triglycerides and, to a lesser degree, blood pressure. Type Aness does not automatically mean poor health or stress, nor does Type Bness mean good health and low stress. More correctly, having a Type A personality is one very important risk factor.

Why are Type A individuals more prone to stress and coronary heart disease? Type A individuals may be more likely to overwork and less likely to relax and take vacations. They may be more likely to expose themselves to a range of stressors. Type A individuals are encouraged by others who have a similar orientation. They energize themselves through their competitive exploits and achievements. Type A behavior was originally described by the following characteristics.

Hyperaggressiveness

The aggressive drive of a Type A individual is often associated with a sense of anxiety. Type A people seem to express their anxieties in the form of aggression. Any possible feelings of anxiety or insecurity are expressed by taking action and competing. One of the indicators of this aggression is the tendency to compete with or challenge other people in various activities, including business, sports, or discussions. In this sense, achievement may not be the prime measure of Type A behavior; however, the person is constantly at war with others and trying to win over them at all costs.

Time Urgency

A Type A individual does not have enough time to do all the things that he or she would like to do or believes should be done. This person strives to keep accomplishing more and undertakes many events and tasks. The Type A individual lives with a belief that he or she *can* do more and will seek to do so within the limited time available. To be effective, this person sets schedules, deadlines, goals, and standards and constantly imposes internal pressures to work at a faster pace. This is characterized by a tendency to race against the clock even when there is little reason to do so. This restless, impatient rush has been called "hurry sickness."

A Tendency to Overachieve and Self-Destruct

The Type A person is driven by an ungovernable drive to achieve more and more, accompanied by a diminishing capacity to feel good about what has been accomplished. An innate quest to acquire things probably is part of all of us. Children express this by the desire to collect anything from toys to marbles to stamps. As adults, people accumulate art, wine, furniture, and cars. Many people are able to manage this impulse, but the Type A individual develops an obsession with making more money, getting a bigger house, or exhibiting a standard of excellence expressed in numbers. University academics measure the number of publications, real estate people calculate the volume of their sales, and marathon runners count the number of seconds off their previous records. The drive for self-destruction sets in when the Type A person receives less and less enjoyment from these accomplishments.

The value of success is measured in achievements and accomplishments. To achieve more, the person will usually have to work harder, meaning longer hours and over a longer life span. The Type A individual is insecure with measuring life by its quality, by the beauty of the experience, or by enjoyment. Such criteria are not tangible, and the Type A individual is more secure with concrete measurements.

TEST 1. THE A INDEX

The questions in this test attempt to define your behavioral orientation. There are no right answers. The more honest you are the more valid will be the results of this questionnaire. It is *important* that you respond to *all* statements. For each statement, place a number from 1 to 4 on the line to the left of the item. The numbers mean:

1	2	3	4
Very Untrue	Somewhat Untrue	Somewhat True	Very True

_____ 1. Whenever I undertake a task, I try to work as quickly as I can to complete it.

_____ 2. I seem to never have time to enjoy some of the things that I have accomplished.

_____ 3. Even though I may not show it, I like to win.

_____ 4. I tend to undertake a number of tasks or assignments at the same time.

_____ 5. I get impatient whenever I listen to a conversation or speech that does not interest me. I get the feeling that I am wasting my time.

_____ 6. I often compare myself with others in terms of my accomplishments, income, performance, achievements, or value of property.

_____ 7. I enjoy competition.

_____ 8. I sometimes do other work (for example, write letters or notes or make mental plans) when I am in a meeting, working on the computer, answering the telephone, or listening to others.

_____ 9. I feel impatient when other people do not carry out their tasks quickly.

_____ 10. I often find myself analyzing how I could have done a task better.

_____ 11. I become irritated when others show no interest in working hard to achieve things.

_____ 12. I rush into tasks or make decisions quickly. Sometimes, I feel like I have been too hasty in making decisions.

_____ 13. I feel that I could never complete the many tasks I have to do.

_____ 14. My standards for success are extremely high. I find that my expectations are getting increasingly higher.

_____ 15. When I meet aggressive people, I usually feel compelled to compete with them.

_____ 16. I rarely find myself sitting around doing nothing. I often do many related tasks (for example, write letters or notes or make mental plans) at the same time.

_____ 17. Time is quite important to me. I do not like wasting time when I could be doing something productive.

_____ 18. I sometimes review my day and ask myself how I could have accomplished things more effectively.

_____ 19. I enjoy being in good arguments or debates.

_____ 20. I often find myself in situations where people say, "You are just doing too much."

SCORING TEST 1. YOUR TYPE A PERSONALITY

The test on type A characteristics is made up of four subscales representing hyperaggression, time urgency, overachievement, and polyphasic behavior. The questions representing each subscale are listed below. Add up the items for each subscale. This will give you an indication of the range of Type A behaviors you exhibit.

Hyperaggression	Time Urgency	Overachievement	Polyphasic Impulsive
3._____	1._____	2._____	4._____
7._____	5._____	6._____	8._____
11._____	9._____	10._____	12._____
15._____	13._____	14._____	16._____
19._____	17._____	18._____	20._____

Totals	_____	_____	_____	_____
	B1	B2	A2	A1
	0–25	26–50	51–75	76–100

B1 is strong Type B behaviors.
B2 is moderate Type B behaviors.
A2 is moderate Type A behaviors.
A1 is strong Type A behaviors.

Impulsiveness and Polyphasic Behavior

Impulsiveness is the tendency to jump into something without having a full understanding of its complexity. It is an eagerness to get involved and failure to prioritize and see the total picture. Impulsive people are overly willing to get started and will often fail to listen for important clues or directions. It is like taking medicine without looking at the directions or assembling a household item without reading the instructions. A polyphasic ("poly" meaning many and "phasic" meaning phases) person undertakes two or more tasks simultaneously at inappropriate times. This person might complete a report while listening to complaints of an employee, or make serious deals on the phone while working on the computer. These people shave and shower at the same time and watch TV while eating or working. The results are usually ineffective use of time due to inability to concentrate on one task.

Any one of these four personality traits could result in high stress levels, even though they probably evolved out of what was once reasonable business behavior—time consciousness, high motivation, the desire to do more than one thing at a time, and being a "go-getter." Collectively, these traits refer to the Type A personality, or coronary-prone personality. The traits are highly correlated with premature heart disease.

An individual's personality type can be an important contributor to an individual's health as well as his or her performance. Type A can be characterized as overly competitive, an achiever, aggressive, a fast worker, impatient, restless, explosive in speech, tense, always under pressure, and, according to Dr. Friedman's recent studies, insecure and unaware of his or her limitations. Type B behavior is the mirror opposite: easygoing, seldom impatient, taking time to enjoy things in life besides work, not easily irritated, not preoccupied with social achievement, and moving and speaking more slowly. The following table summarizes the characteristics of Type A and B personalities.

Type A	Type B
▪ competitive achiever	▪ relaxed
▪ more aggressive	▪ easygoing
▪ fast worker	▪ seldom impatient
▪ impatient	▪ taking time to enjoy
▪ restless	▪ not easily irritated
▪ hyperalert	▪ working steadily
▪ explosive in speech	▪ seldom lacking time
▪ tense	▪ not preoccupied with social achievement
▪ social climber	
▪ always feeling pressure	▪ moving and speaking more slowly

Type A personalities are more likely to develop heart disease. They are both males and females who are obsessed with getting ahead. They work longer hours, travel more days per year, work in high-growth companies, have supervisory responsibility, have heavy workloads, and work in competitive environments. The Type A person not only harms himself or herself, but the company as well. In addition to such direct costs as medical payments and lost time and productivity, there are indirect costs, such as causing stress for other non–Type A employees.

BECOMING LESS TYPE A

Enjoy the present hour,
Be thankful for the past,
And Neither fear nor wish
Th' approaches of the last.

—ABRAHAM COWLEY

Becoming more Type B and less Type A is a desirable objective in preventing or reducing the possibility of becoming stressed. Type B individuals are less likely to compete in such destructive competitive and time-urgent environments.

The quickest way to reduce one's Type A orientation is to quit associating with other Type A individuals. This is a desirable objective that is easier to suggest than to practice, as it involves a change in values and attitudes. We have learned to like Type A personalities. They are fun to be with, they talk a great deal, and they are involved in endless tasks. They are most often rewarded and promoted in organizations. On the other hand, they also run out of steam or burn out.

Commitment to change grows from a person's need for change and the ability to act. Some general steps for reducing Type Aness involve an assessment of one's behavior and then taking steps to change. *Aggressiveness, time urgency, the drive to overachieve,* and *polyphasic behavior* are characteristics that can result in the need to make an endless series of decisions on very small and large issues. The small issues sometimes take on a higher priority, resulting in rushing to meet constant deadlines and insufficient time for other important matters or for personal relationships.

One of the most important first steps is to slow down and schedule less. Say "NO" and delegate those tasks that you do not value or are not of high priority. This involves revising your daily schedule and learning to work within priorities that recognize your life values and career needs.

Effective time management is one way to minimize the anxiety and fatigue resulting from Type A behaviors. The initial step involves assessing the tasks and activities that you carry out over the week. Then you can make a log of each hour of the day, including the hours for recreation, hygiene, and sleep. The log should describe the whole day in as much detail as possible.

Midnight–6:30 A.M.	Uninterrupted sleep
6:30–7:00 A.M.	Morning shower and hygiene
7:00–7:45 A.M.	Help children get ready for school, breakfast on the run
7:45–8:00 A.M.	Read paper
8:00–8:30 A.M.	Travel to work
8:30–9:15 A.M.	Informal social meeting with people in office, respond to phone calls from friend
9:15–9:30 A.M.	Check mail and talk to colleague in mail room

The next step is to identify those tasks, activities, or interruptions that might be least desirable or less productive. What activities are viewed as "time wasters," low priority, or unimportant? What activities are useful and stress reducing and should be maintained?

The assessment should help you identify your priorities and goals. These can be further refined by responding to questions such as: What are my values and life priorities? What are the most important things I want to do in my work and my life? What are my objectives regarding relationships, health, exercise, and contributions to others?

The next step is to develop a more realistic schedule that blocks out important times for exercise, family, and certain work tasks. It is also feasible to schedule time for relaxation or for cleaning up the office.

Many time-pressured people are very unorganized and spend hours looking for documents or notes that are mislaid and lost. The "office cleanup" is a useful exercise to do at least once a month. It is important to develop a system for prioritizing daily work. Classify all your incoming material into three drawers or piles.

The "A" Drawer. These are the materials you receive daily that you can easily deal with or are of very high priority.

The "B" Drawer. This is the material that needs to be filed or worked on by someone else. It is the material that you require for financial and legal reasons. You should periodically file this material.

The "C" Drawer. This is the drawer where the bulk of your material should end up. When you are in doubt about something's importance or think you might want to look into it more when you have time, throw it in the "C" drawer. You will find that much of your material goes into this drawer. You will also find that you seldom open it, but just in case you do, you have it. At the end of a period of time, throw the contents of your "C" drawer away.

Objective setting is a device for becoming more efficient and productive, and it can also be helpful for establishing realistic and relevant priorities. It allows people to say "no" to tasks or requests that are not within an objective or set of priorities and focus more specifically on higher-order priorities. Another approach to setting objectives or priorities is the following: Imagine yourself at the end of a party celebrating the success of things you have accomplished over the last year. Looking back, what tasks did you accomplish? Express these in behaviorial terms.

Overachieving is an expression of anxiety that is common for people who measure life success in material terms such as wealth, the size of one's house, or the type of car owned.

What makes overachieving stressful is that the person is never satisfied, and the subject of every conversation is a monologue on "how much I have done" or "how hard I work." The person is saying, "Please tell me how nice my car is or how much you like my house." Being secure with one's status in life is really being at peace with oneself. Why should a person always seek to measure one's achievements in the eyes of others? An appropriate first step toward becoming more secure with one's status is to learn to be content with what one now has. Learn to express your feelings about nonmaterial things such as relationships, relaxation, life, enjoyment, and love. Quit talking so much about material things and, when you do, recognize that you are asking for attention.

When you catch yourself being materialistic or not satisfied with your accomplishments, ask yourself what life is all about. Think of the analogy of the race between the turtle and the hare. The Type A hare will go off in a hundred different directions during the race, while the more organized, directed, and relaxed turtle continues on her slow pace. Who is going to win the race in life?

The analogy should illustrate that Type B personalities still work hard but they are more directed and, hopefully, less stressed. A Type B personality is not a relaxed person who does not work. He or she works more efficiently and is more focused. The following questions might help in rethinking or reframing how you can become less Type A.

Questions to Ask Yourself

- Why is time so critical; what is the rush?
- Why do I have such high expectations of myself?
- Why do I feel I need to be such a superhuman person?
- Why are certain stressors so bothersome to me? Why should they be so important and take such a high priority?
- How can I feel better about myself?

HOSTILITY, A KEY DIMENSION OF THE STRESS-PRONE PERSONALITY

Hostility may be one of the most serious elements of the stress-prone personality and may present more health-related problems than being hurried or time obsessed. Hostility is a key personality variable in the link with coronary heart disease.

ANGRY, HOSTILE PEOPLE ARE FIVE TIMES MORE LIKELY TO DIE BEFORE THE AGE OF FIFTY, COMPARED TO THOSE WHO ARE CALM AND TRUSTING.

A constant state of anger causes severe physiological reactions. The bloodstream is more likely to receive infusions of stress hormones and raise blood pressure, gearing up the muscles and constricting blood supply to the internal organs. The resulting changes to the blood, including higher cholesterol and clotting factors, have a long-term adverse effect on the coronary arteries.

A person who is angry generally has feelings ranging from intense fury to rage. Hostility usually involves angry feelings, but it also involves a set of attitudes that motivate aggressive behavior directed at destroying or injuring people or objects. When a nonhostile person is aroused, their parasympathetic nervous systems (the stomach, gut, and bowel) act like a "stop switch" to calm things down. Hostile types seem to have weak parasympathetic nervous systems. When they get fired up, they stayed unpleasantly aroused, and interact differently with the world. These differences exist even in infancy.

Reducing hostility in a constructive manner involves channeling it more appropriately through calming techniques (for example, reading a newspaper while waiting in a line or meditation) and modifying one's attitude. Bottling up feelings of anger and hostility is a very harmful way of responding to stress. This tendency is often associated with a person's unwillingness to trust others. Such people are walking "time bombs."

TEST 2. THE AT INDEX

The questions in this test attempt to define your behavioral orientation in your unique setting. Think of the setting that most demands your time, such as your work, your school, on your relationships with people in the community. Keep this in mind when completing the test: There are no right answers. The more honest you are, the more valid will be the results of this questionnaire. It is *important* that you respond to *all* statements. For each statement, place a number from 1 to 4 on the line to the left of the item. The numbers mean:

1	2	3	4
Very Untrue	Somewhat Untrue	Somewhat True	Very True

_____ 1. When someone is hogging the conversation, I tend to feel quite angry and upset.

_____ 2. I tend to believe that the people who I am most responsible to (supervisors, teachers, or spouse) honor our collective interests rather than their self-interest.

_____ 3. When something goes wrong when I am in a hurry, I have been known to lose my temper and swear.

_____ 4. I have, on at least one occasion, broken or thrown something in anger during the last six months.

_____ 5. I tend to believe that the people I work most directly with (colleagues or fellow students) are interested in our collective interest rather than their self-interest.

_____ 6. I believe that many of the top people in government are honest rather than corrupt.

_____ 7. I tend to believe that the people I most relate to are by and large honest and sincere in their dealings with me.

_____ 8. When someone has treated me unfairly and I feel angry, I am more expressive rather than reserved in stating my feelings.

_____ 9. When I get angry with someone, I let them know about it immediately.

_____ 10. My personal feelings are something that I share with others rather than keep to myself.

_____ 11. I have been told by others to "cool it" or "calm down."

_____ 12. I tend to feel annoyed at those who do not carry out their fair share of work.

_____ 13. When I remember something that has made me very angry previously, I feel angry all over again.

_____ 14. If I lost my wallet in a supermarket, I believe that there is a very good chance that it will be returned intact.

_____ 15. I generally believe that the people I work with are basically honest.

_____ 16. I feel annoyed when someone criticizes something I have done.

_____ 17. When there is a really important job to do, I delegate it and count on other people rather than doing it myself.

_____ 18. When something goes wrong and I get really angry, I sometimes wake up at night thinking about that situation.

_____ 19. I generally believe that people will tell the truth about themselves.

_____ 20. I often feel I'm working with people who are incompetent.

SCORING TEST 2. THE AT INDEX:
RATING YOUR ANGER AND TRUST

Anger	Expressed Anger	Trust
1. _____	3. _____	2. _____
12. _____	4. _____	5. _____
13. _____	8. _____	6. _____
16. _____	9. _____	7. _____
18. _____	11. _____	10. _____
		14. _____
		15. _____
		17. _____
		19. _____
		20. _____

TOTALS _____ ÷ 5   _____ ÷ 5   _____ ÷ 10

The test is a measure of the anger within you. It provides you with only a rough indication of whether or not you are generally hostile.

Interpreting Your Score

Anger:

A tendency to feel quite annoyed and upset when things go wrong.

2.5+ A higher score on this dimension suggests that you have a tendency to feel annoyed and angry when things go wrong or when something happens with which you do not agree.

Expressed Anger:

>2.5 Expressed anger is a tendency to express one's anger and annoyance by lashing out.

<2.5 A lower score on this dimension suggests that you have a tendency to be more reserved.

Trust

A tendency to trust others and feel that people are honest.

>2.5+ A higher score on this dimension suggests that you have a tendency to trust others. This is generally a healthy strategy.

<2.5 A lower score on this dimension suggests that you have a tendency to be rather cynical and mistrusting. You may be in an environment where people are highly distrustful of others. Ideally, you should have low scores on anger. If you have high scores on anger, how do you express it? Do you share your feelings with others?

People who are most in danger are those who have high scores on expressed anger and low scores on trust. These people are angry and tend to keep their feelings to themselves. They may be in environments where there is a great deal of mistrust and cynicism.

Expressing one's feelings is a catharsis that clears the air. It releases energy and frustration. It is always healthier to be open and communicate one's feelings.

Expressing one's anger, however, can be extremely stressful. I once participated in a experiment where people were encouraged to get mad and throw things around. Then, we were asked to get in touch with how this felt. It took many of us a long time to calm down. We were tense, full of emotion, and could feel the strain on our bodies. When someone tells you to express your feelings, this does not mean that you should go out and beat up the world.

The critical personality traits are a combination of being unable to trust others and being angry and hostile. Mistrustful people who are angry and hostile seem to have fundamentally different nervous systems.

Becoming Less Hostile

Most people create a great deal of stress by burdening themselves with unnecessary worries that are based on incorrect assumptions. This "self-talk" is the way that we learn to describe and interpret the events around us.

If the self-talk is untrue or unrealistic, a person will experience stress or an emotional disturbance. For example, a person might feel that "my boss is angry with me and will fire me when she gets the chance." On average, very few people get fired in most organizations. So, what is the probability of getting fired (what percentage of people got fired over the last three years)? Being fired may be uncomfortable, undesirable, and frustrating, but most people can live through it, and many people learn a great deal from such an experience and are more prosperous as a result. Years later, some people describe this as "the best thing that could ever have happened to me." So, why get so worked up by such fears?

Albert Ellis developed an approach to help people replace these irrational beliefs and ideas with more realistic statements. He suggested that many emotions are triggered by interpretations, not actual events. Many feelings have little to do with actual events; rather, they result from either rational or irrational self-talk. A person's thoughts are what create anger, anxiety, and hostility. The following figure illustrates the relationship between an event, self-talk, and emotions.

FIGURE 5.1 THE RELATIONSHIP BETWEEN EMOTIONS AND EVENTS

IRRATIONAL SELF-TALK

Event———>	Self-talk———>	Emotion
Lack of communications from a supervisor	"The supervisor does not like my work." "The supervisor is untrustworthy."	Hostility, Anger, Depression

RATIONAL SELF-TALK

Event———>	Self-talk———>	Emotion
Lack of communications from a supervisor	"The supervisor does not have time to talk." "I have not made myself available for communications."	Disappointment, Need to Change

When you are feeling hostile or angry, ask yourself, "What is my self-talk?" This self-talk, and not the event, is what produces the emotions. To assess one's self-talk, ask yourself the following questions:

- Is there any rational support for the thought?
- What evidence exists for the incorrectness of the thought?
- What evidence exists for the correctness of the thought?
- What is the worst thing that might happen to me? Is this so bad?
- What good things might possibly occur if the worst case actually happens?
- Identify self-talk that you might view as more realistic.

Fighting angry or hostile emotions involves a commitment to follow the above steps whenever such emotions arise. Certain rules can assist in promoting rational thinking.

Tell yourself, "It does not bother me." This involves telling oneself that the situation does not make you feel anxious or angry and recognize that the self-talk creates the emotion. For example, the next time that a driver cuts you off in traffic, ask yourself why you are angry. Is it the other driver or the self-talk that describes the other driver as an "inconsiderate moron"?

1. Tell yourself, "Everything is exactly the way it should be." Most of the time, we think we would feel a lot better "if only" things were different. In fact, things are not different and they are exactly as they should be. To keep hoping for a magical transformation is unrealistic. Things are like they are because of a long series of events that have made them that way, and there is little that we can do to change them. All that we can do is affect the events in our immediate surroundings, including our self-talk.

2. All humans are fallible creatures. Trial and error and success and failure are important aspects of our human existence. Everyone makes mistakes and everyone should realize that they are allowed a reasonable quota of them. If you do not allow for some errors, you will have a greater than average number of disappointments.

3. It takes two to have a conflict. Most conflicts involve two parties who are working against each other. Any party to a conflict is contributing at least 30 percent of the fuel to keep it going. The key to resolving conflict is to identify the issue and work toward a solution in which each party can resolve some of his or her interests.

4. The original cause of your anger will eventually be lost in antiquity. It is a waste of time to continue to seek reasons why certain things occurred the way they did. The best strategy is to resolve the problem and to prevent others from happening in the future.

5. We feel the way we think. Becoming less hostile and angry involves changing our self-talk. Instead of labeling a driver who has cut you off as an inconsiderate moron, it is more appropriate to think that there are always going to be drivers who are discourteous or bad-mannered. Because of your capability, you can thank your good driving skill for preventing an accident. More importantly if you did not get angry, your ability to continue this behavior will add years to your life.

OTHER DIMENSIONS OF THE STRESS-PRONE PERSONALITY

Several other personality characteristics are part of the stress-prone personality, including self-esteem and anxiety, locus of control, and perfectionism.

Anxiety and Self-Esteem

Large numbers of North Americans are anxious or fearful. This has led to our time being described as the Age of Anxiety. To help deal with anxiety, North Americans typically fill over 100 million prescriptions for drugs per year, swallowing tons of Valium and Prozac each year. Fear triggers the endocrinological and physiological systems to prepare the person for survival (fight-flight response). The extra wear and tear on the body shows up in a number of psychosomatic disorders, from ulcers and headaches to hypertension and CHD.

ANXIETY IS A HYPERSENSITIVE SET OF EMOTIONS THAT DRIVES US TO BE PERFECT.

Anxiety can be expressed as fear of losing, or a fear of having someone else get ahead of you. Anxiety is most often driven by being overly conscious of the criticisms and judgments of others. Or it may be stirred on by unrealistic drives to be perfect. Anxiety is an emotional response resulting from an overexposure to criticism or judgments of others. Anxiety is associated with hypertension.

Why do Type A people struggle endlessly and senselessly to accomplish more and more things or involve themselves in more and more events? While some environments demand it of them, more often it is because they demand this of themselves.

Many famous people exhibit these tendencies. For example, most of us believe that presidents like Johnson and Nixon were secure individuals with high self-esteem and low sense of insecurity. There is much evidence to the contrary. These presidents, and many others, were constantly measuring themselves against others, in terms of how history would remember them. Even President Clinton likes to compare himself to John F. Kennedy.

Anxiety and self-esteem are very much related. People who have poor self-images and low self-esteem perceive a greater number of situations or conditions in their lives as potentially threatening (psychologically and physically). High self-esteem individuals have healthy self-images with corresponding high levels of self-esteem. They rarely feel threatened.

A person's self-esteem is not determined by one's accomplishments, no matter how brilliant these may seem to other people. Self-esteem is a measure of a person's sense of comfort with one's life and accomplishments.

People with high self-esteem may work just as hard to meet goals and objectives as others. However, if they do not succeed, they do not collapse and feel insecure. They do not feel compelled to prove themselves just to satisfy others.

> **SELF-ESTEEM IS AN INDICATION OF A PERSON'S PRIDE, SELF-CONFIDENCE, AND SELF-RESPECT.**

An individual with low self-esteem might perceive a greater number of situations or conditions in life as potentially threatening (psychologically and physically). High self-esteem individuals have healthy self-images and are rarely as threatened by life's troubles.

Self-esteem is directly related to expectations for success. Individuals with high self-esteem are more likely to feel that they will succeed and will take greater risks. People with low self-esteem are more susceptible to external influences and are dependent on others for approval. People with high self-esteem have a tendency to be involved in life's full range of activities and have a generalized purpose or understanding that allows them to find meaning and value in who they are and what they are doing.

HIGH ANXIETY

High Scorer

- Tends to worry
- Easily upset
- Apprehensive about the future
- Usually composed
- Tense
- Nervous
- Preoccupied
- Anxious
- Edgy
- Fearful
- Distressed
- Agitated

LOW ANXIETY

Low Scorer

- Calm
- Takes things as they come
- Can relax in difficult situations
- Easygoing
- Patient
- Calm, serene
- Tranquil
- Contented
- Placid

HIGH SELF-ESTEEM

High Scorer

- Confident in dealing with others
- Not easily embarrassed
- Not easily influenced by others

- Self-assured
- Composed
- Egotistical
- Poised
- Self-sufficient

LOW SELF-ESTEEM

Low Scorer

- Feels awkward among people
- Ill at ease socially
- Prefers to remain unnoticed at social events
- Has low opinion of self
- Lacks self-confidence
- Easily embarrassed
- Self-deprecating
- Timid, humble, self-conscious

Self-esteem is the ability to feel good about oneself. It usually results when people are able to understand and express feelings. Such people are proud of their beliefs, are self-confident, and feel they are free to act.

Assess your self-esteem and anxiety by completing Test 3.

TEST 3. THE AE INDEX

This test assesses some of the things you think about. It is *important* that you respond to *all* statements. For each statement, place a number from 1 to 4 on the line to the left of the item. The numbers mean:

1	2	3	4
Very Untrue	Somewhat Untrue	Somewhat True	Very True

_____ 1. Before an important meeting, I have difficulty concentrating on other things.

_____ 2. I generally feel my views are important, and I am confident in sharing them.

_____ 3. If someone says something negative to me, I may not get over it right away. It might bother me later.

_____ 4. I am usually quite confident when taking on new tasks.

_____ 5. The mistakes and crises I have gone through often bother me for a few days afterwards.

_____ 6. I am the informal leader in my work.

_____ 7. I have lost sleep worrying about others' criticisms or judgments.

_____ 8. I have a very positive attitude toward my future career.

_____ 9. I find that when waiting to speak in a group, I feel nervous.

_____ 10. If I die tomorrow, I would feel proud of my accomplishments.

_____ 11. I often cannot sleep when I have something important the next day.

_____ 12. I would be very confident about getting a job, even in difficult times.

_____ 13. I sometimes relive my past mistakes when something goes wrong.

_____ 14. I am quite confident when meeting new people. I do not tend to guard what I say or do.

_____ 15. I frequently worry about my ability to do new things.

_____ 16. All in all, I am inclined to think I could be successful in most situations.

_____ 17. I worry about whether others' decisions or mistakes might affect me.

_____ 18. I have a great deal of pride in what I do.

_____ 19. I sometimes worry about whether I can do all the things I have to do in my schedule.

_____ 20. I am very happy about the success I have made so far in life.

SCORING TEST 3. THE AE INDEX:
MEASURING ANXIETY AND SELF-ESTEEM

Anxiety	Self Esteem
1. _____	2. _____
3. _____	4. _____
5. _____	6. _____
7. _____	8. _____
9. _____	10. _____
11. _____	12. _____
13 _____	14. _____
15. _____	16. _____
17. _____	18. _____
19. _____	20. _____

Total _____   _____

Anxiety scores greater than 22 indicate that some of your stress may come from feelings of anxiety. Self-esteem scores lower than 18 indicate that you lack self-esteem. A stress-prone personality has high anxiety and low self-esteem.

Developing Self-Esteem and Reducing Anxiety

How we interact with others can be a source of considerable stress. Anxiety and low self-esteem are a major cause of the feelings of uneasiness and inadequacy that many people experience. Self-esteem and anxiety are products of our past experiences. We have learned these attitudes. That is the bad news.

The good news is that these attitudes can be changed. We can teach people to stand up for themselves and feel confident. In the same way, anxiety can be reduced. A person with low anxiety is not fearful of people, ideas, or change. He or she is more relaxed and able to deal with situations without feeling nervous, agitated, or concerned.

Respond to the following questions. Later chapters will offer other steps for developing self-esteem and reducing anxiety.

- What are your priorities and values?
- What are some of your basic fears?
- What are some of the obstacles to reducing these fears?
- What are some ideas for reducing these fears?
- What makes you feel good?
- What are some of the obstacles to improving your self-esteem?
- What are some ideas for improving self-esteem?

Locus of Control

Some people believe that they are in control and are masters of their own destiny. Others see life as being determined by the randomness of external events, believing that what happens in life is due to chance or circumstance. An individual who believes that his or her life is controlled by outside forces is said to have an external locus of control. The person who believes that life's directions can be controlled by one's actions is said to have an internal locus of control.

TEST 4. THE LC INDEX

This test assesses how you view the opportunity to take control of the events around you. Respond to *all* statements. For each statement, place a number from 1 to 4 on the line to the left of the item. The numbers mean:

1	2	3	4
Very Untrue	Somewhat Untrue	Somewhat True	Very True

_____ 1. I believe that my success in this organization depends solely on my abilities.

_____ 2. The influence of certain people might be extremely helpful to me in getting ahead.

_____ 3. If I look back at my career, I would say that it was largely shaped by opportunities that appeared rather accidentally.

_____ 4. Using one's entrepreneurship and creativity is the surest way to get ahead, rather than luck or timing.

_____ 5. I feel that business clubs are very important to my success, much more than entrepreneurship and creativity.

_____ 6. I believe that the right environment is much more important than just having persistence and entrepreneurship.

_____ 7. My persistence and hard work are key in determining my performance, much more than the assistance of others.

_____ 8. The leadership and assistance of others is much more important to me than my persistence and hard work.

_____ 9. Receiving rewards for one's efforts is often a result of the influence of others and luck.

_____ 10. The quality of one's work is more important than the influence of others.

_____ 11. Politics is often very important in the judgment of one's work.

_____ 12. Getting people in this organization to listen to my ideas involves luck and politics.

_____ 13. I believe that rationality and merit are important to getting things accomplished.

_____ 14. My success or failure depends on those who work with me.

_____ 15. Most matters in this organization are beyond the control of the people who work here.

_____ 16. The quality of my work influences how other people in this organization view my suggestions.

_____ 17. Interest groups are more powerful than individuals are, and they control more things than individuals do.

_____ 18. The degree to which things get changed depends more on chance than logic.

SCORING TEST 4. LOCUS OF CONTROL

(Internal) (I)	(External—Others) (EO)	External—Chance) (EC)
1. _____	2. _____	3. _____
4. _____	5. _____	6. _____
7. _____	8. _____	9. _____
10. _____	11. _____	12. _____
13. _____	14. _____	15. _____
16. _____	17. _____	18. _____
Total _____	_____	_____

The locus of control questionnaire provides an assessment of your ability to control certain issues. Each of the pairs of alternatives reflects one dimension—either external or internal local of control.

Interpreting Your Scores

Your scores reflect the way you view what happens in your organization or life. No score (or view) has to be permanent. If you are not happy with your view, you may want to create an action plan that will help you change the way you look at things.

I Internals: Belief that the future can be controlled and that you are responsible for it.

18+   Very high internality suggests self-confidence in your ability to control what happens to you. High internality may be realistic at times, especially when a person ascribes personal failure to situations over which they have no control.

14–17   High trust in your ability and effort.

10–13   Lack of trust in your ability to control situations.

<9   Represents very little self-confidence in your ability to handle external situations.

EO Externals—Others: Belief that the future is controlled by powerful others.

18+   Very dysfunctional dependence on other people for achieving.

14–17   Realistic dependence on supervisors, peers, and subordinates.

10–13   Independence orientation.

<9   Indicates counterdependence.

EC Externals—Chance: Belief that the future is controlled by luck or chance. The lower the score, the better.

>13   May reflect problems in coping with frustration when unforeseen factors prevent achievement of goals.

Events that are outside an individual's control might provoke feelings of helplessness and powerlessness. People who believe that they cannot control life events (externals) are less satisfied with their jobs, have higher absenteeism rates, and are less involved. They are less satisfied and more stressed because they perceive that they have little ability to affect outcomes. They may persist in carrying out their work even though they feel that they cannot do much about it.

Internals and externals will handle stressful situations differently. Internals believe that they can have a significant effect on results and will act to control events. Externals are more likely to be passive and defensive and will usually give in or comply as a method of reducing stress. They feel helpless in stressful situations and are more likely to experience stress. Externals are likely to perceive situations as stress inducing, while internals will assume that their own behaviors can control and handle different situations. Internals are more creative, resilient, and capable of handling stress. They confront stressful experiences with vigor and energy, while externals might feel depressed and angry.

Assume that you are an individual facing a stressful situation that requires that a number of projects be completed over a short period of time, or you are facing time pressures because you are constantly inundated with new requests or tasks. If you are an external, you may feel that you can never fully take control of the situation. You feel overwhelmed and incapable of handling the problems you face. Each situation is perceived as a minor crisis. You have difficulty taking control and dealing with these crises.

If you are an internal, you will take steps to reduce the threats and establish control. You might delegate work, assign priorities, and establish deadlines and schedules. To the extent that you take control, stress will be reduced. Taking control means setting priorities, asking for additional help, saying "no," setting schedules, taking time to examine the process (even when you are in the midst of a crisis), or taking preventive action.

PERFECTIONISM AND THE NEED FOR STRUCTURE

Perfectionism and the need for structure are illustrated by phrases such as, "If you want something done right, you have to do it yourself," "You've got to dot all the i's and cross all the t's."

The pursuit of excellence and success is not a characteristic to be questioned. Excellence and perfection is called for in several situations, such as when an engineer builds a bridge, a brain surgeon performs an operation, or a pilot flys a jumbo jet.

PERFECTIONISM GOES FAR BEYOND THE HEALTHY PURSUIT OF EXCELLENCE OR THE DESIRE TO ACHIEVE HIGH STANDARDS.

Perfectionism is a compulsive obsession with standards that are unrealistically high and beyond reach or reason. It is experienced by those who measure their worth entirely in terms of productivity and accomplishments. These people are inclined to set unrealistic and impossible standards while becoming obsessed with details and facts.

Perfectionists set idealistic and critical standards for the people they work with and the jobs they undertake. They set unrealistic goals in sport, diet, appearance, and for life in general. Such a drive is a self-defeating obsession. The cost is stress and impaired health, poor self-control, troubled personal relationships, and low self-esteem. The perfectionist is also vulnerable to serious mood disorders such as depression and anxiety. People who have this trait are more likely to respond to their inability to be perfect with a loss of self-esteem.

This is a vicious circle. The low self-esteem leads to withdrawal, pessimism, and an external locus of control, or increased perfectionism in an attempt to avoid criticism and rejection and gain approval and acceptance. Perfectionism is a recipe for low self-esteem when people do not reinforce us the way we hope.

Because of a fear of making a mistake or appearing foolish, a perfectionist is more unwilling to share his or her feelings and thoughts. Perfectionists fear and anticipate rejection when they are judged to be imperfect and will react defensively to criticism. They have an excessive sensitivity to real or imagined disapproval.

Perfectionists often apply their excessively high standards to others and are inevitably disappointed. They may react with annoyance and resentment and become more demanding when others do not meet their expectations.

Perfectionism can affect performance. For example, a study of life insurance agents showed that perfectionists who linked self-worth and achievement earned an average of $15,000 less a year than nonperfectionists.

Studies of highly successful athletes have documented an absence of perfectionistic styles; they more easily underemphasize little mistakes and difficulties. Those who failed tended to rouse themselves into near-panic states during competition. Perfectionists may also experience more stress in schools and universities; they often wish to leave school and may suffer depression and anxiety.

Why are perfectionists more vulnerable to emotional turmoil and impaired productivity? Three characteristics common among perfectionists: all-or-nothing thinking, the tendency to overgeneralize, and the tendency for critical self-evaluation and improvement.

Perhaps the most common mental distortion among perfectionists is "all-or-nothing" thinking. They tend to evaluate experiences in dichotomous terms, as either black or white, with no shades of gray. The perfectionist A student cannot tolerate getting a B. Thus, he or she may fear mistakes and overreact to them.

Perfectionists do not believe in moderation. When perfectionists begin a diet, they have either "off" or "on" behavior. This means total abstinence and rigorous standards of control. The first time a perfectionist falters on the diet, the diet is over and the period of "sainthood" ends. A period of "sin" begins, characterized by guilt, moralistic self-deprecation, and binges.

Perfectionists tend to overgeneralize and jump to dogmatic conclusions that negative events will be repeated endlessly. When perfectionists make mistakes, they make statements such as, "I'm taking too much time off," or "I'm not trying hard enough," or "I'll never get it right." They have a very narrow threshold of error in making judgments of their adequacy. Because of a compulsive drive to achieve a flawless result, the perfectionist has trouble sensing when something is "good enough."

A third distortion is the tendency to be overly critical and demanding of self-improvement. When a goal is not met, perfectionists make statements such as, "I shouldn't have taken time off," or "I should have worked harder." Such attitudes create feelings of frustration and guilt that cause them to focus on their errors even more. They perceive themselves as inefficient because they imagine that successful people achieve goals with minimal effort, few errors, and maximum self-confidence. As they dwell on their shortcomings, they feel inferior and underrewarded.

TEST 5. THE P INDEX

The following is a list of attitudes and beliefs that people sometimes hold. Decide how much you agree or disagree with each of the statements, and fill in the blanks preceding each statement with the number best describing you.

1	2	3	4
Very Untrue	Somewhat Untrue	Somewhat True	Very True

_____ 1. I define myself through my ability to achieve high standards in my work and life.

_____ 2. I feel people will think less of me if I make a mistake.

_____ 3. Doing things really well is very important to me. If I cannot put the time into doing something well, I would choose not to do it.

_____ 4. I believe that people tend to judge you on the basis of simple mistakes such as punctuation, spelling, and grammar.

_____ 5. People I work for demand perfection.

_____ 6. I make sure that I do not make the same mistake twice.

_____ 7. I feel pressured to meet the standards I have set.

_____ 8. When I go someplace, I tend to make sure that there are no loose ends. I plan the trip in detail.

_____ 9. I often find myself looking for mistakes in projects that others have completed.

_____ 10. I tend to be very good at completely finishing and perfecting the jobs I start.

_____ 11. When something is unfinished, it bothers me.

SCORING TEST 5. PERFECTIONISM

Add up the scores on all items (except number 5) and divide by 10.

1. _____	7. _____
2. _____	8. _____
3. _____	9. _____
4. _____	10. _____
6. _____	11. _____

Total _____ ÷ 10 = _____

Interpreting Your Scores

3.1–4.0   A high level of perfectionism

2.1–3.0   Moderate level of perfectionism

1.1–2.0   Nonperfectionionist mind-set

Research indicates that approximately half the population scores between 3.0 and 4.0, indicating high levels of perfectionism.

How do perfectionist characteristics originate? It is unclear why people have this obsessive desire to be perfect, although extreme desire for approval and acceptance may be a major precursor. It may arise in children with obsessively perfectionist parents, especially when the parents react to a child's mistakes and failures with anxiety and disappointment. This is likely to be understood as punishment or rejection. The child begins to fear making mistakes and to avoid failure.

Dealing with Your Perfectionism

> *The first problem for all of us,*
> *men and women, is not to learn,*
> *but to unlearn.*
>
> —GLORIA STEINER

The notion that "we are our own worst enemy" coincides with the idea that the "dragon (the enemy) is within us." Anything learned can be unlearned and to unlearn is to change. The following steps encourage you to unlearn some of your old habits, reframe your self-concept, and take control of a more desired behavior.

When you eliminate the idea of trying to be a perfectionist, you lose your fear of being criticized. Perfectionists don't enjoy the real world because they are so critical of it. Perfectionism is the death of spontaneity, creativity, and good fun.

Unlearning involves discarding the old habits. It involves:

- **Awareness**: Complete Test 5 and become aware of your own perfectionism. Ask others about your behaviors. How does this affect your enjoyment, stress, happiness, and overall effectiveness?

- **Acceptance:** According to C. G. Jung, we cannot change anything unless we accept it. Self-acceptance is the acid test of your willingness to change. If you are not aware that perfectionism truly is dysfunctional, you will have little chance of changing. Thus, if it is an issue, recognize how it affects you.

  Reframing your self-concept involves taking control and identifying the new behaviors that are more desirable. This involves making the shift from "I am defined by my successes and achievements" to "What I do (accomplish) and who I am (my essence) are different." In short, one begins to take control of one's identity or essence by stating, "I define me" and "My essence resides inside me and not external with you."

- **Will:** Do you have the will or commitment to change your style?

- **New Habits:** Involve others in defining the new habits to which you will subscribe. For example, how can you define your own sense of worth internally rather than externally? When your sense of worth is defined by others, you are more likely to be a perfectionist. Define your personal worth, assuming that no one would ever judge you. You should define habits relating to relaxation, enjoyment, and so forth. Develop a list of do's and don'ts. *Do's* might include: taking time to relax, letting others finish a few projects, leaving a typing mistake just to test other people's reactions. *Don'ts* might include a list of things such as: don't stay late at work more than once per week, don't take work home on certain evenings.

Reinforcement involves developing ways to assure that you are setting forth a program for changing yourself.

- **Involve Others**: When you tell other people about what you plan to do, you are more likely to get their help. In addition, you may be more motivated to change.

- **Continual Reassessment**: Check yourself against your list of do's and don'ts.

Reassess Yourself

IT'S THE MIND THAT NEEDS TO BE HEALTHY.

I constantly run into people who seem to be doing everything right to be healthy—they watch their diet, they exercise, they are thin, and do not smoke or drink—but they are examples of poor health. On the other hand, I know people who are quite healthy and seem to observe questionable practices. Here are two cases that are illustrative.

Ted is a sixty-six-year-old male, a former archictect who weighs about 130 to 140 pounds. He jogs, is compulsive in following a strict no-fat diet, and is constantly reading books and articles on stress and health. Ted has experienced some problems throughout his medical history. He has had three strokes, two heart attacks, and a quadruple bypass heart operation. His arteries are now just as clogged as they were several years ago, and he is awaiting an operation to relieve a 5-millimeter aneurysm in his stomach. Ted's personality is that of a very stress-prone individual. He is vindictive, negative, skeptical, pessimistic, and critical. He lacks any sense of humor. Three wives have left him, two adult children refuse to talk to him, and he has few friends.

Tom is an eighty-year-old male, a former electrical lineman who has smoked for over fifty years. He never has really exercised, except to walk to and from the coffee shop. Tom has always had an apprentice who did all the hard work. Tom is at least 40 pounds overweight. He just bought a camper van so that he can tour the southern states during the winter. Tom's personality is that of a very kind person. He is optimistic, interested, and analytical. He is positive and warm. He is the neighborhood listener and spends endless hours listening to others. I go to see Tom at least once a week. He often buys me coffee and a muffin. He calms me down when I begin taking life too seriously.

Ted and Tom are just two cases, but they illustrate an important principle. You must refocus your stress-prone personality traits. I am not suggesting that you should ignore other important facets of stress management such as diet, relaxation, and exercise. But, as this book will illustrate, the mind is key in any transformation.

As individuals, we are all different. One person might become angry, while another might see the same situation as humorous. Your personality is important in diagnosing whether a situation is potentially harmful or threatening. What is clear is that individuals may consciously and unconsciously decide what is threatening and what is not. In the same way, we decide whether to be angry or not.

The first step in this book should help you assess who you are.

PRINCIPLE 2:
Control Your Organization: Don't Let It Control You

KNOW HOW TO MANAGE YOUR STRESS-PROMOTING ORGANIZATION

I like my job and am good at it, but it sure
grinds me down sometimes, and the last thing
I need to take home is a headache.

—TV COMMERCIAL FOR ANACIN

Many stressful organizational events and relationships—the pace of work, constant change, career blockages, retiring, losing one's job, taking on a new job, and so forth—are hard to avoid. Principle 2 encourages you to understand those issues and events in the organization that seem out of your control. It highlights how to deal with the stress of organizational change, career and environmental issues, and life events. Subsequent chapters illustrate other aspects of stress that come from the way the job is designed, unfriendly co-workers, and working with a harassing boss.

THE TYPE A ORGANIZATION

Many health problems, such as coronary heart disease, are a result of environments that encourage people to act like Type A individuals. They may not, in fact, have a natural personal style that is Type A, but their environment encourages people to have the same emotional responses. A Type A organization encourages people to respond like Type A individuals. People become more competitive, angry and hostile, perfectionistic, and so forth. If they don't, they feel that they will not be effective.

For many employed individuals, the organization occupies far more than a mere forty-hour week. Organizational-related tasks, such as preparing for work, commuting to work, lunches, and discussions about the job after hours can increase the workday to a minimum of ten hours, and sometimes eleven or twelve. Many people stay long at the office, take work home in the evenings, and regularly return to work on weekends. The organizations we work for may consume 70 percent of nonsleep time for some individuals.

We spend a great deal of time in our organizations, and many people find a substantial proportion of their lives consumed by the activities of administration, management, or simply surviving at work. Organizational stressors are usually extrinsic to the job itself and arise from issues relating to policies and procedures, pay, fringe benefits, general safety, and the way the organization is managed.

A "DOG-EAT-DOG" ATMOSPHERE MAKES IT DIFFICULT TO DO THE REAL WORK THAT IS PART OF THE JOB.

People are constantly responding to changes in policies, supplying information for others, or answering complaints and intrusions by personnel and financial administrators over getting paid and redefining their authority and responsibilities. Many are involved in equity disputes, pay disputes, grievances over poor management, and suggestions by financial managers to justify the existence of certain programs or plans. As a result, the organization is like a battlefield where the players are fighting over turf, territory, and jurisdiction.

The pressures in an organization are further complicated by pressures from the home and family. Organizational deadlines put stress on the family while personal and family events create demands at work. Conflicts arise among our various roles and are often stress evoking, as when problems at work clash with those of a sick parent or child, or when a supervisor is divided between loyalty to her superiors and to fellow workers and subordinates. Given these pressures, there is little employer sympathy for stressed workers in a time of worldwide budget restrains. Even co-workers may complain about those who take time off for sickness or holidays.

PERSPECTIVE 6. STRESS AND DOWNSIZING A WORKFORCE

Bill Smith was a midlevel office worker at an electric power company until his position was eliminated during the height of a recent restraint program and downsizing. Smith took sick leave when he was threatened with a job change, claiming he suffered from stress. Since then, he has been collecting disability benefits payments and suggesting that he is unable to return to work. He may very well be on long-term disability for the rest of his life. After two years of stress leave, the company hired a psychologist to assist him to return to a new job with many members of his former work team. In the midst of the return, team members said they would refuse to work with him.

John Dobson, an engineer with the Department of Transportation, was faced with working long hours to keep up with the extra demands from downsizing and privatization. He had just taken over the position of acting planning director, as the previous director had been moved to another position. John was a conscientious engineer who took pride in his work and was generally liked and respected by his colleagues. He was somewhat of a perfectionist and liked to make sure the plans of his department were well done. To complete his assignments during this period of demand, John worked into the late evening hours and on weekends. John Dobson was found dead at the bottom of an open stairwell in the Department of Transportation. The death was diagnosed as a suicide, and the government department began an investigation on stress among its workers. The investigator reported that many workers in the department of 4,000 workers were experiencing alarming levels of stress, the highest he had seen in all the studies he had conducted.

Jane Brown, a former director of a national social program, didn't fit into her department's restructuring plans. Brown wasn't cast out of the public service altogether, just demoted and stripped of her management pay. She's at home now, claiming illness, and marking time on temporary sick leave payments until she qualifies next year for the long-term disability plan.

In the above perspective, Smith, Dobson, and Brown are borrowed names for three employees who illustrate some of the repercussions of occupational stress during a time of restraint and downsizing in some organizations. Many of these employees pay their rent and buy groceries with sick-leave benefit checks instead of salaries. Most have legitimate illness or injuries that prevent them from doing their jobs. Many others are in a gray area. They are displaced, demoted, and disenchanted and have sought refuge in their organizations' generous disability programs.

Since organizational downsizing and restraint programs began, employee rolls have declined steadily and disability claims have increased by over 100 percent. The director of a life insurance company that manages one program suggests that stress is second to heart disease in conditions that lead to long-term disability. A displaced employee experiences severe mental anguish, frustration, and lack of support. Some depressed employees stay at home, some take to drinking, while others take out their frustrations on family members. Physicians argue that disorders such as loss of appetite, sleeplessness, alcohol abuse, disinterest in sex, and irritability are just as legitimate occupational health problems as a broken arm or a slipped disc.

These cases illustrate how stress affects people in organizations. Stress occurs when an issue or person (such as a loss of a job or a supervisor) is perceived as presenting a demand that threatens a person or exceeds his or her capability for meeting it. In this definition, stress is largely perceptual—different individuals may react to the same situation with entirely different stress levels. However, certain organizations and environments are more likely to be stress promoting.

THE STRESS OF A TYPE A ORGANIZATION

Among other things, the stress of a Type A organization might be described by work overload, unclear and unrealistic goals, career blockage, and unresponsiveness to individual needs and values. Type B environments encourage individuals to prioritize their workload within clear goals and objectives based on individuals' career objectives and values.

TABLE 6.1 TYPE A AND B ORGANIZATIONAL ENVIRONMENTS

Type A Environments	Type B Environments
■ Organizations where tasks are overloading or underloading	■ Organizations where tasks are carried out within clear priorities
■ Environments where goals are unclear or unrealistic	■ Environments where goals are clearer and important
■ Environments where one's career is blocked	■ Environments where one's career can develop
■ An organizational hierarchy that is unresponsive to individual needs and values	■ An organizational hierarchy that is responsive to individual needs and values

Work Overload

The pressures of having too much work to do or feeling that one has too much to do is an obvious stressor. It is most evident in the effect of working long hours. In one study of heart attack patients, 25 percent of them had been working two jobs and an additional 45 percent had jobs that required them to work more than sixty hours per week. Another study reported that employees in light industry who worked more than forty-eight hours a week had twice the risk of death from coronary heart disease as a similar sample of employees working forty hours or less.

OVERLOAD CAN BE BOTH QUANTITATIVE (HAVING TOO MUCH TO DO) OR QUALITATIVE (HAVING TASKS THAT ARE TOO DIFFICULT OR CHALLENGING).

Quantitative overload may be simply long work hours without adequate rest periods, excessive overtime, or taking on more than one job. It can be created by too many phone calls, meetings, and work interruptions or by the imposition of unrealistic expectations or deadlines. Most recently, it has been creeping into organizational environments that require employees to do more with less. Fewer people are available to do the work, and the demand for services is increasing.

Qualitative overload is experienced by people whose work demands continuous concentration or who are exposed to situations of intense emotion and feelings. Air traffic controllers and surgeons who are required to perform concentrated operations or procedures may experience such stress. Nurses and social workers may experience intense emotional drain from disappointments over the failure of some patients to respond to their concentrated efforts.

OVERLOAD, WHETHER QUANTITATIVE OR QUALITATIVE, LEADS TO BREAKDOWN.

TEST 6. THE O INDEX

This questionnaire asks about the stress you experience in your work environment. Please think about present and recent complaints, not those that you had in the distant past. It is *important* that you answer *all* the questions.

1	2	3	4
Very Untrue	Somewhat Untrue	Somewhat True	Very True

_____ 1. I tend to set a number of deadlines that I cannot always meet.

_____ 2. I am generally dissatisfied with my career progress.

_____ 3. I feel I have little control over my work because of the procedures and regulations required.

_____ 4. I tend to feel that there is little challenge in the goals and tasks I undertake.

_____ 5. I often feel emotionally drained from the work that I have to do.

_____ 6. I work over forty-eight hours per week.

_____ 7. I feel I am hurting my career by staying in this organization.

_____ 8. I feel I am part of a large impersonal bureaucracy.

_____ 9. I feel that the goals I set are vague and ill defined.

_____ 10. I often wish I did not have so much to do and that someone would relieve me of my workload.

_____ 11. All in all, the number of tasks that I have to do each day can not be completed within the normal working day.

_____ 12. I feel that I cannot progress in this organization no matter how effective I am.

_____ 13. The size of this organization makes it very difficult to take on personal ownership for any task.

_____ 14. I am often blocked in the pursuit of my work-related goals (by conflicts, implementation difficulties, and so forth).

_____ 15. I often feel that I need a break from the action.

_____ 16. I often feel compelled to take work home or stay late in the evening to complete my work.

_____ 17. I have few opportunities to move ahead in my job or career.

_____ 18. I tend to find it very difficult to be loyal to this organization.

_____ 19. The goals and tasks I undertake are rarely my own or are set by others.

_____ 20. Much of my work involves me in tasks that require intense periods of concentration.

SCORING TEST 6. UNDERSTANDING YOUR ORGANIZATIONAL STRESSORS

The questionnaire measures five aspects of organizational stress: work overload, qualitative overload, pay and career stress, change and lack of control, and lack of clarity of policies and procedures. The item numbers and appropriate categories are listed below. Add your responses for each category and arrive at a total for each one.

QUANTITATIVE Work Overload	QUALITATIVE Work Overload	Unresponsive Hierarchy	Unrealistic Goals	Career Stresses
1. _____	5. _____	3. _____	4. _____	2. _____
6. _____	10. _____	8. _____	9. _____	7. _____
11. _____	15. _____	13. _____	14. _____	12. _____
16. _____	20. _____	17. _____	18. _____	19. _____
Totals _____	_____	_____	_____	_____

Overall total _____

Interpreting Your Score

The significance of each score will vary from individual to individual. As a general guide, high scores for each subcategory would be greater than 10. A overall score of greater than 40 would be considered high.

Responding to Work Overload or Underload

WORK OVERLOAD IS LIKE "BATTLE FATIGUE." YOU BEGIN TO WEAR DOWN. YOU ARE TIRED AND YOU DO NOT REALLY KNOW IT.

When you perceive that work overload or underload is a problem, you might take the following steps:

■ Develop a record of the types of activities you do each day. Be very clear on those activities you can plan for and those that are interruptions, those that are mundane, and those that are critical.

- Which activities are most important to your organization, your career, and your personal priorities? Which can you drop?.

- Define your job expectations and requirements. Are they realistic? Do you need to reclarify or rearticulate them? Should you talk to your supervisor and indicate the overload problem and the priorities you are suggesting?

Unclear and Unrealistic Goals

Most organizations have stacks of policies and procedures concerning assignments and goals for carrying out the work. Some policies, procedures, and goals are very loose and flexible, while others provide a firm set of guidelines that must be followed. Other organizations do not have clear policies either because they are not plainly outlined or because they are inconsistently administered.

Strictly defined policies and procedures create certain types of stress from red tape, bureaucracy, paperwork, forms to complete, and procedures to follow. There are rules for parking a car, using office equipment, talking on the telephone, and taking lunch breaks. Unwritten rules, or norms, dictate what to wear, how to address a supervisor, or the need to work long hours. These rules and norms dictate practices that provide a maze of standards by which to abide. While certain policies and practices might be seen as stressful because they are restricting, it may also be stressful to have no set of guidelines at all. In some cases, employees will not know how to behave or which rules apply. Some people choose to observe a more flexible work schedule while others choose to punctually report for work at 8:30 a.m. One person may wish to smoke in the office while others feel that smoking should not be permitted. Such situations, where there are no clear rules and direction, are more stressful than where rules and procedures are overly restrictive.

Lack of clarity about one's role, job objectives, and the scope of responsibility is called role ambiguity. Almost everyone experiences some degree of role ambiguity relating to promotion or transfer, the first job, a new boss, the first supervisorial responsibility, a new company, or a change in the structure of the existing organization. No company can be structured or managed in a way that will eliminate ambiguity. Usually, such ambiguity relates to lack of definition, challenge, and input and difficulties in implementing policies, goals, or procedures.

Those people who experience ongoing role ambiguity report less productivity, more job dissatisfaction, more job-related tension, and low levels of self-confidence. This ambiguity may be associated with indicators of poor physical and mental health such as elevated blood pressure. It has also been linked to depressed moods, low self-esteem, decreased life satisfaction, low levels of work motivation, and expressed intentions to quit an organization.

Responding to Unrealistic and Unclear Goals

When you perceive that role ambiguity or lack of clarity is a problem, you might take the following steps in responding:

- Define your priorities and objectives. Be very clear on what is of most value to your career, organization, and personal priorities.
- Define your job expectations and requirements. Are they realistic? Do you need to reclarify or rearticulate them?
- Ask questions of others. What do they think are the most important priorities? What are norms that we should follow?

Career Blockages

In order for a person to become self-motivated and responsible, he or she must first be able to respond to the basic demands of existence. In other words, it is difficult to think of long-term career needs if a person does not have some degree of economic security and safety.

Extrinsic motivations are derived from sources other than the job itself and are concerned with pay, fringe benefits, general safety, and supervision. Pay and other extrinsic factors are not stressful unless there is a perceived inequity or the individual has high expectations of achieving a reward, promotion, or benefit. Pay, general safety, working conditions, threats of work loss, supervision, holidays, and pensions are all potentially stressful. The stress may result from the ability of informal groups or unions to emphasize higher expectations or perceived inequities. Thus, laborers usually experience a great deal of stress during labor-management conflict over demands for greater pay. Regardless of pay increases, it is unlikely that performance or satisfaction will increase or overall stress will be reduced significantly unless other workplace stressors are dealt with.

My Days are phantom days, each one
The shadow of a hope;
My real life never was begun
Nor any of my real deeds done

—ARTHUR UPSON, *PHANTOM LIFE*

A person's career can be a source of anxiety and frustration. Stress results over issues of job security, promotions being blocked, or being unable to realize one's career aspirations. Career stressors can affect anyone at any time. However, they seem to be more prevalent for people between the ages of forty to fifty. It is during this period that many individuals experience doubts about the quality of their careers and the likelihood of significant future contributions. This stress shows up in a variety of ways at work:

- reduction in the quality or quantity of work produced
- increases in accident frequencies
- alcoholism or drug abuse
- declining interpersonal relations in the job
- unwillingness by the individual to perform certain tasks
- the tendency to question and challenge previously accepted management practices
- a renewed interest in nonjob activities; for example, real estate, private business, or personal activities.

The vanity of human life is like a river,
constantly passing away,
and yet constantly coming on.

—ALEXANDER POPE

Organizational changes can create a great deal of turmoil, and workers often express concern and anxiety about their careers. Managers may implement new ideas without appropriately communicating their goals and plans.

As a result, employees feel uncertain about their futures, which is likely to encourage a range of rumors about what managers are planning to do. Even where there are attempts to communicate the progress of a change, managers have been criticized for not recognizing the fears, stress, and human needs of people who are facing a potential job loss.

The impact of many organizational changes often requires workers to transfer to new jobs and locations, learn new skills, and carry out more specialized work. Impending transfers cause workers to express considerable anxiety; for example:

- It is just not possible to sell our house. I would have to sell at a loss.

- The moves they are planning are part of a cold, calculated strategy to get rid of as many employees as possible.

- A move to a new location may not be so bad, but what if they ask me to move again and again?

Workers may express dismay about the financial losses they are facing:

- We have worked our asses off for twelve years to buy a trailer and a lot to sit it on; it's all we have. . . . It's worth nothing if we have to move. . . . I feel like I've worked myself into a corner and there is no way out.

When a change is introduced, existing patterns and values may be disrupted. The degree of personal trauma is associated with how people adjust to the uncertainties they face. Reactions during a period of change range from rejection and withdrawal to fundamental shifts in thinking and behavior.

Changes are consistently seen as sources of uncertainty for organizations. When they are originally conceived, they can create a stage where anticipations run wild. Uncertainty and anxiety can lead to such dysfunctional outcomes as stress, job dissatisfaction, low trust in the organization and lack of commitment, and increased desires to quit. Workers fear job loss and the costs of relocation and generally mistrust management motives. Some people feel more dissatisfied, express more job tension, and spend more of their time than others worrying and talking about management motives and potential.

Organizational changes alter tasks and skills. New technologies provide new equipment designs that reduce the amount of knowledge and discretion employees need to perform their work. Tasks may become more predictable, specific, routine, and reliable. These changes, in turn, may alter the individual's desire to work and may have long-term effects on his or her contribution to the organization.

In some ways, career stresses from organizational changes are the most difficult to deal with because they are the hardest to control. The strategy for dealing with these stressors depends on our ability to plan our future.

Responding to Perceived Career Blockages

When you perceive that you are blocked in your career, you must evaluate whether it is possible to unblock yourself. The ideal solution would be for you to adjust to your deficiencies or have your organization develop a commitment to your career development.

Some organizational situations are unlikely to change. Or, you may find it very difficult to change your style. In such cases, you might be better off in some other organization. But before you quit, consider that you might be able to continue to work for your organization and still find fulfillment in a career.

Many people choose to fulfill themselves outside their places of employment. Volunteer organizations and community groups need help. If you are not spending time with your family, you might evaluate how important your family is to you. Other people find fulfillment in developing a business that they can work at on the side.

Here are some questions you might consider if you are blocked in your career:

- Define what is blocking you. Is it organizational politics? In most cases, interpersonal issues are the dominant factor.

- Reassess your skills and career goals. What do you want to do in life? What are your values? Can you fulfill your values and expectations in ways other than work?

- Ask questions of others. What do they think are the most important priorities? What are norms that people should follow?

- If you perceive you are blocked in your career, you must take some action by either changing your style and getting more involved in your organization or finding extraorganizational ways to fulfill your interests. People who feel fulfilled live longer.

An Unresponsive Organizational Hierarchy

In common conversation, the word *bureaucracy* is often used to denote endless amounts of red tape and an unresponsive organizational hierarchy.

Classical sociologists use the term to point to a phenomenon of growing importance—the large organization with fixed positions linked together in a hierarchical pyramid, with specialization and division of labor, and with established rules and regulations governing behavior.

Administrative acts, decisions, and rules are formulated and recorded in writing, even in cases where oral discussion is the rule or is even mandatory. Actually, a bureacracy can be any administration that has certain degrees of complexity.

In a bureaucracy, authority is legitimized by a belief in the correctness of the rules, and the loyalty of the bureaucrat is oriented to a superior position, not to the person who holds it. What makes an organization more or less bureaucratic is not simply the existence of rules, but the dominance of the rules and the extent to which they are proceduralized and formalized.

Organizations become more impersonal as they become increasingly proceduralized and formalized. They become more hierarchical as they become more sophisticated, automated, and specialized.

> **AS ORGANIZATIONS BECOME MORE IMPERSONAL AND HIERARCHICAL, WE CAN EXPECT MORE EMPLOYEE DISSATISFACTION AND STRESS. THE STRESS IS GREATEST FOR THOSE WHO ARE AT LOWER LEVELS.**

The hierarchy may play an important part in generating social inequalities in people of working age. Michael Marmot and Martin Shipley at University College London's Medical School studied more than 18,000 men who worked in the British Civil Service.

> **THOSE AT LOWER GRADES DIED SOONER AFTER RETIREMENT THAN THOSE WHO REACHED HIGHER RANKS.**

Overall, 30 percent of those in the administrative grade died during the twenty-five year follow-up compared to 69 percent of those in the lowest grade.

This study and others clearly show the costs of being caught up in a hierarchy and being unable to rise to the higher ranks.

The negative effects of the hierarchy occur because people cannot control their lives and are not sure what to anticipate. Uncertainty is more disruptive and controversial than the jobs that people are doing. The resulting deterioration in morale is fed by an informal atmosphere of negativism and anger. Such an atmosphere is likely to increase rather than reduce uncertainty and the inaccurate flow of information, which leads to increased anxiety and a range of counterproductive behaviors.

Responding to an Unresponsive Organizational Hierarchy

The facts are clear. People in low-level bureaucractic positions die younger. This is why many very competent people are leaving bureaucratic organizations. At the very least, they are recognizing the need to find fulfillment in extraorganizational activities.

Here are some questions you might consider if you are working in a large hierarchical organization:

- How would you describe the organization in which you are working? Is it highly formalized, proceduralized, and impersonal?

- What are your opportunities to move up the organizational hierarchy? What are your aspirations?

- Reassess your goals and values. Can you find ways to fulfill your interests outside large hierarchical organizations, where you can have more control?

CONCLUSION

This chapter outlined many of the organizational stressors that may provoke you. In organizations, the most important stressors are:

- qualitative and quantitative overload
- unclear and unrealistic goals
- career blockages
- a hierarchy that is unresponsive to individual needs

The importance of understanding individual differences is one of the key elements of stress management. One person's stressor is another person's stimulus. Because of this, your stress plan is a very personal document that evolves from your personality and unique interactions.

The planning process outlined in this chapter is only a starting point to help you focus your attention on developing your stress management plan. It should help you respond to some of your key organizational stressors. It can assist you to respond to the stressors that are bothering you now. Subsequent chapters will provide more information on how to respond to stress by developing a clear idea of your personal mission, values, and vision.

PRINCIPLE 3:
Establish Winning Relationships

COPING WITH STRESS-PROMOTING RELATIONSHIPS

A loving person lives in a loving world.
A hostile person lives in a hostile world:
everyone you meet is your mirror.

—KEN KEYES

PEOPLE CAN BE A MAJOR SOURCE OF STRESS.

One of the most serious types of stress we face comes from our relationships, whether they are with supervisors, work colleagues, close friends, neighbors, or community members. Most of us have interacted with at least one person we dislike or with whom we disagree. Disagreeable people are seen as controlling, caustic, and negative. Interactions will likely disturb us, bother us, affect our sleep, or consume a great deal of energy, thought, and time.

INTERPERSONAL STRESS AND HARASSMENT

Interpersonal stress results from the tensions of working with or for other people. Stress is as much a part of our intimate relationships as with those of work colleagues, clients, and customers.

PERSPECTIVE 7. A PERSONAL STORY

It is late at night, 3:23 A.M. to be exact. I cannot sleep. Again. Every time I close my eyes, I think about what happened to me yesterday. The scene is alive in my mind where a colleague (Brad) suggested that I had been manipulative. He said that I had written the report and that I had lied and was trying to exclude his work from our project.

I was helpless at first, mute and extremely hurt. I strive very hard to be principled, to be honest and integrative rather than conflictive and divisive. Why must he treat me this way? I was unable to express myself. Other people tried to help and deflate his comments and support me. But Brad kept speaking, and he pointed his finger at me. He was threatening me.

Finally, I lost it. I let go and called him a little fool, among other things. I told him that his ego was getting in the way of his logic. I'm afraid I went on a bit.

I try to take my thoughts away from this event and look again at the clock. Thirty minutes have passed. I try to meditate but my mind keeps coming back to this incident. I think of things that I could have done to be a good facilitator and problem solver. These are brilliant ideas that would have moved Brad to speechlessness, or, better yet, recognition that I am right and he is wrong. I see them now.

But when a person acts like Brad, I cannot let him get away with it.

My breathing slows a bit, and I get up and go downstairs and make myself some green tea.

I again return to bed and tell myself to think of relaxing, breathing calmness in and tension out.

I still cannot sleep.

Employees complain that their bosses play favorites, are autocratic and unresponsive, or are untrustworthy. They also complain about their co-workers, indicating that they are uncooperative or dishonorable. Clients are often thought of as overdemanding, selfish, and uncompromising.

On the job, pressures grow from working with others, from disagreements among co-workers, and from complaints from clients, managers, union officials, or interest groups. Public servants dislike having to face a cranky public in places like unemployment offices, police stations, and tax departments. The public is often angry at what they perceive to be unresponsive government workers. Business managers complain about overly demanding consumers and unmotivated employees, while consumers feel angered about what they perceive to be shoddy products and services.

Differences between men and women have as much to do with how we are raised as they do with the biology of the brain.

Pressures in the home can involve children. Children fight with parents over family issues ranging from television habits and staying out at night to taking on more responsibility in the home. For example, Sharon was a single mother with a seventeen-year-old son. "I didn't say anything when he came home with purple hair and earrings on various parts of his body. I accepted that and felt that this was his way of asserting himself. But I finally blew up when he put a tattoo on his arm with the "F" word. This marked him. . . . He said I was trying to control him, so he left home. He came back three days later, and I told him he would have to change. We have some rules now. We'll see how this works."

The stresses encountered in interpersonal relationship are worse today than they have ever been. They will be even worse in the future as society grows more complex and we are forced to respond to an ever-increasing number of challenges in work and the home.

PERSPECTIVE 8. WHO'S THE MOST DIFFICULT PERSON YOU ENCOUNTER?

1. List three people you find most difficult to relate to and who bother you, frustrate you, and use up a great deal of your mental time and energy.
2. As specifically as you can, write down what makes each person difficult.
3. Write down how you respond to these people. Do you fight back and argue? Do you withdraw? How much time do you spend thinking about them?
4. What would you want to happen differently?

What do most people say when they talk about the difficult people they encounter? Phrases that describe these people include:

■ He's terribly uncommunicative. He doesn't talk to people. His wife often asks me what he's thinking.

■ I can't trust her. She is very pleasant on the surface. But she has her own interest that she is serving.

■ He simply doesn't listen. He's always talking about himself.

■ It's a political game with her. All she wants is power over me. She wants me to do what she wants and to serve her interest.

■ Whenever something goes wrong, he has to find someone to blame.

What is the basis for these comments?

HOW DO INTERPERSONAL RELATIONSHIPS DETERIORATE?

When we depend on others to complete a task, there is a potential for conflict. Conflict is a statement of the relationship between people. It seems very easy to move from a positive, reinforcing relationship to a negative, angry relationship. When relationships deteriorate, it is sometimes very difficult to reinvigorate them. Damaged relationships are like a cancer. A surgeon might cut out the cancer in one part of the body, only to watch it grow in other parts. In the same way, once a relationship begins to deteriorate, it is difficult to stop it.

TEST 7. THE IS INDEX

This test asks you to respond to questions about your work environment. Please answer *all* the questions using the following scale.

1	2	3	4
Very Untrue	Somewhat Untrue	Somewhat True	Very True

_____ 1. I tend to feel that I am being watched closely by my supervisor.

_____ 2. The morale of my peer group creates extra tensions in my work.

_____ 3. I have more responsibility for the supervision and guidance of people than for things.

_____ 4. I have the feeling that I will be unjustly criticized for a job failure that may not be in my control.

_____ 5. My co-workers are very unfriendly.

_____ 6. I am responsible for the development of others.

_____ 7. I feel I do not get the support that I deserve from my supervisor.

_____ 8. There is a low level of trust among my co-workers.

_____ 9. I tend to meet informally with others to assist them with their careers.

_____ 10. My duties and tasks are not clearly laid out for me so that I can do my job well.

_____ 11. I cannot count on my team members for support and guidance when I have difficulties.

_____ 12. When others have problems, they usually come to me.

SCORING TEST 7. THE IS INDEX: ASSESSING THE INTERPERSONAL RELATIONSHIPS IN YOUR WORK ENVIRONMENT

The item numbers and appropriate categories are listed below. Add your responses for each category and arrive at a total for each one.

Responsibilities for Others	Interpersonal Support	Managerial Support
3._____	2._____	1._____
6._____	5._____	4._____
9._____	8._____	7._____
12._____	11._____	10._____
_____ +	_____ +	_____ = _____ Totals

Interpreting Your Score

The significance of each score varies from individual to individual. As a general guide, high scores for each subcategory would be greater than 10. An overall score greater than 24 would be considered high. Environments that are more likely to provoke stress are those where you have responsibility for supervising others and where colleagues and supervisors are not supportive.

A supportive and positive interpersonal relationship is created by:

▪ the interpersonal support you have from others
▪ your responsibilities for others
▪ the style of your supervisors or managers

Stress from Lack of Interpersonal Support

Interpersonal support binds people together, just as lack of trust can break people apart. It is the cement that is the foundation for interpersonal integrity.

A supportive environment is not some 1960s dream of a loving, trusting commune of people who thrive on self-awareness, openness, and intimate feelings. Rather, support and trust is best illustrated in an environment where we feel bolstered by others, whether they are managers, work colleagues, spouses, or family members. When interpersonal support is absent, we may still be willing to help because of work attitudes and general professionalism, but we have no commitment to go the "extra mile."

How does interpersonal support deteriorate? We are sometimes hard pressed to define the details underlying feelings of lack of support and mistrust. Most people use terms such as *harassing, oppressive, dishonest, self-serving, back-stabbing, political,* and *selfish.* The true facts behind these labels may be hard to find.

Interpersonal support grows in settings where people are committed to relationships as the most important objective. Commitment to a relationship involves a willingness to be more concerned with people than with tasks. I learned a great deal about this principle when working with a colleague on a joint consulting project. I knew what we had to do, and I wanted to get on with it. He chose, however, to spend the time talking philosophically about relationships, values, and what he liked and disliked. We went for a walk and even drank a few beers at a bar. I was quite frustrated at the time. But, years later, I began to appreciate this. We have a very strong relationship. Whenever I have doubts about what we are doing, I remember our joint commitment to the relationship, no matter what the task.

Lynda offered the following comment about a friend who lied to her. "I was very shocked when I found out that she had lied to me. I just couldn't believe it. When I talked to her the next day, she denied it and acted like nothing had happened. I talked to others about it, and they said the same thing had happened to them."

Interpersonal support and trust develops when people feel they can rely on you for help and assistance. Help comes in many forms. Some people just want someone who is a friend.

A supportive environment, at home and in the workplace, can help people deal with stress. Interpersonal support might help people deal with potentially stressful situations at work or at home. It can buffer the effects of potentially stressful work problems, such as a boring job, a heavy workload, or fears of unemployment. When Janice was told she might lose her job, she spent many hours talking to me. I listened and offered to help. Frankly, I couldn't really do anything, except offer suggestions from time to time. When she left, I felt I had helped her and that Janice was going to do something to help herself.

A supportive relationship with spouse and family may help a person recognize that the job is not so important in the total context of life, and that stress on the job might be compensated for by satisfactions and accomplishments outside work. Support from co-workers can also buffer the stressful effects of crisis situations.

Interpersonal support and trust can also be used for dishonorable purposes. During the stress of conflict in a workplace, the support of others might serve to exaggerate feelings toward the opponents. Often, people who have unjustifiable causes have strong relationships that are fueled by their opposition to others rather than positive concerns for them. Criminals also have strong relationships with fellow criminals, just as terrorist groups are bonded together in their desire to accomplish a mission.

The point of developing interpersonal support and trust, in my view, is to gain help for yourself and to be helpful to others who need you.

Stress from Your Responsibilities for Others

All people have acted in some managerial capacity in one way or another. Managerial tasks are not only organizational but are also found in the home, community, and schools. They are performed by front-line workers in a street shelter for the homeless as well as an executive in charge of a large multinational corporation. The manager, either implicitly or explicitly, is responsible for the goals, standards, and contributions of others.

> **THE MORE A PERSON HAS RESPONSIBILITIES FOR MANAGING PEOPLE, IN COMPARISON TO MANAGING THINGS, THE MORE LIKELY HE OR SHE WILL FEEL STRESSED AND HAVE HIGH BLOOD PRESSURE AND ELEVATED CHOLESTEROL COUNTS.**

When you manage others, whether you are a parent or chief executive officer, you are likely to feel some pressure and stress. Any type of responsibility can be a burden, but, for people who are quite sensitive, responsibility for others is likely to be particularly stressful.

> **WE PROBABLY ALL KNOW SOMEBODY WHO SEEMED TO AGE AS A RESULT OF THE PRESSURES AND RESPONSIBILITIES OF A NEW MANAGEMENT JOB.**

Individuals who have significant levels of responsibility for people are more likely to suffer from heart disease than those who have responsibility for things. The pressures of interpersonal responsibilities frequently mean more meetings (that contribute to work overload and deadline pressures) and lack of control of one's agenda. When things go wrong, your role as parent or manager is the focal point for grievances and resolutions of problems. You are the person other people look to for solutions. You are often a dumping ground for complaints, concerns, and expectations.

Stress from Your Supervisors

People in organizations spend a great deal of time and energy discussing their managers, and many of their comments are not very positive. They talk about lack of recognition and direction as well as back-stabbing and favoritism. Many comments relate to the interest and support displayed by managers, and cover issues related to priorities, roles, purposes, goals, and identity. Many people say their managers are not interested in or support-ive of them. Some typical comments from employees include the following:

- I get the feeling we are pretty low on the priority list of the managers. To me, this indicates lack of interest and support.

- Some managers have never visited the job site and have little or no idea about what goes on.

- I have the perception that managers are not interested in worker happi-ness and welfare generally, they don't appear to be informed about what is happening with workers, and they don't seem to be concerned about asking us how we can help improve the organization.

How do you better manage relationships? Whether you work as a parent or a manager in a hospital, government agency, or labor union, positive rela-tionships with others are important in defining whether your life is stressful.

DEVELOPING MECHANISMS FOR COLLABORATION IS A BASIC STRATEGY FOR RESPONDING TO A STRESSFUL ENVIRONMENT.

Working life can become more humanized and less stressful if extreme com-petitiveness is counteracted and a more communal approach is favored. Iso-lated and negative people have nearly twice the risk of early death as others, and not just because they're sicker or antisocial. In general, social involve-ment reduces risk. Death is more likely among those people who are single because of divorce or a spouse's death, do not participate in organizations, lack regular interactions with people or are hostile toward others and give and receive little social support.

STRATEGIES FOR REDUCING THE STRESS FROM INTERPERSONAL RELATIONS

THINK OF ONE OF YOUR MOST CONFLICTED RELATIONSHIPS. HOW CAN YOU MAKE THIS RELATIONSHIP LESS STRESSFUL?

Reducing stress from interpersonal conflict involves making choices among a number of strategies. Some strategies suggest ways of understanding dif-ferences and creating win/win solutions, while others are methods of coping.

Strategy A: Exploring the Origins of Stressful Relationships

Knowing why people cause you stress prepares you to take action.

Everyone brings to an interpersonal interaction a basket full of assumptions, values, and beliefs. Some of these might engender congenial, comfortable, productive discussions while others might lead to frustrating, conflicting, unproductive disagreements.

> **THE STRESS OF INTERPERSONAL RELATIONSHIPS COMES FROM ONE THING.**
> **PEOPLE ARE DIFFERENT IN FUNDAMENTAL WAYS.**

As individuals, we all want different things and have unique motivations, purposes, needs, values, beliefs, and impulses. Sometimes, these differences are hard to see; we tend to make judgments that others are mad, mean, stupid, or sick or that they are old, young, male, or female. In other words, we account for the variations we see in others in terms of their flaws, afflictions, race, age, or gender.

> **WE THINK, IF ONLY THEY WOULD BE MORE LIKE US. IF WE COULD PERSUADE**
> **THEM TO CHANGE, WE WOULD ALL BE BETTER OFF.**

It is very difficult to change people's values and beliefs. Getting another person to change is as difficult as asking a devout Muslim to accept Christianity, or vice versa. Most attempts to change spouses, offspring, or others result in resistance. The outcome is usually begrudging acceptance rather than transformation.

The belief that people are alike and can change is a neoclassical notion that is related to the idea that people in democratic societies are fundamentally equal. If they are equal, then we must be alike.

TEST 8. THE R INDEX

For each statement, place a number from 1 to 6 on the line to the left of the item. The numbers mean:

1	2	3	4	5	6
Definitely Not True	Not True	Tends to Not Be True	Tends to Be True	True	Especially True

_____ 1. I feel I am rather creative and imaginative.

_____ 2. I am generally outgoing in seeking people with whom to be friends.

_____ 3. I like to develop plans and programs much more than carry them out.

_____ 4. I prefer to work with others rather than by myself.

_____ 5. I find myself beginning my sentences with "I feel" rather than "I think."

_____ 6. I tend to be quite organized.

_____ 7. I would rather spend time meeting and working with others than be alone.

_____ 8. I often find that I have already made a decision while others are still considering the options.

_____ 9. I feel I would be called imaginative or intuitive rather than factual and systematic.

_____ 10. I like people who express their feelings.

_____ 11. I do not consciously try to control my feelings and hunches when making decisions.

_____ 12. My vision of what I want to do is quite important to me.

_____ 13. I do not like people who keep their private feelings to themselves.

_____ 14. Everything in my work space is neatly arranged.

_____ 15. I am not inclined to carry out an extensive analysis of trends.

_____ 16. I am a sensitive person.

_____ 17. I like to do things with others much more than doing them by myself.

_____ 18. I like to make sure things are really clear before I start them.

_____ 19. I see myself as more outgoing rather than reclusive.

_____ 20. Predictability is quite important me.

SCORING TEST 8. THE R INDEX

The purpose of this inventory is to give you a picture of your interpersonal style. Are you intuitive or sensing? Are you an extrovert or an introvert? Are you a thinking or a feeling person? Are you a judging or a perceiving person? Your style dictates how you relate to others. You may find that your style is quite different from others with whom you deal. This may be why there is conflict in your relationships.

Enter your scores below and total the results:

(N) Intuitive or (S) Sensing	(E) Extroversion or (I) Introversion	(F) Feeling or (T) Thinking	(J) Judging or (P) Perceiving
1. _____	2. _____	5. _____	6. _____
3. _____	4. _____	10. _____	8. _____
9. _____	7. _____	11. _____	14. _____
12. _____	17. _____	13. _____	18. _____
15. _____	19. _____	16. _____	20. _____

Total your scores

N _____   E _____   F _____   J _____

Interpreting Your Scores

(N) Intuition versus (S) Sensing. The N score reflects your intuitive style. Scores of 15 and higher suggest you are intuitive. Scores lower than 15 suggest you are more sensing than intuitive. High scores are greater than 24 (high intuition). Low scores are less than 12 (high sensing).

(E) Extrovert versus (I) Introvert. The E score reflects your extrovert style. Scores of 15 and higher suggest you are an extrovert. Scores lower than 15 suggest you are more introvert than extrovert. High scores are greater than 24 (high extrovert). Low scores are less than 12 (high introvert).

(F) Feeling versus (T) Thinking. The F score reflects whether you use a feeling style more than a thinking style. Scores of 15 and higher suggest you are a feeling person. Scores lower than 15 suggest you are more thinking than feeling. High scores are greater than 24 (high feeling). Low scores are less than 12 (high thinking).

(J) Judging versus (P) Perceiving. The J score reflects your judging style. Scores of 15 and higher suggest you are judging. Scores lower than 15 suggest you are more perceiving than judging. High scores are greater than 24 (high judging). Low scores are less than 12 (high perceiving).

In 1920, Carl Jung illustrated how people are fundamentally unique and different. Even though they have a multitude of instincts and preferences that drive them, he offered a typology to describe these differences. He suggested that we think of four basic preferences; extrovert/introvert, intuitive/sensing, thinking/feeling and judging/perceiving.

WHY DO EXTROVERTS AND INTROVERTS CAUSE EACH OTHER STRESS?

Extroverts have a high need for sociability. They appear to be energized or "tuned up." The extrovert is more likely to say, "I am outgoing, I like to go to parties, I like to do things in a group, I like to start conversations with strangers."

While the extrovert seeks contacts with others, the introvert is energized by solitude. The introvert prefers to be alone and says, "I like to be by myself, I am more reserved, I seldom start conversations, I avoid parties."

Extroverts, with their need for sociability, are energized by talking, playing, and working with people. They experience loneliness when they are not in contact with people. The introvert, on the other hand, is territorial, desiring private places in their minds and the environment. They like solitary activities and working alone. They experience a sense of loneliness when surrounded by people they do not know.

About 75 percent of the population is more extrovert than introvert.

Extroverts look down at introverts for being unsociable, while introverts feel threatened by extroverts.

Extroverts can reduce their stress from introverts by trying to encourage them. Introverts will not initiate an interaction, but they go through life trying to be extroverts.

Extroverts are always talking and socializing and it is difficult for the introvert to get involved. Introverts can reduce their stress from extroverts by seeking to slow them down by asking questions to control some of the direction of a conversation.

WHY DO INTUITIVE PEOPLE AND SENSING PEOPLE CAUSE EACH OTHER STRESS?

A person who has a natural preference for sensing often describes himself or herself as wanting facts and other verifiable information. This person is concerned with what actually happened rather than worrying about what might happen in reality rather than the future. The intuitive person views the sensing person as plodding and exasperatingly slow. The intuitive person lives in anticipation, with visions, hunches, and the unconscious.

Alan described himself as a practical, factual person, and he loved to gather information on his favorite topic of automobile parking in the downtown core. He had details on parking rates, use of street parking and parking lots, and the average number of cars that used each of the central downtown streets. It was very hard to interest Alan in anything else. Jim was a very intuitive person who was full of ideas and visions of what might be done. His creativity was very motivating and inspiring.

When Allen and Jim tried to work together, very little was accomplished. Jim would often develop a great idea for how to improve things, and Alan would take on the task of gathering information to carry it out. When Alan reported back with the information in his usual boring and systematic fashion, Jim appeared disinterested. He was thinking of other ideas and had lost interest.

Sensing thinkers tackle information in a systematic manner. They excel in planning and organization, and they like to work according to an outline. Intuitive thinkers excel with elusive, hard-to-define problems. They may avoid committing themselves, and they may use a strategy of solution testing and trial and error. They may jump from one method to another, may discard information, and will make decisions based on intuition or "gut feel." They frequently redefine the problem as they proceed and try out one idea after another.

People collect information in different ways. Intuitive people focus on details and will digest and ponder individual facts and clues without trying to categorize them or fit them into conceptual schemes. Sherlock Holmes, an intuitive information gatherer, is always at odds with Dr. Watson and the detectives at Scotland Yard, who zeros in on the "obvious" suspect and fit the facts to build a case against him. Holmes is more an intuitive thinker who zeros in on odd, individual facts and details, eventually building a hypothesis and linking it to others.

The sensing person wants facts, trusts facts, and remembers facts. Experience that is anchored in the real world is critical.

About 75 percent of the population is more sensing and 25 percent is more intuitive. Women are described as being more intuitive than men.

The intuitive person prefers the future rather than the past, ideas rather than facts, and broad concepts rather than details.

The intuitive person can skip from one task to another, while the sensing person likes to make sure that each job is finished. The sensing person appears flighty or impractical or unrealistic. The intuitive view the sensing type as plodding and exasperatingly slow.

The best way for intuitive and sensing people to deal with each other is acceptance of the merits of each perspective. Both perspectives are extremely valuable, and any approach that recognizes and balances each one will be harmonious.

WHY DO THINKING PEOPLE AND FEELING PEOPLE CAUSE EACH OTHER STRESS?

Thinking people are impersonal in their relations with others. They are less emotionally sensitive than the feeling types and respond more positively to objectives, principles, policies, laws, criteria, and firmness. They tend to be good at arguments and try to persuade others using logic rather than emotion. Feeling people tend to be more subjective and make decisions on the basis of their personal impact on others.

There seems to be as many thinking people as feeling people in our population. Women are often more concerned with feelings than men.

A feeling person begins statements with "I feel we should . . ." and prefers to make decisions using his or her gut feelings and emotions. These persons use statements such as, "I would love to go there," or "I follow my passion."

Thinking people begin their statements with "I think we should . . ." and prefer to use logic and facts rather than emotions in making their decisions. They will use statements such as, "I think that is a logical way to proceed," or "Let's analyze all the alternatives."

Feeling people have a great deal of difficulty handling the emotions and stress of conflictive situations, while thinking people are more logical and do not emotionalize their conflicts or problems.

These differences are very fundamental and often lead to conflict. The best way for thinking people to deal with feeling people is for each to respect the perspective of others.

WHY DO JUDGING PEOPLE AND PERCEIVING PEOPLE CAUSE EACH OTHER STRESS?

People who prefer closure in their choice of options are likely to be the judging type. They tend to establish deadlines and to take them seriously and expect others to do the same. Judging people tend to use words that are associated with making a decision, planning ahead, completion, urgency, and deadlines. Perceiving people tend to take longer in making decisions and to keep options open for a longer period. They like to use words such as flexible, adaptable, variation, and open search. A curious conflict often exists between perceiving people who are responsible to judging supervisors who want to impose strict deadlines.

Perceiving thinkers suspend judgment and avoid preconceptions, and insist on a complete examination of a data set before deriving conclusions. Judging people filter, arrange, and weigh information on the basis of their mental frameworks. It is as if they had a mental picture that described, at the outset, the kinds of information that are important. They start right off looking for facts that fit their mental pictures. Judging thinkers are quick to make decisions and have a sense of urgency.

There seem to be as many judging people as perceiving people in our population.

Judging people have a strong work ethic and tend to describe perceiving people as indecisive, procrastinating, and critical. Perceiving people are often frustrated with judging people because they are hurried, have a tendency to jump into things too quickly, and are inflexible.

Judging people are often too quick to make judgments. Be careful with them, as they will form quick first impressions. They will make decisions on the basis of very little information, and it is very difficult to change their minds. Give them precise information. Deal with judging people by asking questions that illustrate other points of view.

Your preferences may be in conflict with others who are demanding that you be different. This causes the stress and conflict that sometimes exists between the planner and the engineer, the management professor and the manager, and the psychologist and the accountant. No organization or group is immune to conflict. Personalities clash over the smallest of issues. People battle openly and spend a great deal of energy trying to figure out ways of winning or getting even.

Several psychologists have used Jung's preferences to illustrate why people do not get along. When people understand their own styles of interacting, they may begin to recognize how this might affect other people. They might also begin to be more accepting of the differences of others.

PERSPECTIVE 9. REVIEW YOUR BASIC PREFERENCES

Are you an:

Extrovert	or	Introvert
Intuitive	or	Sensing
Judging	or	Perceiving
Thinking	or	Feeling

Review the Basic Preferences of a Person with Whom You Are in Conflict.

Underline His or Her Preferences

Is he or she an:

Extrovert	or	Introvert
Intuitive	or	Sensing
Judging	or	Perceiving
Thinking	or	Feeling

Does this help you understand why you are in conflict?

Battles over individual differences need not result in situations where people lose trust and commitment toward others. Conflict between individuals can be a healthy way of relating. What would your life be like if you never had a conflict? Some of the most intense conflicts in North America have been over race and gender. Some of these have been bitter and vicious but they have resulted in change.

Conflict is an opportunity to learn because it forces one to see another point of view. It offers the opportunity for personal growth and development in seeing things in different ways and in being creative.

Conflict can also be stressful and alienating. Such conflicts have tremendous costs on all of us and are destructive.

Conflict is not bad. It is the way that we deal with it that can be stressful and destructive. The key to diminishing the costs of destructive conflict comes from understanding what it is that makes people different. Know yourself and your opposition.

Strategy B: Creating Integrative Solutions

The stress from an interpersonal conflict is an indication of a difference or disagreement, a statement that something might be ineffective or problematic for one person or another. The stress might provide the seed for change.

> **PEOPLE ARE MORE LIKELY TO CHANGE DURING A PERIOD OF STRESS. THEY ARE ALSO QUITE LIKELY TO RESIST. THIS IS THE 50 PERCENT RULE.**

You have a 50 percent chance of continuing a conflict and a 50 percent chance of resolving it so that each person can win something. I was involved in a conflict with my daughter who had just returned from a party where people were smoking in an enclosed room. She has allergies and is potentially asthmatic. I questioned her about this and the importance of thinking of values of health. She immediately responded by saying I was trying to pick her friends for her. The conflict escalated, and both of us used words that we regretted afterwards. I thought that I had lost that battle and a lot of respect. She never talked to me about this issue again. However, over the following months, Julia quit going to those parties and has taken on a different group of friends. She never said anything to me about this. In her private moments with her mother, she admitted she was lonely and wanted to meet new people. Over the next year, she made a new set of friends. It has been hard for her.

Had it not been for this conflict, we might not have been able to focus this issue. The goal in a positive conflict resolution process is to encourage good disputes that allow people to focus on problem solving. The process encourages:

- a healthy relationship
- statement of emotional feelings
- focus on common goals
- statement of a range of alternatives

A HEALTHY PROBLEM-SOLVING RELATIONSHIP HAS CLEAR RULES THAT ARE NOT BASED ON INCOMPLETE INFORMATION OR ASSUMPTIONS.

If we do not have a clearly defined understanding of a relationship, we will make assumptions about others based on tidbits of information such as their mannerisms and posture, the ideas they express, and their facial features and disposition. These perceptions emerge very early in a relationship, often during the first four minutes or so. Often, these initial perceptions do not change; new information is often used to support initial judgments.

THINK OF THE LAST TIME YOU MET SOMEBODY NEW. HOW LONG DID IT TAKE TO KNOW WHETHER YOU WOULD LIKE OR DISLIKE THIS PERSON?

All people are unsure about a relationship at the beginning of an interaction. Even boxers entering a fighting ring have a better understanding of the rules. However, when a professional boxer meets a street fighter, the rules are not clear. A street fighter might feel that kicking and pulling hair is appropriate while the trained boxer expects that the fight would be carried out using the rules of the boxing ring. A willingness to fight fair will not establish a clear set of expectations because different people will have unique opinions of what is fair.

Even in wars, there have been attempts to establish rules for fighting fair. There are expectations that nuclear weapons and poison gas should not be used and that civilians and prisoners should be humanely treated. While our world leaders have tolerated war as a necessary evil, they have tried to establish codes of being fair and just. There has been stiff moral condemnation of those who have broken the rules of war, such as Hitler's killing of the Jews during World War II, and Saddam Hussein's rape of the environment and fire bombing of the Kurds.

If the relationship is not defined, people will make assumptions that are likely to be incorrect. The breakage of these expectations, whether they are articulated or not, is more serious than the dispute itself. A well-defined relationship has clearly understood guidelines for cooperation. People are clear on the rules, codes, and norms to be practiced in resolving a disagreement.

Joanne and Bob began their relationship in a bar. They immediately liked each other and, after a short, happy courtship, they decided to live together. Before they took the plunge, they met with a friend, a psychologist, who encouraged them to become clear about their relationship. Here are some questions the psychologist encouraged them to answer:

■ What are the long-term interests you share in this relationship?

■ What are some things that Bob might do to contribute to the relationship?

■ What are some things he might do to hurt it?

■ What are some things that Joanne might do to contribute to the relationship?

■ What are some things she might do to hurt it?

In response to the first question, they indicated they wanted to have a long-term relationship where they both grew together, where they could talk and share interests, and where they would develop a home and family.

They came up with a long list of do's and don'ts that covered topics of loyalty, spending time together relaxing, and so forth. Bob also mentioned that he really wanted Joanne to help him complete a book. Joanne took exception to this at first, but grew to like the idea. The book was later published with Bob and Joanne as co-authors.

I have used a similar set of questions to build a relationship between union executives and managers who were undertaking a more positive approach to labor relations. The questions are as useful for initiating a marriage or labor relations as they are for assisting cooperation in families or organizational teams.

IN MOST CONFLICT SITUATIONS, ESPECIALLY DURING THE EARLY STAGES, FEELINGS AND EMOTIONS MAY BE MUCH STRONGER THAN LOGIC OR FACT.

Feelings during a conflict may manifest themselves in tactics for getting even or doing battle in some form. In a conflict, we often react rather quickly to statements such as "You are wrong," "You don't have all the facts," or "I disagree." Some of us use more illustrative statements such as "You're crazy," "You don't know what you're talking about," or "You're in a different time zone."

Such statements usually evoke a range of defensive responses that rarely get the conflict resolved effectively. Roger Fisher and William Ury's book, *Getting to Yes,* reminds us that "negotiators are people first," and we are very often dealing with emotions resulting from breaches of trust and misunderstandings. People also need to save face, to look good, and to win.

Feelings tend to become entangled with a problem or issue. When a person states that there is a problem, there is often an assumption of blame. Problem statements such as "the video you sold me does not work," "I don't agree with this promotion decision," or "you're late" are often viewed as personal attacks. The assumption of blame implies the other party is responsible for fixing the problem. Getting beyond emotion is extremely important but very difficult to do. During the heat of conflict, we need to understand how our emotions are entangled with the issues or problem.

In most conflicts, people have strongly felt positions, things that they want to achieve. One person's or group's position is at odds with those held by others. One cause of many conflicts is that parties get caught into extreme positions to which they are personally committed. My wife and I became involved in a dispute over where to go on vacation. She wanted to go to Las Vegas to see some shows and to do some gambling. I hate gambling and wanted to spend the time together on the ski slopes of Aspen or Whistler. Each of us had a strongly held position.

Whenever she came up with logic to defend her position, I had a rebuttal. So we were at a stalemate. The tactic for resolving this conflict was to get beyond our positions and recognize our interests. Interests are needs that we both have in this dispute. My needs were:

- to go skiing
- to spend some time with my wife
- to do what I really wanted

Her interests or needs were:

- to spend time watching a show and gamble
- to spend time with me
- to do something she really wanted

Interests are best focused by asking, Why? Why do you need to go Las Vegas? Why do I need to go skiing? The answers to such questions begin a process of discovery.

If we are creative in looking for solutions that respond to our interests, we might come up with a number of options, such as going to Reno or some other place that allows both of us to meet our needs.

The process relies on an accurate definition of interests and the ability to revisit and understand the real interests. Such real interests are often concealed, and only after a great deal of probing can they be uncovered. For example, two parties were deadlocked over the price of a car the owner was selling. The buyer recognized that the seller could use the car for another month before he left the country. Thus, he calculated his price to be somewhat lower and indicated that he was willing to take delivery on the car a month later. This could save the seller the price of renting a car for the one-month period of time until he left. This interest—here, of needing the car— is easier to uncover in a healthy relationship where parties are willing to share and where one party has the ability to ask, Why? For example, Why are you selling the car at this time?

The best alternatives require creativity and brainstorming. This is a process in which parties are encouraged to see creative ideas.

Strategy 3: When Differences Cannot Be Overcome

People are different and it is not always possible for some to work together. We will always find ourselves in situations where these differences are hard to overcome, because of lack of time or because of the ulterior motives of the people involved.

Opposites attract, but they sometimes don't get along. Tensions exist between extrovert and introverts, between thinking and feeling people, between intuitive and sensing people, and between judging and perceptive people. When two people decide to get into a relationship, they often do so because they admire something in the other person that is lacking in themselves. These differences later give rise to tensions.

When forming business partnerships, we often seek people with different talents. One person may be very creative and imaginative while the other has an apptitude for detail and is systematic and factual. The tensions between these styles often frustrate them.

Individual differences become overwhelming when you cannot trust other people, and clearly, some people cannot be trusted. It is very hard to deal with the Saddam Husseins and Adolf Hitlers of the world, and we may be rather foolish to continue trying.

PERSPECTIVE 10. WORKING WITH A DIFFICULT PERSON

This is the story of John Low, an accountant in a large firm of two hundred and forty professional workers. A relentless manager, John was a hard worker and surrounded himself with a group of loyal lieutenants who would implement his orders and ideas. John Low would spend hours each morning carrying out a number of regular tasks such as approving project proposals, leave applications, and requests to make international telephone calls.

John Low constructed several control systems that forced his staff to complete regular progress reports on their work. He often called his employees at odd hours of the day. Sometimes, there were calls directly to people's homes, and at other times, there were messages left on the office answering machines at 8:10 in the morning or at 5:10 in the evening. There seemed to be an implication that good workers report early and leave late.

John began using the employees' own computers for surveillance. He monitored the number of hours an employee was logged on the computer network, and kept a record of E-mail and fax machine transmissions.

John's style had many effects on his employees. While they greeted him in a jovial manner and told him exactly what he wanted to hear, they feared what he would do if they complained or disagreed with him. There were stories of people whose contracts were not renewed or who had been stalled in their promotions.

No one dared to demonstrate their anger in a visible way, as they feared for their jobs and for the possibility that they might be formally charged. So the protests were silent. One person wrote a "poison letter" to all staff members. The unsigned letter was a critical account of John Low using words like incompetent, stupid, and beyond his level of competence. After this letter was distributed, John Low went on a hunt to try to find the person who sent it.

Staff had other tactics as well. They would insert plastic in the copying machine, causing a $200 repair bill. They would not be available for social functions like meetings with the president. Even personal requests from John Low were met with excuses such as, "I'd like to come, but I have a meeting at that time."

Some people are inherently conflictive and, even if you are skilled and well intentioned, you may find it difficult to develop a positive, let alone trusting, relationship. The survival tactics for dealing with the interpersonal stress from being around such difficult people include:

- Developing a support system
- Working within your values
- Developing strategies that reduce the conflict

Developing a Support System

> A SUPPORT SYSTEM PROVIDES EMOTIONAL ENCOURAGEMENT DURING DIFFICULT TIMES AND AN OPPORTUNITY TO RETHINK ONE'S IDEAS.

People who are part of your support system should not be selected just because they agree with you. This is like "fanning the fire." You could be wrong. You might need to change.

Never enter into a conflict with a difficult person by yourself. A support system helps you deal with the stress of a conflictive relationship as well providing a perspective to help you strategize. Most importantly, it helps you identify how you might change, if change is necessary.

Working Within Your Values

People seem to have a universal human tendency, common to all places and cultures, to exhibit in both verbal and nonverbal behavior some preferences and aversions, some obligations and prohibitions, some hopes and fears, some satisfactions and disappointments. People feel, express, and act on these values or concepts of good and bad.

In defining your values, you should respond to a range of questions relating to the people that stress you.

- What are some things that you feel especially good about doing when you are with these people?

- What are some things that you feel bad about when you are with these people?

- What are some things that might happen with these people that make you feel good?

- What are some things that might happen with these people who make you feel bad?

- What are some things that this person might do that would please you?

- What are some things that this person might do that would displease you?

After answering these questions, you might come up with a list of things that you value.

Your statement of values should help you focus on things you should do and not do for coping with these difficult people. Some things that you might do to develop a more positive environment might include the following:

- Be true to your values. Just because others cheat doesn't mean you should do it yourself.

- Meet weekly with somebody to talk and reflect on this conflict. Be careful to use the session for being positive rather than negative.

- Be sociable but detached.

Some things that you should do to help deal with seemingly impossible situations include:

■ Try not to work with people who are not trusting.

■ When in doubt about what to do with difficult people, don't get provoked. Say nothing.

■ If you must say something, ask a question.

■ When other people begin talking about this untrusting person, indicate you have no desire to talk about him or her.

■ Don't let difficult people control you. Whenever you are in direct conflict, strategize how to respond.

Where Do You Go From Here?

■ Develop a support system of one or two people you can trust. Define these relationships in terms of what you both can gain from them. Be explicit in that what you want to do is use the relationships to provide you with feedback, help you handle stress better, and so forth.

■ Begin to analyze those relationships that stress you and then develop values for how you should respond.

PRINCIPLE 4:
Enrich Your Job

AVOID BURNOUT AND RUSTOUT

There is dignity in work only when
it is work freely accepted

—ALBERT CAMUS

Work, according to Studs Terkel, is akin to violence against the spirit and the body. We find ulcers, accidents, shouting matches, and fist fights, nervous breakdowns as well as physical abuse. Above all, people feel frustrated, humiliated. To survive the day is triumph enough for the walking wounded among the great many of us.

The work that a person does is much more than the job that a person has to do. Work is affected by the organization and the way people are treated as much as by interpersonal relationships on and off the job. A range of stressors exists in any work setting.

■ Our postindustrial society has fostered much mechanization and automation, and workers' tasks have become increasingly specialized. An organization is like a machine that has many individual parts and functions, each of which has to be coordinated. As such, managers set objectives, standards, and measurements, and errors are caught and corrected by specialists who play a role in training and coordinating employees to work within defined roles and responsibilities.

■ New technologies provide new equipment designs that reduce the amount of knowledge and discretion employees require in performing their work. Tasks are more standardized and routine.

■ In today's economic upheavals, downsizing, layoffs, mergers, and bankruptcies have cost hundreds of thousands of jobs. Such upheavals are catastrophic for those who are forced to find new jobs and careers. Those who are left in the organization face similar dramatic changes in the way they carry out their work. Their jobs are very different. Millions of workers have been shifted to unfamiliar tasks within an organization and wonder how long they will continue to be employed. Adding to these pressures, workers face new bosses, computer surveillance of their work, fewer health and retirement benefits, and the feeling that they may have to take on even more responsibilities to survive.

Whether you are forced to take on a new job in a new organization, or whether you have to adjust to the effects of others leaving, the results are the same. You will suffer stress caused by a sense of powerlessness and lack of control. These types of stress cause burnout.

THE POTENTIAL FOR BURNOUT

They intoxicate themselves with work so they won't see how they really are.

—ALDOUS HUXLEY

The feeling of powerlessness and lack of control is a universal cause of stress and burnout. Administrative assitants, food servers, middle managers, police officers, and professional athletic coaches are among those who are in the most stressful occupations; these are marked by the need to respond to others' demands and schedules. They have little control over their environment.

MANY OF US WORK TOO HARD BECAUSE WE FEEL WE HAVE TO DO SO.

Our jobs demand that we work hard. Our personalities are geared for achievement and for doing more in less time. Added to this, we face many activities that are unanticipated and unplanned for and that often overtax our personal energy and resources.

A colleague gets sick and you have to take on his assignments in addition to your own. On a rainy day, your car will not start and the taxis are too busy to respond to your calls. Your spouse indicates that he or she will not be able to pick up the children after work.

Such extra demands are stressful because they block our ability to satisfy our basic needs. Many stressors act in the same way. Feeling harassed by a boss or fellow employee may impact feelings of satisfaction. Working long hours may affect the body's ability to rest and regenerate. The burden of taking care of a close friend or relative can bother us emotionally.

Various stressors we face can wear us down or "burn us out" over a long period of time. That is, stress can affect our emotional health and create emotional exhaustion, or burnout.

Leading to Burnout

Dr. Hans Selye, an endocrinologist at the University of Montreal who is frequently referred to as the "father of stress," provides a definition of how stressful conditions cause exhaustion and burnout. Selye first described stress as outside forces acting on the organism, or the general wear and tear of life on the body.

Later, he suggested that stress was an internal condition of the organism that results from a response to evocative agents. These external agents might be called stressors.

> STRESS OCCURS WHEN ENVIRONMENTAL SITUATIONS (SUCH AS AN ARGUMENT WITH A SUPERVISOR OR FRUSTRATION OVER A COMPUTER FAILURE) ARE PERCEIVED AS PRESENTING A DEMAND THAT THREATENS OR EXCEEDS A PERSON'S CAPABILITY OR RESOURCES FOR MEETING IT.

Perception of a stressful event or situation is extremely important, as different individuals may react to the same situation with entirely different levels of stress. Stress results from a person's appraisal that the event is potentially dangerous or threatening. Thus, stress is a function of how important the situation is perceived to be in personal terms, and individuals are not bothered by situations that are unimportant to them.

PERSPECTIVE 11. BIG BROTHER'S PRESENCE IN THE WAY THAT JOBS ARE DESIGNED

We have to be impressed by the increased capacity of computers to store information, record measurements of inventory, and assess the efficiency and the effectiveness of various operations. However, such highly mechanized technical and computer jobs have been called the "Trojan horse for Taylorism," in that they have ushered in a style of work that is very mechanized, specialized, mindless, and boring. The logic underlying the new technologies is strikingly similar to Frederick Taylor's scientific management. Taylor, the father of scientific management, is known for practices such as piece work, time-and-motion studies, and stopwatch production.

These fears are most pronounced in modern-day offices and factories where new technologies have permeated every routine activity and profoundly affected the nature of work and its skill requirements. In many cases, automation, computerization, and the use of robotic devices has created monotonous and simple jobs. These mindless jobs do not rely on individual skill, ingenuity, and enthusiasm. The craft of work has disappeared. Employees perform simple manual operations that no longer require discretion, self-control, or brain power.

This is the way some workers describe their jobs:

■ I used to come home and have a drink to toast a job well done; now, I come home to have a drink so I can better cope with the day I have just finished.

■ The job is thankless, boring, valueless; I hate it. . . . Where is there to go?

■ I am really confused about some of the new technologies they are introducing.

■ I feel that the company is only training the people who were sympathetic to the company cause.

In one case, a telephone operator complained that the company was using the computer to monitor her work. She pointed to the fact that the computer was able to identify the exact time she spent on each phone call, as well as the number of minutes she was not available because of going for lunch or going to the bathroom. She said that her supervisor was spying on her and plugging in to listen to whom she was talking and what she was saying.

How do people respond to stress? Selye's description of the stress response is called the "general adaptation syndrome." He called it *general* because the stressor had effects on several areas of the body. *Adaptation* refers to the stimulation of defenses designed to help the body adjust or deal with the stressors, and *syndrome* indicates the individual factors in the reaction occur more or less together, and in fact are at least partially interdependent.

Three distinct phases of the stress response are:

- alarm
- resistance
- exhaustion

THE ALARM STAGE OCCURS WHEN A THREAT OR STRESS IS ENCOUNTERED, EXCITING THE BODY'S ENTIRE STRESS RESPONSE SYSTEM.

During the alarm stage, the body's energy reserves are activated. Adrenaline acts upon muscles and fat tissues, causing them to release various stored chemicals. The alarm stage is also characterized by increases in respiration, heart rate, blood pressure, and blood cholesterol, decreases in digestive processes while blood is diverted to the needed areas, and activation of blood-clotting mechanisms (a safety device in case of injury), and pupil dilation.

The alarm stage can be exciting, and people might feel challenged and enthusiastic. It might occur when a person takes on a new job or a task. In one case, Tom got a new job and was excited because of its many opportunities. Like most of us under stress, Tom may be keenly aware of feelings, thoughts, and actions and be more sensitive when his supervisor yells at him and tells him to get to work. His body goes through a range of changes that are stirred on the endocrine and autonomic nervous systems. Tom's body consumes a great deal of energy during the alarm stage.

The second stage, the resistance stage, is where the stress of other incidents and events in the new job might begin to become more taxing and, perhaps, overwhelming. During this stage, certain organs and bodily functions will adapt to respond to the stress. The heart rate might increase, and more adrenaline might be provided.

DURING THE RESISTANCE STAGE, A PERSON CAN BECOME FRUSTRATED AND FULL OF ANGER.

A person might question the job, his or her effectiveness, and the effectiveness of others. He or she might begin to manifest some behavioral problems. During this stage, the person might become more anxious, frustrated, or fatigued. The person might find his or her sleep interrupted and may display anger or irritation. It is during this stage when an individual begins to see some personal effects of stress.

THE FINAL STAGE IS EXHAUSTION, WHERE PROLONGED AND CONTINUED EXPOSURE TO A RANGE OF STRESSORS EVENTUALLY USES UP THE ADAPTIVE ENERGY AVAILABLE.

The system fighting the stressor eventually becomes exhausted. One consequence is that the effects of stress begin to be felt by other body systems, such as the heart and arteries. It is this stage that might be labeled overload or burnout. The body's systems are overworked and exhausted.

PERSPECTIVE 12. CASES OF BURNOUT

We've all heard about the popular cliches related to stress and overwork: "Don't work so hard, you'll burn yourself out." "You are burning the candle at both ends." "If you don't take some time off, you will wear yourself out." "To a certain extent, we can overwork."

Howie is a cable splicer with an Electrical Power company who was able to double his yearly salary because of overtime. His colleague commented, "He had a heart attack the next year." Another said, "I told him he was going to have problems if he did not take some time off."

Donna Uchuck works a regular day at the telephone company and then hurries home to help her children with their homework. She has little trouble adjusting to family routines, but stressful events sometimes occur. One day, a teacher called indicating that Ryan, her son, was acting up in class, and she should come to the school to discuss how to deal with the problem. Her supervisor, however, had warned her about taking extra time off work to deal with family. These extra demands create stress that is possibly overloading.

Flight or Fight?

Through our evolution as human beings, we have developed psychological and biochemical ways of reacting to the many stressful incidents and events we encounter. This basic response plan is deeply engrained in our genetic systems. It developed over several thousands of years from the time when the human species lived and worked first in cave and nomadic societies and then in rural, agrarian societies. Stressful events of agrarian society involved many tasks related to protection from animals and other tribes and securing food by fishing, gardening, or hunting. When faced with a threat, our bodies automatically mobilize and consume energy to respond physically in a fight-or-flight manner.

While we are conditioned to respond in this way, most of the stressors we face today are very different, as well as more numerous than just fifty years ago. Automation has created jobs where machines have replaced much of the physical activity, and the typical blue-collar worker is turning knobs and valves rather than lifting a shovel or fork.

> *Workaholics commit slow suicide by refusing*
> *to allow the child inside them to play.*
>
> —DR. LAURENCE SUSSER

The stresses of today's society involve workplace boredom, sex discrimination, overwork, long hours with little variety, and the emotional problems of unfriendly co-workers or difficult bosses. These stressful events cannot be dealt with by a fight-or-flight response. As a result, we do not relieve much of the stress we face.

Some jobs create more stress of this sort, including police work, air traffic control, and customer relation. When police are asked about their stress, they rarely discuss the dangers of the job; instead, they mention the court system and their frustration in not being able to deal justly with criminals. Air traffic controllers are required to be vigilant in responding to a range of incidents. The job requires little muscular activity, except for pressing buttons, focusing the eyes, or speaking on the radio. The customer relations clerk is responsible for satisfying customers who may be impolite and untruthful.

> **OUR "STONE AGE" GENETIC SYSTEM IS NOT EQUIPPED TO RESPOND TO "SPACE AGE" STRESS AND, BECAUSE OF THIS, WE FACE THE DANGER OF LIVING WITH A LARGE AMOUNT OF UNRELIEVED STRESS.**

Instead of reacting physically to the stress we encounter, we internalize our responses. Work stress goes unrelieved. These feelings go on year after year, and an individual has no opportunity to let off steam. The modern workplace allows little opportunity for the same level of physical activity that we grew accustomed to as we evolved. Instead of the one or two stressful incidents that used to take place, the modern organization offers a wide range and variety of stressful incidents to which we have no way of responding physically.

While there are many strategies for coping with stress, we often ignore them or do not use them to their full potential. These techniques encourage people to take control of their jobs and of their thoughts and actions. When we do not respond appropriately, we feel angry, frustrated, and dissatisfied. Secondary responses include depression, burnout, sleeplessness, and withdrawal. There are also physiological responses, such as high blood pressure and high cholesterol.

PERSPECTIVE 13. THE SABER-TOOTHED TIGER SYNDROME

Throughout our evolution, the body has learned to deal with threats with a fight-or-flight response. This fight-or-flight response was perfectly suited to tribal society or the cave existence. When a man or woman faced a threat, such as a saber-tooth tiger, he or she would respond by fighting or running away.

Faced with modern threats, our bodies exhibit the same coping responses as they did during our tribal existence.

- Heart rates increase and extra oxygen and nutrients are delivered to the bloodstream and assist a quick flushing of waste materials from our bodies.

- Blood pressure increases to assist circulation.

- Hyperventilation occurs to increase availability of oxygen.

- Adrenal glands pump extra adrenaline and nonadrenaline.
- Sugar and fats spill into the blood to generate fuel for immediate energy; the digestive system slows down the rate of absorption of food and increases the manufacture of energy producing substances.
- Blood flow to the hands and feet is reduced.
- Hormones are released that quicken blood clotting, more blood is sent to the brain and major muscles.
- The spleen contracts, the senses become more alert.
- Muscles become more tense.

While our bodily systems become conditioned for fight or flight, in most cases, there is little movement. We repress our feelings and no action is taken. This could happen five to ten times a day. Our innate bodily responses are conditioned to answer threats, such as saber-tooth tigers. This event might occur two to three times a week. However, in today's office world, most of us are facing a number of minor saber-tooth tigers each day and we cannot act. These false alarms create a stress buildup that affects our overall tension and capacity to respond in the long run.

HIGH STRESS LEVELS MAY BE FOUND IN THOSE WHO FEEL OVER- OR UNDEREXPOSED TO STRESSFUL CONDITIONS.

In general, deprivation or excess of almost any influence is stress provoking. High stress levels may be induced by sensory deprivation and also from sensory overload. Stress is higher under conditions where there is too much stimulation, responsibility, variety, information, and the like. Stress is higher under conditions where there is too little stimulation, responsibility, variety, and information as well.

BURNOUT CAN BE LONG LASTING.

The longer a person's body is affected by stress (duration) and the greater the amount of stress from what has grown to be normal (degree or intensity), the more likely we are to experience ill effects. The effects of stress during military combat illustrates how serious health problems result. Without any sign of external injury, soldiers simply could not continue fighting.

During the Civil War, this syndrome was called "nostalgia," during World War I, "shell shock" or brain damage from the blast of explosives. During World War II, hundreds of soldiers were diagnosed as being mentally ill, or having combat psychoneurosis. It was later called "battle fatigue." During the Vietnam War, experts began suggesting that burning out on the battle-field resulted from unrelieved stress. To deal with this, soldiers were given shorter tours of duty, spending only a few days in the combat area before those suffering from exhaustion were moved by helicopters to a base where they could have a hot shower and meal.

In work settings, stress rarely reaches the level that we would expect in combat situations. However, it goes on year after year without relief in most cases. The continuous onslaught of stress depletes a person's energy and leads to symptoms such as those found with combat fatigue. By taking the pressure off for short periods, it is possible to restore one's reserve of energy.

A long string of stressful incidents may cause paralysis, or an inability to carry out the work. In addition to frustration, the anxiety and depression that may be experienced by those under a great deal of stress may manifest itself as alcoholism (an estimated 15 percent to 20 percent of the adult population in the United States are problem drinkers), drug dependency (over 150 million tranquilizer prescriptions are written annually), and hospital-ization (over 25 percent of the hospital beds are occupied by people with psychological problems) and can end, in extreme cases, in suicide (one of the most rapidly increasing causes of death in the last twenty-five years).

DIAGNOSING BURNOUT

Is there any way to diagnose the problems of stress before they produce such traumatic outcomes as stress leave, alcoholism, drug dependency, hos-pitalization, and death? In most cases, the conditions are the result of extreme depression or exhaustion from instense stress or burnout.

Hans Selye's second stage of stress, the resistance stage, is really a pre-burnout stage. It is during this time that various organs in the body are beginning to be taxed. Minor mental disruptions, such as the inability to concentrate, reduced attention span, and impaired decision-making abili-ties, are indicators that something might be wrong.

In some organizations, we see employees expressing their frustrations with the workload, a supervisor or employee, or a customer or client. For some people, the most vivid behavioral effects of such stress-related events are fatigue, loss of sleep, inability to relax, and a loss of confidence. These are indicators of stress and strain and an early warning sign that a person should take some corrective action.

TEST 9. THE PB INDEX

Answer "Yes" or "No" to the following questions.

_____ 1. Have you recently found it more difficult to concentrate on the main tasks you were doing because you felt distracted by anger or worry?

_____ 2. Have you recently lost sleep because of worry?

_____ 3. Have you recently felt you lacked energy?

_____ 4. Have you recently found yourself being snappy and irritable when dealing with others?

_____ 5. Have you recently felt that you were really having difficulty in dealing with some of your work?

_____ 6. Have you recently felt depressed?

_____ 7. Have you recently felt that you wanted to quit?

_____ 8. Have you recently felt insecure about life or your self-worth?

SCORING TEST 9. THE PB INDEX: ASSESSING YOUR POTENTIAL FOR BURNOUT

This questionnaire provides a rough indication of the level of strain you are feeling. It will indicate the many ways you might be overtaxed. Many "Yes" answers to the questionnaire illustrate that you have a wide range of symptoms. The number of "Yes" answers is an indicator of the strain you are feeling. Strain is the outcome (breakdown) of stress over time. Greater than 4 is cause for concern.

Symptoms of Burnout

Burnout is exhaustion or overload and typifies Hans Seyle's third stage, in which continuing exposure to stressors eventually overtaxes various organs in the body.

BURNOUT IS SOMETHING LIKE A SEVERE DEPRESSION THAT AFFECTS A PERSON'S APPETITE, SLEEP, AND SELF-ESTEEM.

People who manifest signs of burnout may exhibit one of the following profiles:

- unassertive, timid and submissive, anxious and irritable; they may feel sad or lonely and may have lost interest in many of life's activities
- impatient and intolerant, easily angered and frustrated
- lacking confidence and self-esteem, with no desire for autonomy or control
- authoritarian with an excessive need for control, a tendency to want to do it all, and inability to delegate

People experiencing burnout may wake up often in the early hours of the morning; have difficulty concentrating; withdraw from others; feel lonely, worthless, and helpless; and may turn to alcohol or drugs. Burnout has been associated with great work stress and may be causally related to job satisfaction. It is also likely to affect a person's physiological health, as it is a generalized state characterized by a depletion of energy and significantly lessened personal effectiveness. When you are less effective than you used to be and you have less energy available, you are to some degree burnt out.

Burnout may seem very much like a cold at first. A person might feel more easily tired or weary. He or she might feel frustrated and have minor hostile reactions. This short-term burnout may go completely unnoticed, and people will go through their routines in a somewhat normal way. They might simply say that they feel rundown. Often, they blame this feeling on a cold or lack of sleep.

ONE SYMPTOM OF BURNOUT MAY BE EXTREME EXHAUSTION.

A person experiencing emotional exhaustion feels drained or used up. He or she might lack energy and feel emotionally depleted. The person becomes uncommunicative and unable to understand his or her own feelings. Friends may say the person is aloof, distant, or uncommunicative. Once emotional exhaustion sets in, a person feels unable to give to others and may respond by cutting off involvement with others.

A SECOND MAJOR SYMPTOM OF BURNOUT IS INTERPERSONAL STRAIN, A GROWING NEGATIVITY TOWARD OTHERS.

Interpersonal strain is demonstrated by office conversations that are critical and hostile of others. The anger may seem like a passionate hatred and, at the minimum, an overzealous effort to be critical of others. Such actions reflect a lack of trust and a general negative or hostile view of others that separates "me" from "them." To fight off feelings of personal failure, people who exhibit depersonalization will blame others for their problems by seeing them as untrustworthy, devious, unmotivated to change, bad, or weak. Cynicism, disappointment, and frustration describe some of the feelings expressed.

TEST 10. THE B INDEX

Write a number in the blank to the left of each statement below, based on this scale: To what degree is each of the statements *like* or *unlike* you?

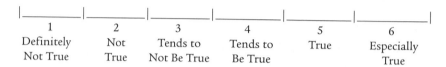

_____	_____	_____	_____	_____	_____
1	2	3	4	5	6
Definitely Not True	Not True	Tends to Not Be True	Tends to Be True	True	Especially True

Make certain you use *low* numbers to describe statements that are *unlike* you and *high* numbers to describe statements *like* you.

_____ 1. I dread going to work lately.

_____ 2. I feel irritated with some of my co-workers.

_____ 3. I find myself getting behind in my work lately.

_____ 4. I feel used up at the end of the day.

_____ 5. I feel like withdrawing from people lately.

_____ 6. I need much more time to sort things out.

_____ 7. Lately, I have felt tired and drained.

_____ 8. Working with people all day is a strain on me lately.

_____ 9. I feel overwhelmed by what I have to do.

_____ 10. I often feel like I do not have the energy to carry on.

_____ 11. Lately, I have been more irritated by certain people.

_____ 12. I feel that my responsibilities are overwhelming.

_____ 13. I feel like quitting.

_____ 14. Lately, I have been rather impatient with certain people.

_____ 15. I worry that I do not have more time to deal with what I have to do.

_____ 16. I feel emotionally frustrated by my job.

_____ 17. Lately, I have had little time for close relationships.

_____ 18. I never seem to have time to enjoy what is important to me.

SCORING TEST 10. THE B INDEX: ASSESSING THE BURNOUT YOU ARE EXPERIENCING

The B index suggests that burnout is best understood in relation to the strain that a person exhibits. Often, people feel stressed and frustrated from their work. The prolonged stress results in strain.

Burnout may be a response to chronic, everyday stress rather than occasional stress. The emotional stress of working closely with people is a constant part of the daily routine. What changes over time is one's tolerance for this continual stress, a tolerance that gradually wears down under the never-ending onslaught of emotional tensions.

There are three critical components of the burnout syndrome—emotional strain, interpersonal strain, and task strain.

Emotional strain reflects a person's psychological condition. This is described by statements such as, "I feel emotionally drained from my work," "I feel used up at the end of the workday," and "I feel fatigued when I get up in the morning and have to face another day on the job."

Interpersonal strain is described as seeing people in negative terms. This is demonstrated by statements such as "I don't really care what happens to my co-workers," and "I feel I treat my co-workers as impersonal objects."

Task strain is described by statements indicating that a person does not have time to physically handle life activities and tasks. Examples include, "I find that I need time to myself to work out personal problems," or "I wish I had more time to catch up."

The following scores describe various symptoms of burnout.

Emotional Strain	Interpersonal Strain	Task Strain
1. _____	2. _____	3. _____
4. _____	5. _____	6. _____
7. _____	8. _____	9. _____

10. _____	11. _____	12. _____
13. _____	14. _____	15. _____
16. _____	17. _____	18. _____

Total   ES = _____   IS = _____   TS = _____

Add the scores in each of the columns.

■ Scores higher than 25 in each area indicate a high degree of strain.

■ Total scores higher than 75 indicate that you may be feeling intense strain or burnout.

Your scores will give you an indication of the level of burnout you are feeling.

ANOTHER SYMPTOM IS INABILTY TO COPE. IT IS A FEELING OF BEING OVERWHELMED.

Inability to cope is illustrated by nurses who are unable to feel any sadness for a dying patient; police officers who become frustrated with police work and take out their anger on society; teachers who are unable to understand how a person learns; or social workers who use all the correct phrases but are unable to feel or cry.

Some people see their inability to perform the job as a personal failure and seek therapy to understand their inadequacy. They might be very unwilling to talk about this because it reflects, in their eyes, a personal weakness.

The burnout syndrome is a response to chronic, everyday stress rather than occasional stress. It indicates that a person is less able to tolerate prolonged, continued stress. The smallest little aggravation will unleash some very hostile responses. In one case, John Ho exploded at an employee, saying, "You guys better start getting your act together. I'm wasting my time in trying to fix up all the mistakes you are making." When the employee indicated that it was a mistake made by central administration, John yelled back, "You are playing with fire when you are dealing with me," and continued to tell the employee he was incompetent and irresponsible. The employee finally walked away, but John went into his office and slammed the door. Here was a person whose anger and hostility were simmering below the surface. The smallest incident would unleash an unpredictable reaction. He seemed to display many of the symptoms of burnout. He was releasing his pain and anger by attacking others.

Burnout is not just anger that is created from a situation or anger that is ready to explode for no apparent reason. Sufferers perceive that others are frustrating their ideals. They become angry at their jobs, their bosses, and their colleagues. They hate everything, and anger and hostility is directed at anyone who is in the way.

ONE REACTION TO BURNOUT IS TO BURN.

The term *burn* suggests the anger, heat, or hostility of a person who strikes out at others. While some people burn, others are just out of it. They have nothing left.

While some strike out with anger and hostility, others are alienated and depressed. They detach themselves and simply will not provide any energy to help others. These people hang on and put in their time, but expect nothing will change.

AN ENVIRONMENT THAT HAS THE POTENTIAL FOR CREATING BURNOUT IS ONE WHERE THERE ARE HOSTILE AND ANGRY INTERACTIONS WITH PEOPLE.

Environments where other people are angry, cynical, or emotional, or where there is frustration, crises, or pain can create burnout. These environments provide little support or positive feedback, where people hear little praise when things go well but constant criticism when something goes wrong. Some environments put people in constant touch with those who are upsetting, depressing, or disagreeable. Examples might be environments where people are abusive or sick. Imagine working as a nurse in a hospital where people are suffering and dying from pain.

An overloading environment also promotes burnout Emotionally or physically overloading environments challenge a person's ability to cope. In these situations there are too many demands for the person to do a competent job. The immediate reaction to an overloaded situation is to provide a quicker and more impersonal response. The job is still completed but it is done in a qualitatively different way, with emotional detachment. Some people become so overwhelmed by the intensity of the emotional contacts that they get irritated and frustrated and lash out at the situation. They might throw things, hit the computer, or have a tantrum.

Why do people experience burnout?

> **PEOPLE EXPERIENCE BURNOUT WHEN THEY HAVE UNREASONABLY IDEALISTIC EXPECTATIONS OF ACCOMPLISHING SOMETHING.**

Many people have very firm views of what the world should be like. They fail to recognize that things do not change because of logic, fairness, and justice. It is not hard to imagine why people with idealistic goals get frustrated when they encounter people who are unwilling to be fair and just.

> **PERHAPS PEOPLE ARE IDEALISTIC BECAUSE THEY ARE UNABLE TO GROW AND ADAPT TO LIFE.**

PERSPECTIVE 14. DEATH VALLEY AND THE DEAD SEA

The desert in Death Valley was once an ocean full of life. The waters supported an array of life forms and creatures that are no longer present on Earth. Then the water that fed it ceased to do so. The array of species in the ocean died. As a phenomenon of nature where there was an outlet and no inlet, Death Valley simply gave up. It died because it had nothing new coming in.

Like Death Valley, there are people who are asked to give up their energy day after day. Teachers, nurses, social workers, and ministers all have excessive demands made on them by others. They drain themselves of their energy and emotion. Many of these people have no sustenance and stimulation coming in from outside. Like Death Valley, they lose their capacity to provide energy for life.

The Dead Sea is a body of water that is stagnant. Its main inlet is the Jordan River, but it has no outlet. The waters of the Jordan River provide a variety of stimulus for life. However, the Dead Sea doesn't have an outlet to let things out. The Dead Sea has become a stagnant storage tank for all sorts of life and waste.

Like the Dead Sea, there are people who, for one reason or another, are unable to let anything out. They take things but do not let them go. They take in the tensions and frustrations of the world without letting them out. Like the person who overindulges at meal time, they have more than they need. Waste and toxins fester, become cancerous, and eat away, so that the person becomes devoid of life.

Burnout is as much a result of the inability to take in new energy as it is the inabilty to let out negative feelings and emotions. Death Valley and the Dead Sea both suffer from lack of energy and stagnation. We struggle in the same way. We need energy to nourish us, and we need ways to release our waste.

TAKING CONTROL

There has been a growing interest in how emotional burnout is triggered in people with emotionally charged job situations. Burnout can also result from the loss of a loved one, marital problems, job loss, working too hard, or from work pressures and is both a cause and effect of job satisfaction.

People suffering from burnout feel helpless and unable to take control of their lives. Lack of control may stem from a supervisor who is very demanding and inflexible. It can result from having no impact on the procedures defining one's job or from feeling trapped by institutional rules that determine what the job should be. Who wants to be an administrative assistant who has to constantly cover up for a boss's mistakes or a sales clerk who is always listening to customers who are frustrated with poor-quality products?

> BURNOUT SIGNALS THAT YOU HAVE BECOME POWERLESS AND UNABLE TO TAKE CONTROL OF MANY OF THE FORCES THAT ARE STRESSING YOU.

The decision to take control is one of the prerequisites to dealing effectively with burnout. Effective treatment of burnout requires diagnosis of the problems affecting you, recognition of the need for change, and development and employment of effective strategies for improvement.

The first step in responding to job burnout is diagnosing why you may be prone to it. The questionnaires in the previous section are a way to understand the level of burnout you are now experiencing. However, it is also necessary to identify some of the stressors that are unique to your job.

One immediate way to take action is to diagnose the things that are bothering or overloading you. An inventory of the work stress of a college professor, Jim, revealed the following general list:

TABLE 8.1 INVENTORY OF WORK STRESS

Tasks	People	Conditions
Teaching	Office workers	Noisy classroom
Grading	Demanding students	Poor equipment
Motivating	Affirmative action	Little support
Research	Lazy students	High expectations
Library work	Administrative	High criticism
Data gathering	incompetence	
Analytical problems	Back-stabbing colleagues	
Administration	Little cooperation	
Meetings		

To create a general list similar to the above, begin writing down, on a daily basis, some of the things that bother you, where and when they happened, who is annoying you. The list should identify specific people and events that caused you stress. This will give you a perspective on what is affecting you most. During a one-week period of time, a college professor noted the following stressful people and events:

- He spent over two hours listening to a faculty colleague who was making an appeal to have a hiring decision reviewed on the basis of unfairness. Over that week, the thought of how this would affect the long-term working climate in the department continued to bother him.

- He had a discussion with the former tenant of his home. The tenant had not made the final month's payment. He said that he incurred expenses. The college professor was upset by the pressures of returning to his house after it had been rented for three years. There were demands to purchase a car and buy new appliances. The lawn mower needed repair, and there were several household items that had been neglected by the renters.

- He had an argument with his wife. There was the stress of completing a book. His wife had promised to help but had not been able to spend any time on it because of her own demands.
- He met with a bank official over finances. Financial problems were a concern. Because of all the new purchases, there was little money left.

Look at your list and respond to the following questions: What was frustrating? What made me angry? What made me nervous?

BEING POSITIVE ABOUT STRESS

Instead of thinking about events as stressful and dysfunctional, it is productive to see them as an opportunity to find a more comfortable direction.

> IF YOU DO NOT FIND A PLACE WHERE YOU WANT TO GO, YOU WILL NOT KNOW WHAT YOU WILL DO WHEN YOU GET THERE.

Knowing where you want to go allows you to get away from those things that are stressful to you now.

Instead of fighting changes that might be inevitable, we should define how they can benefit us. For example, many people resisted the introduction of computers in their lives while others saw them as an opportunity to be more productive.

Organizational strategists often use what is called an OPEN analysis to aid the process of understanding how best to respond to the stress around us. Such a technique is helpful for people who are involved in the process of change.

OPEN is an acronym that stands for (O)pportunities, (P)ositives, (E)nvironmental issues, and (N)egatives. Together, the process provides a perspective on how we might respond to the stress around us.

The first step in making stress more positive is to define what opportunities you feel are important. Jim's list of (O)pportunities for his job as a college professor suggested that he had several chances to pursue his work, including teaching and administration and writing research articles or for popular publications.

Those things that Jim found most (P)ositive were his relationships with his students and his popular writing. He wanted to write books that were less academic and were more widely read. In addition, he found it extremely positive to work as a consultant and to assist clients in improving their organizations. He also had some extremely positive working and social relationships with others, which he felt were especially helpful in dealing with his stress.

Jim began identifying the (E)nvironmental issues on which he should focus more specifically. He asked himself what he could do to work more effectively as a consultant and to publish books that were read by a wider audience. After considerable thought and discussion, he began working more closely with some of the people with whom he already had good relationships. They formed a consulting firm and began meeting with clients. He also contracted with a literary agent who helped him focus and market his books.

Those things that Jim found most (N)egative came from the relationships he had with his colleagues. He sought to resolve this by asking himself how he could reduce the stress he felt and began to outline things he could do with others where he could feel more positive. His tactic for resolving his stress amounted to forming new relationships and minimizing his relationships with the colleagues who were stressing him the most.

In carrying out this OPEN analysis, the understanding and imagination of others is particularly useful in identifying the opportunities, positives, environmental issues, and negatives. Brainstorming and other idea-generating activities are useful. Brainstorming can assist in establishing an atmosphere where ideas are encouraged and supported.

WHEN YOU'RE WORKING IN A NONCHALLENGING JOB

MOST INDIVIDUALS FEEL LESS STRESS WITH JOBS THAT HAVE SOME MEANING AND SIGNIFICANCE.

Meaningful jobs are challenging and offer an opportunity to learn. A person might perceive the work as worthwhile or important. What is done will "count" and is rewarding and meaningful.

The human organism needs a certain level of stimulation from the environment, not too high but not too low. In cases of prolonged overstimulation, the effects may be fragmentation of thought, loss of integrating ability, and what is called tunnel vision, in which we perceive only small parts of the processes going on around us and miss essential information. In the case of understimulation, we become mentally impoverished, bored, and alienated. We are easily distracted and lose initiative and capacity for involvement.

Many of the features of a stressful job grow out of a design that restricts control, reduces initiative, and allows for close supervision. They evolve from managerial assumptions that workers need close supervision and control. They define jobs within principles that minimize skill requirements, restrict individual responsibility for specific tasks, and specify uniform work procedures and standards.

PERSPECTIVE 15. OFFICE WORK

Kelly Egbert was really fed up with her department's performance and morale. She knew that office work can be very boring and that her administrative assistants had responded by spending many hours chatting and socializing.

The managers who work in the office indicated that the socializing had gone too far. They have no desire to ask the administrative assistants to do anything as they respond with seemingly joking statements such as, "Can't you send your own fax?" "You mean that I have to do that?" "Well, don't you know how to type this?" "I took on this job because I did not expect to do typing." Clients made statements such as, "I've never seen such a poorly managed office," "Do they ever do anything?" "I was never treated so rudely in all my life."

Three other administrative assistants in the next office work extremely hard and have little time to socialize. They are demoralized as a result of the director's unwillingness to deal with the poor performance of the chatty workers.

Some aspects of the job are rather boring, but the workers seem to have no desire to improve the situation. Their most innovative idea for improving their work was to begin working flex-time. Two of them come to work earlier, and while eating breakfast, have a chance to socialize when no one is around. A third worker stays later and does much of her own personal work.

Kelly Egbert was convinced that there must be some way to make it more interesting to do a dull job and hopefully improve the commitment of the workers. "At least I want to try to enrich their work and encourage their learning. I might possibly improve their performance," she thought.

The employees in Kelly's department admit people to a program of studies and help the managers train this select group. They are also responsible for helping managers carry out their work, by preparing reports and managing programs. Each employee has his or her own assigned workstation and stays at that particular place for the entire day.

Kelly decided to try a couple of things to improve performance. First, she organized the department into work groups and asked each group to define the tasks they are responsible for and then share the work. Next, Kelly developed a feedback system for all employees. When clients wished to offer comments and feedback to the office workers or managers, the comments were posted, along with a response by the person(s) involved. She also helped the employees develop a program for rotating their work.

So far, the results of the changes have been encouraging.

The nature of a job's design can affect the productivity of an organization as well as the stress and satisfaction of employees. In enriching a job's design, a manager has a smorgasbord of approaches to choose from—ranging from Japanese management and quality circles to more general applications of organizational development and job enrichment.

Some jobs can be enriched by allowing workers to be involved in teams. In this sense, an individual can understand how each task relates to the final output and appreciate his or her contribution to the whole project. It is easier to identify with a job that allows a person to work on a team and complete an entire project, rather than doing a few tasks that are performed all day long. This allows for more opportunity for managing the work. Such approaches seek to improve coordination, productivity, and overall quality and respond to employees' needs for learning, challenge, variety, increased responsibility, and achievement.

Jobs can be designed so that they more fully utilize individuals' capabilities. Simplified and highly specialized jobs are less motivating because they require little human talent and effort. On the other hand, overly complex jobs are not motivating if they require more skills and abilities than the individual possesses.

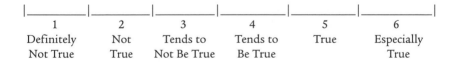

THE ELEMENTS OF THE JOB SHOULD BE SUCH THAT THE INDIVIDUAL CAN LEARN, GROW, DEVELOP, AND ADJUST.

In a highly automated organization, the role of the individual depends on the learning and challenge in the job. Learning and challenge enhance an employee's commitment and intrigue with the work assignments or tasks.

TEST 11. THE JD INDEX

This questionnaire assesses how your job is designed. For each statement, place a number from 1 to 6 on the line to the left of the item. The numbers mean:

1	2	3	4	5	6
Definitely Not True	Not True	Tends to Not Be True	Tends to Be True	True	Especially True

_____ 1. My job requires me to work closely with other people, either customers or people in related jobs.

_____ 2. I have a great deal of autonomy in my job; that is, my job permits me to decide on my own how to go about the work.

_____ 3. My job involves a whole and identifiable piece of work; that is, the tasks are a complete piece of work that have an obvious beginning and end.

_____ 4. I experience a great deal of job variety; that is, the job requires me to do many different things at work, using a variety of skills and talents.

_____ 5. In general, I feel my job is significant or important; that is, the results of my work are likely to significantly affect the lives or well-being of others.

_____ 6. My managers or co-workers let me know how well I am doing on the job.

_____ 7. The job itself provides me with information about my work performance; that is, the actual work itself provide clues about how well I am doing, aside from any feedback co-workers or supervisors provide.

_____ 8. The job requires me to use a number of complex or high-level skills.

_____ 9. The job requires a lot of cooperative work with other people.

_____ 10. The job is arranged so that I do not have the chance to do an entire piece of work from beginning to end.

_____ 11. Just doing the work required by the job provides many chances for me to figure out how well I am doing.

_____ 12. The job is quite simple and repetitive.

_____ 13. The job can be done adequately by a person working alone without talking or checking with other people.

_____ 14. The supervisors and co-workers on this job almost never give me any feedback about how well I am doing.

_____ 15. The job is one where a lot of people can be affected by how well the work gets done.

_____ 16. The job denies me any chance to use my personal initiative or judgment in carrying out the work.

_____ 17. Supervisors often let me know how well they think I am performing the job.

_____ 18. The job provides me the chance to completely finish the task I begin.

_____ 19. The job itself provides very few clues about whether or not I am performing well.

_____ 20. The job gives me considerable opportunity for independence and freedom in how I do the work.

_____ 21. The job itself is not very significant in the broader sense of things.

SCORING TEST 11. THE JD INDEX: ASSESSING THE JOB'S POTENTIAL FOR ENRICHMENT

The Job Diagnostic Index describes the motivation potential of your job, based on its degree of variety, task identity, task significance, autonomy, feedback from the job, feedback from others, and ability to deal with others. You are more likely to experience job stress and dissatisfaction in jobs that are not designed to recognize these factors. In developing an understanding of your job, add the scores for the questions associated with each factor.

Note: The items in brackets ( ) are reverse scored

- 6 should be scored as a 1.
- 4 should be scored as a 3.
- 2 should be scored as a 5.
- 5 should be scored as a 2.
- 1 should be scored as a 6.
- 3 should be scored as a 4.

➡ **Skill variety:**

Add the scores for questions: 4, 8, (12)   _____

➡ **Task identity:**

Add the scores for questions: 3, 18, (10)   _____

➡ Task significance:

Add the scores for questions: 5, 15, (21)   _____

➡ Autonomy:

Add the scores for questions: 2, 20, (16)   _____

➡ Feedback from job:

Add the scores for questions: 7, 11, (19)   _____

➡ Feedback from others:

Add the scores for questions: 6, 17, (14)   _____

➡ Dealing with others:

Add the scores for questions: 1, 9, (13)   _____

Interpreting Your Score

The highest possible score for each factor is 18 and the lowest is 3. If you scored 12 or above on a factor, your job has a high motivating potential on that dimension.

If your total score on a dimension is less than 8, you need to think of ways to enrich your job. Such jobs have a very high possibility of being dissatisfying and stressful. If your total score on a dimension is between 9 and 11, things could be improved.

Review the scores for all the dimensions. Identify those areas needing enrichment and then follow the steps outlined in the chapter.

___

Stress might be reduced by redesigning a job by taking into account its basic characteristics. Code the results of Test 11. You should be able to describe the features of your job. Indicate those features below 2.5 that might be improved; that is, those features below 2.5 that might produce stress for you because they are boring, insignificant, and give you little control and feedback. Put a check mark by those that do not need change.

	Need Change	Do Not Need Change
▪ Skill Variety	_____	_____
▪ Task Identity	_____	_____
▪ Task Significance	_____	_____
▪ Autonomy	_____	_____
▪ Feedback from the Job	_____	_____
▪ Feedback from Others	_____	_____
▪ Dealing with Others	_____	_____

You can encourage positive stress in your job by enriching it and recognizing the principles of horizontal loading, vertical loading, and career learning.

Horizontal loading suggests that a person might take on additional responsibilities at the same level. A worker at Disneyland might spend two hours collecting tickets, another two hours guiding guests, two hours cleaning tables, and another two hours doing general duties.

Vertical loading means assigning higher-level tasks to a person. Responsibilities and controls formerly reserved for higher levels of management are added to the job, giving the employee discretion in setting schedules, checking on quality, granting additional authority, deciding when to start and stop work, trouble shooting and crisis decisions, and establishing financial controls.

CAREER LEARNING PROVIDES FOR DIFFERENT TYPES OF EXPERIENCES AND OPPORTUNITIES.

Career growth allows opportunities for advancement or fulfillment of one's aspirations, with some level of security.

ENCOURAGING POSITIVE STRESS

Find a job where you can control your destiny and you'll never work another day in your life. Your job will be fun, challenging, and interesting, rather than stressful and harassing.

Rethink the Way You Do Your Job

Although certain jobs are potentially more stressful, much can be gained through understanding the way the job is designed. Job stress is less when people have control of their lives and work. Those who control what they do, when they do it, and how they do it exhibit lower levels of distress than those who have minimal control over their work. Those who have minimal control of their tasks, such as food servers, administrative assistants, assembly-line workers, and file clerks, have a higher incidence of ulcers, CHD, absenteeism, and hypertension.

> STRESS OCCURS WHEN THE JOB'S DESIGN CREATES CONDITIONS THAT ARE THREATENING, AMBIGUOUS, AND THAT DO NOT RESPOND TO AN INDIVIDUAL'S EXPECTATIONS AND NEEDS.

Employers and workers can change the way the job is designed and reduce the effects of stress. A person's stress is closely tied to how much control an individual has in completing some of the job's tasks, the interpersonal environment, and the way the organization is managed. The criteria describing these major interactions are displayed on the next page in Table 8.2.

Reducing Job Stress

Here are some steps that managers and employees can use to develop a less stressful and more motivating job environment. The ideas can be applied by managers in consultation with employees, or by either group acting independently. Obviously, the involvement of others is most important if the ideas are to be applied to them. The following are a set of steps for helping managers and employees understand and respond to stress on the job.

- Review Table 8.2 and ask yourself if you are stressed because of any of the criteria identified. For example, does a lack of job variety cause you stress? Are you stressed because of increased responsibilities?

- Brainstorm a list of changes that may reduce the stress from these criteria. You might wish to enlist the assistance of other people in creating ideas. Remember, brainstorming is an uncritical, creative process of thinking about a number of ideas or options. When you first begin, simply list all the ideas you can possibly think of without any concern for practicality. You can then use the criteria in Table 8.2 as a checklist to enhance your creativity. That is, how can we increase or reduce the vari-

TABLE 8.2 CRITERIA FOR REDUCING STRESS AT WORK

Job Enrichment Criteria

Horizontal and Vertical Loading

- Job variety
- Task identity
- Task significance
- Autonomy
- Feedback

Vertical Loading

- Increased responsibilities
- Increased opportunities for advancement

Career Learning and Progression

- Different opportunities and experiences
- Opportunities for advancement
- Feelings of job security

Interpersonal Criteria

Interpersonal Trust

- Ability to rely on others for accurate and honest feedback
- Confidence that others will be truthful and honest

A Positive Organization Climate

- Positive method of providing feedback and comments
- Positive outlook or enthusiasm about the organization and life

Collaboration and Support

- Encouragement to work together in a productive and supportive manner
- Support and assistance is provided in a positive and willing manner

Managerial Criteria

- Co-operation between management and employees
- Common goals and values
- Increasing autonomy through group work
- Group responsibilities
- Sharing responsibilities
- Responsibilities that an employee can meet

Opening Feedback Channels

- Job-related feedback
- Clarity of communications and feedback

---

ety in this job? How can we increase the significance of the tasks with which people are dealing? How can we improve the level of task identity? Are there ways we can reduce or increase people's responsibilities?

- Screen the list of suggestions to eliminate those that are not practical.
- Screen the list of suggestions to eliminate those that are too general and offer vague ideas for change. For example, discard those ideas that simply say "get more involved." Alternatively, try to make the vague items more specific.

- Finally, eliminate those suggestions that contribute to either rustout or burnout, or that are mechanisms to compensate or "buy people off" for the stress they encounter. Tasks that encourage rustout are those that provide no stimulation and learning. Those that contribute to burnout are those that are overloading.

- The initial attempts to define a number of strategies might be carried out alone so that you can see how to reduce the level of stress in your own job. However, most changes will involve other people. For this reason, it may be advisable to involve others who are working in similar jobs.

- In the initial attempts to define a number of strategies for reducing job stress, set up a controlled experiment to observe the effects. You might do this on a scientific basis by using experimental and control groups. Alternatively, you might begin a process of evaluation where people are actively involved in understanding how their jobs are being changed to reduce the level of stress. Both types of evaluation are valuable for different purposes; the former is a traditional scientific evaluation, while the latter is more useful for assisting people in a process of change.

There may be some adjustment problems, as people may feel that the changes are not working. Indeed, change itself may be a stressor. Anxiety over the changes may lead some people to feel that the only way to reduce stress is to reduce the workload.

CONCLUSION

PEOPLE WHO ARE BETTER AT DEALING WITH STRESS AND BURNOUT SEEM TO THRIVE ON JOBS THAT WOULD BURN MOST OF US OUT.

Some people have developed good strategies for responding and might be able to survive in almost any stressful job. They seem to be able to alter the nature of the work to reduce stress. They change schedules, rearrange tasks, and offer suggestions to their bosses for improving work. They have ways of relieving stress through exercise, meditation, and nonwork pursuits. Most of all, they do these things naturally, not because they were told to do them to relieve stress. Rather, they use these coping strategies as if they are a natural part of their lives.

Over the last thirty years, we have witnessed vast changes in the way that work is designed and carried out. There have been diminished opportunities for work autonomy, resulting from the shift to large impersonal corporate and government bureaucracies. As organizations continue to get bigger, they become more mechanized and specialized and require standardized performance. A change in attitudes and values among many members of the workforce—youth, minority members, and women—exacerbates these problems. With higher expectations generated by increased educational achievement, these groups are placing greater emphasis on the intrinsic aspects of work and its inherent challenge and interest, and less on strictly material rewards.

The nature of work, and its demands on the workers, undoubtedly is affected by a worker's abilities, needs, and expectations. Thus, a harmonious work environment may be affected by discrepancies between the stress of work and a worker's expectations and needs. The institution of work has to be questioned, especially in the way it is organized, its adequacy in meeting human needs, and the effects of work on other dimensions of human welfare.

PRINCIPLE 5:
Control Life's Trials and Tribulations

MANAGE THE STRESS-PROMOTING LIFE

Life is full of stresses, and they are all very different for each of us. The stresses of life are unique to each individual's personality, job, and lifestyle, among other things.

We experience different stresses as we grow older. Each time we move from one stage of our lives to the next, we face a transition, according to Daniel Levinson's *The Seasons of a Man's Life* and Gail Sheehy's *Passages* and *New Passages*. Transitions describe how our lives evolve as we move from adolescence to adulthood to old age. Transitions occur when we become teenagers, when we get married, when we become thirty, forty, fifty, and so on. Each stage is a transition.

Gail Sheehy's *Passages* popularized the concept that adulthood continues to proceed by stages of development throughout the life cycle. Stages of adulthood are characterized, not by the physical growth typical in childhood, but by psychological and social growth. Her book, *Passages*, used the analogy of a lobster that grows by developing and shedding a series of hard, protective shells. During each stage of development, it expands from within and the confining shell is cast off, and the body is left unprotected until a new covering grows.

Passages is Sheehy's word for those predictable crises or turning points that usher in a new stage of growth and development. She describes broad stages of development—provisional adulthood (eighteen to thirty), first adulthood (thirty to forty-five), and second adulthood (forty-five to eighty-five plus, with predictable passages between them. In her book *New*

Passages, she describes the stages of second adulthood more fully, as the age of mastery (forty-five to sixty-five) and age of integrity (sixty-five to eighty-five plus).

Typical examples include deaths, marital separations or divorces, personal injuries or illnesses, layoffs, retirements, pregnancy, sexual difficulties, business readjustments, examinations, changes in financial status, and so forth.

Here are some ways people feel during such crises:

- I've lost my wife, and I don't know what I will do.
- I wish I knew what would happen. Hopefully, I'll get a new job after I am laid off at the end of the month.
- This divorce has been really hard on me. The most frustrating part is dealing with the lawyer. I can hardly wait until this is over.
- The doctors are not sure how to respond. Hopefully, the chemotherapy will help me. I've also met with a therapist. I'm getting some advice on diet.
- Just two more months and exams are over. I'll be finished with this degree and out of the university. I can hardly wait.

With every stressful experience we face, we become subject to guilt, doubt, and uncertainty.

- If only I had been more conscious of my lifestyle.
- If only I could get a decent job . . .
- If only my children would help around the house, I could . . .
- If only I had a little more money, I could invest in a house.
- If only my colleagues were more supportive and helpful, I could . . .
- If only I had more time, I could relax.

What are we really doing when we say such things? We are really asking our lives to hurry up so that we can get through our present crises.

WELL-BEING OR STRESS?

The way we adjust to the many unpredictable crises and uncertainties of life is critically important to our growth and development. Some people have used such experiences and learned from them. They have adapted and grown. Others have resisted these experiences, fought them, and have agonized through them.

SOME PEOPLE ARE UNABLE TO ADAPT AND RESPOND TO UNPREDICTABLE CRISES.

When Jackson was told he had cancer, he laid his complete faith in his surgeons, who said that "genetically, you are probably more disposed to these ailments." Jackson did not change his diet or his drinking habits, nor did he try to run away from his stressful job. After his first operation, where a large part of intestine was taken out, he was left with a colostomy. More than half his liver was taken out during a second operation a year later. A third operation, to reduce the blockage in his urinary tract, resulted in a second colostomy. Throughout, Jackson made few changes in his attitude and lifestyle. He ate and drank as he did before. He maintained a positive exterior and returned to work as soon as he could. "A bump in the road," he said.

Eric was shocked about losing his job. "I know I'm capable. I've been very effective in the past and I know I will be able to start a successful consulting business." Eric did not want to work for another large organization again and wanted to be self-employed. He had had enough. Over the next two years, he worked diligently to make contacts and develop programs that might be marketable. However, he did not get much work. At the present time, he is still trying hard to get his business going.

After Luc was terminated, he refused to look for a job for the first year, while proudly suggesting that he could live off his wife's income and his severance package. He spent a second year looking for a job before finally taking a much lower-paying job in another city. His wife later left him. At the present time, he is working in a position that is far below his expectations.

Tom tried to begin a legal action because he felt that his termination was unfair and unjustified. The first part of this process took eight months. The out-of-court settlement guaranteed his employment at the university where he worked. However, he seemed to closet himself away from others and showed an unwillingness to talk to many employees and supervisors. He continued to be angry and adjusted his work habits to do as little as he could. His later performance evaluations discouraged him and gave him even more reason to think that the new managers were as untrustworthy as the former ones.

SOME PEOPLE ARE BETTER ABLE TO ADAPT AND RESPOND TO UNPREDICTABLE CRISES.

Becky was a graduate student who had been going through a messy divorce over the last six months. Her husband had a new girlfriend. One son had left home, while a second seventeen-year-old son was taking the divorce rather hard. He was challenging her, in addition, with rebellious behavior and dress. Then Becky was told she had cancer. "I denied it at first and sought to get another doctor. I cried for a week. But, then, I got over this and said I'm going to beat it." She is the inspiration for many of us.

After being terminated, Mike tried desperately to find a job for over a year without any success. He lost confidence and felt distraught. After a period of rejections, he managed to find a job in another field and indicated to his hiring manager, "I'm interested in taking on your job in the near future." His new job was, at first, much lower in status and salary, although it afforded him an opportunity to get started in another field. He later was promoted and then moved again to a job in another organization and field. As he looks back on it now, he says, "It was one of the best things that could have happened to me."

For a short time, Bret planned to take legal action against the organization that had terminated him. After a month, he met with the new managers and indicated his willingness not to take legal action in return for an opportunity to upgrade his skills for some of the new jobs. He learned from this, and he is now the division chief.

LIFE'S UNPREDICTABLE CRISES

In the 1960s medical researchers Thomas Holmes and Richard Rahe developed a popular scale to summarize the stress people might experience because of change. Conceivably, a person has a higher life stress if he or she is encountering a large number of changes. For example, a higher degree of stress might be experienced by a person who had a lot of changes, such as starting a new semester at college, a mother-in-law's visit, the prolonged illness of one's two-year-old child, and the birth of a new baby. A list of such changes is presented in Test 12. The number and severity of these events, in combination, is an indication of the level of stress a person is experiencing.

TEST 12. LIFE EVENTS

Indicate the number of times any of these life events have happened to you in the last twelve months and multiply by the "Item Value." Add up the scores.

Item Life Event	Times it Happened	Item Value	Your Score
1. Death of spouse	_____	× 100 =	_____
2. Divorce	_____	× 73 =	_____
3. Marital separation	_____	× 65 =	_____
4. Jail term	_____	× 63 =	_____
5. Death of close family member	_____	× 63 =	_____
6. Personal injury or illness	_____	× 53 =	_____
7. Marriage	_____	× 50 =	_____
8. Fired at work	_____	× 47 =	_____
9. Marital reconciliation	_____	× 45 =	_____
10. Retirement	_____	× 45 =	_____
11. Change in health of family member	_____	× 44 =	_____
12. Pregnancy	_____	× 40 =	_____
13. Sex difficulties	_____	× 39 =	_____
14. Gain of new family member	_____	× 39 =	_____
15. Business readjustment	_____	× 39 =	_____
16. Change in financial state	_____	× 38 =	_____
17. Death of close friend	_____	× 37 =	_____
18. Change to different line of work	_____	× 36 =	_____
19. Change in number of spousal arguments	_____	× 35 =	_____
20. Mortgage over $ 150,000	_____	× 31 =	_____
21. Foreclosure of mortgage or loan	_____	× 30 =	_____

22. Changes in responsibilities at work	_____	×	29	= _____
23. Son or daughter leaving home	_____	×	29	= _____
24. Trouble with in-laws	_____	×	29	= _____
25. Outstanding personal achievement	_____	×	28	= _____
26. Spouse begins or stops work	_____	×	26	= _____
27. Begin or end school	_____	×	26	= _____
28 Change in living conditions	_____	×	25	= _____
29. Trouble with boss	_____	×	23	= _____
30. Change in work hours or conditions	_____	×	23	= _____
31. Change in residence	_____	×	20	= _____
32. Change in schools	_____	×	20	= _____
33. Change in recreation	_____	×	19	= _____
34. Change in church activities	_____	×	19	= _____
35. Change in social activities	_____	×	18	= _____
36. Mortgage or loan less than $10,000	_____	×	17	= _____
37. Change in sleeping habits	_____	×	16	= _____
38. Change in number of family get-togethers	_____	×	15	= _____
39. Change in eating habits	_____	×	15	= _____
40. Vacation	_____	×	13	= _____
41. Christmas	_____	×	12	= _____
42. Minor violations of the law	_____	×	11	= _____

Total Score _____

The number of life changes may be an important predictor of a person's health. Dr. Walter Cannon began making this connection between life changes and health as early as the 1920s. This was followed by research in the 1930s by Dr. Adolf Meyer of Johns Hopkins University, who proposed a life chart to assist in diagnosing a person's health.

Thomas Holmes and Richard Rahe at the University of Washington refined the idea of the life chart and developed a list of forty-two common stress-producing experiences, which included change in family, occupation, personal relationships, and so forth.

The life-stress profile in this chapter suggests that both pleasant and unpleasant events are stress provoking. Obviously, each individual's response to each of these changes will be different, although the general principle is that a stressful environment is one in which an individual faces a number of complex changes.

SCORING TEST 12. THE LIFE EVENTS PROFILE

Your score on the test can be calculated by multiplying the *number of times an event happened* by the *item value* to provide the *stress index*. Adding all these stress indexes will give you a total score for the year.

Interpreting Your Scores

■ *A total score of 150–199 indicates mild life change or possibility to be stressed.*

Holmes and Rahe indicated that 37 percent of the people in this category had an appreciable change in their health.

■ *Moderate life change is described by people with scores of 200–299.*

People in this category have a 50-50 chance of experiencing a change in their health.

■ *People with a score of over 300 can be categorized as experiencing major life changes.*

Seventy percent of the people that Holmes and Rahe studied had some illness the following year.

A score on the life-change index does not mean that a person will be ill the next year. There are many limitations to such tests, which rely on memory and which do not take into account genetic differences and personal perceptions of what is stressful.

The test can be used as a general guide to recognizing that an accumulation of stressful events can be overwhelming. It might be used as a way to understand and plan for future events. In this regard, a person might wish to avoid quitting a job or school just after he or she had experienced the death or illness of a close friend.

You may want to take the Holmes-Rahe test to find out how much change you underwent in the past year. You may even wish to include other life events not listed on the test. The scores do not reflect how you deal with stress. They simply show how much change you have to deal with.

When you are faced with a number of stressors at the same time, be aware of their potentially overloading effect. In the same way, certain times of the year—Christmas, for example—are more stressful because they create extra demands on us. For some people, Christmas means an examination period, visits from relatives, and extra financial demands.

The life events in the above test will affect each of us differently. As a result, a high score for one person may be more meaningful than it is for others.

Life's Unpredictable Crises As Transitions

Why are some people more likely to use a stressful life experience to help themselves learn and develop? Those that are more successful have certain characteristics. Think about how you would answer the following questions:

- Have you experienced one or more important life crises, such as taking on a new job, marriage, or divorce?
- Have you learned to deal with such crises as normal challenges? Do you view these crises as something to agonize over and try to defeat them?
- Do you view them as challenges of life?

No one is protected from the crises of life. Crises provoke uncertainty and are characterized by periods of disagreement, internal confrontation, and personal transition. Feelings of uncertainty are not just ambiguous. They are characterized by internal conflict, which often confronts values. The conflict and stress may be so intense that it changes your life, now and later.

Recently, my daughter Julia was a victim of a robbery at the supermarket where she worked. Needless to say, this was a life crisis that completely involved her. When I saw her shortly after the robbery, she was in tears. Before the police brought her home, our family talked about this and how we could help Julia. So, for the first day, we simply listened to her and encouraged her to talk about the experience. Julia was unable to sleep that night, and the experience consumed her for the next few days. We asked a few questions. The purpose was to encourage her to express her feelings and to see something positive in what had happened. "How can I learn from this?" she said. "The only thing that I can learn is to never work alone at night in a place which can be held up." "Yes, Julia, but you are alive, thank the world for that. And, you experienced something that few of us have experienced."

During this period, Julia was very angry and had many questions that bothered her. Why was the videocamera off on this evening? Why hadn't they "stripped" the cash register of the day's revenues before the evening shift? Why were she and another girl the only people there? She seemed to be wanting to say, "I was not the person who was responsible. I am not to blame."

On the third day, I sat with her and sought to do two things. I wanted her to tell me about the feelings that she had during the incident and afterwards. Second, I wanted her to review the facts as she saw them, in terms of what happened during and after the incident. This was a very revealing session, and she found it very helpful. She was past the anger and was beginning to look at the situation more objectively.

We kept talking to Julia, and I and a fellow psychologist, who was a close family friend, sought to encourage Julia into the next stage, of assuring her that what she did was very appropriate. She should be proud of the way she conducted herself. We also encouraged her by saying things such as, "What you did was really smart. You probably saved the other person's life by taking quick action." We also kept encouraging her to view this as an experience from which she could learn how to deal with critical events.

> THE MOST IMPORTANT ELEMENT IN RESPONDING TO A STRESSFUL INCIDENT IS THE WAY YOU DEAL WITH THE UNCERTAINTY AND TRAUMA YOU FACE. THOSE WHO ARE MORE EFFECTIVE IN DEALING WITH SUCH INCIDENTS CAN USE THE EXPERIENCE TO PROPEL THEMSELVES FORWARD RATHER THAN HOLD THEMSELVES BACK.

Those people that are less successful in dealing with a crisis seem to agonize over the stressful experience and to continue the fight after it is over by taking legal action, feeling bitter, and refusing to evaluate their attitudes and behaviors. They never let it go, like many war victims who let their experiences haunt them for the rest of their lives. It becomes part of the subconscious and begins to negatively shape their lives.

A less effective strategy is based on the belief that one can fight life crises and seek to reduce their effects, like a surgeon who tries to cut out an infected part of the body. A more effective strategy is to recognize that life crises cannot be cut out and avoided. Rather, you can become involved with them. Life crises are challenges that call for intense understanding and personal involvement and reassessment.

Developing creative ways to resolve life crises is an important asset in those people who are effective in responding. Effective people are courageous and adaptable. They use uncertainty as an opportunity to focus their reassessment.

Indeed, something more than courage is required. A life crisis may be a stressor, and depending on the individual, different reactions may occur. Some people react with challenge and tension, others with anxiety or depression.

The notion that stress and uncertainty may enhance creativity is expressed by John Dewey's maxim, "We only think when we have a problem to solve." Stress acts as a form of deprivation, which motivates the creative experience. Creative people feel a pressure to create. Problem solving may emanate from deep-seated, unconscious conflicts of great significance in the life of the individual.

Perhaps the creative person's early learning encouraged the conflict, and real creativity may not occur without a compelling awareness of problems and of self-imposed pressure. Uncertainty requires the ability to live with opposition as one lives with nature.

Living with opposition and adjusting to uncertainty may be more valuable than solving a problem by immediately reducing the opposition and uncertainty. Those who are successful in dealing with stressors employ healthy, creative, and productive strategies, while other less effective and healthy people employ maladaptive mechanisms in dealing with opposition. While problems and crises might provoke creativity and innovation, discontent may result from a prolonged inability to adjust to tension.

PEOPLE WHO ARE MORE LIKELY TO DEAL EFFECTIVELY WITH THE STRESSORS AROUND THEM HAVE A MEANING AND PURPOSE IN THEIR LIVES. THE MEANING IS SOMETHING BEYOND THEMSELVES: WORK, AN IDEA, A LEISURE PRODUCT, OTHER PEOPLE, A BOOK, OR A SOCIAL OBJECTIVE.

Debra was very unhappy with her boss but she did her job in a professional manner. She was productive and helpful to everyone in the office and no one knew how her boss treated her. When an opening came up in another department, she was gone. She said, "Life is too short to work for that boss. She has a dark cloud around her every hour of the day. I can't change her but I am sure not going to let her change me. I'm out of here."

Debra got out as quickly as she could and found a job that was consistent with her values and life vision. She liked people and she wanted to be happy around them. It disturbed her that her supervisor was such a negative person.

Debra's commitment to a positive work environment and cheerful people gave her meaning in life. Her personal values expanded to include others beyond her family and the organization. She was not a person who was seeking to change the world. She simply wanted to live and work in a happy environment.

ARE YOU VERY OPEN AND INTIMATE IN TALKING ABOUT THE STRESSES YOU ARE ENCOUNTERING?

The emotional response to stressors—such as an impending death, an impending loss of job, or a divorce—may be denial, rage and anger, bargaining, depression, and even acceptance. Franklin would not accept his doctor's diagnosis that he had cancer. He demanded another opinion and then another. When he finally had the third opinion, he was extremely angry, full of rage and frustration, which he expressed toward his colleagues and loved ones. He later became very depressed and would not talk with anyone, refusing any offer of support and kindness. Most terminal patients who have some time and help can reach a stage in which they are neither depressed nor angry about their fate, and can express less envy and anger toward the living and healthy. In this acceptance stage, the dying patient has found some peace and acceptance, wishes to be left alone, and his or her interests diminish. Those who struggle to keep unrealistic hope alive never really accept their impending death. They continue to fight and view acceptance as being a coward.

A similar response happened when Janice heard about her company's impending layoffs. She denied it. "I'm pretty safe," she said. "I've just developed a new product from which the company will gain immensely." After a time, she became more concerned that she might be laid off. "If only I knew what was going to happen, then I could plan my life." One of the worst problems for her was the rumor mill, which seemed to produce very unreliable information. She was shocked when she got her layoff notice. She swore at her supervisor. The company offered her a job in another location. She refused and walked out. Months later, she thought again about the job offer, but refused to go back.

Why are some individuals less likely to accept the stressors around them while others learn a great deal from them and have the opportunity to grow? Studies show that 90 percent of people who seek medical help are suffering from self-limiting disorders well within the range of the body's own healing powers. Doctors could treat these patients with placebos (drugs that have no medical qualities). The healing process begins because the patient reaches out and puts confidence in others.

PEOPLE WHO ARE EFFECTIVE IN RESPONDING TO STRESSORS ARE VERY OPEN AND WILLING TO TALK TO OTHERS.

People who respond effectively to stress may have experienced denial, rage and anger, bargaining, depression, and even acceptance. Their willingness to talk to others allows them to move quickly to a point where they accept the stressor as a challenge. They then use the support of others to take positive action.

Becky said her cancer was a shock to her. "My lifestyle is generally healthy, and it seemed so unfair. It was pretty bad for me during the first couple of weeks. I guess I dealt with the denial, the anger, the bargaining, the depression. I cried a lot last week. I've got through the anger and depression rather quickly. Now, I'm determined I'm going to beat it."

Everyone knew about the issues Becky faced. She talked about it to anyone who asked, and she was proud of the fact that she was going to respond differently. She developed social support systems with many others, including close friends as well as colleagues who were supportive of her. She sought out the informal support systems that were available from the generosity and kindness of people in general. She had an ability and willingness to communicate her most intimate fears about death. She talked about her family, about her financial difficulties, her divorce, and her difficulty with her son.

HOW DO YOU GATHER NEW INFORMATION THAT MIGHT BRING NEW INSIGHTS AND POINTS OF VIEW ON AN ISSUE?

ALBERT SCHWEITZER ALWAYS BELIEVED THAT THE BEST MEDICINE TO HANDLE ANY CRISIS OR ILLNESS WAS HIS KNOWLEDGE AND HIS ABILITY TO USE HIS KNOWLEDGE CREATIVELY, PLUS A GOOD SENSE OF HUMOR.

Fred and Jackson gathered knowledge about their cancers in different ways. Fred's first step was to gather information from a variety of sources, from experts, colleagues, and personal friends, as well as medical journals and popular books. Yet, he did not grasp onto so-called magical solutions or diet plans. He sought to understand.

After months of study, Fred became interested in a variety of ideas, including meditation, no-fat diets, Chinese medicine, and exercise plans. He even changed his consulting practice to focus on wellness programs and stress management. He continued to study and conduct workshops.

Jackson resisted the invitation of a host of friends who had ideas, anecdotes, and suggestions. Jackson relied on his surgeon, who indicated that "some people were more genetically disposed to cancer."

Fred's story is an inspiration; he has become a resource for others, partially because he encountered and conquered a very stressful situation. The way he gathered information was unique. He talked to others who had similar problems, he consulted popular and academic books, and he even listened to those who might be considered unconventional.

His information gathering was systematic and grounded. From it, he developed his unique perspective on how he would manage his health.

DO YOU SEEK OUTLETS WHERE YOU OBSERVE AND EXPRESS POSITIVE FEELINGS, HUMOR, CREATIVITY, RELAXATION?

JOHANN SEBASTIAN BACH MADE IT POSSIBLE FOR ALBERT SCHWEITZER TO FREE HIMSELF FROM THE PRESSURES AND TENSION OF HIS JOB AT THE HOSPITAL. HE FOUND SPLENDOR AND CREATIVE ECSTASY IN MUSIC. HIS POWERFUL HANDS WERE IN COMPLETE CONTROL AS HE PLAYED. AFTER PLAYING, HE FELT RESTORED.

Many people who become discouraged by the stresses around them do so because they are too tense, lack a sense of humor, and do not have time for relaxation. The costs of being negative are high.

Immanuel Kant wrote in *The Critique of Pure Reason* that laughter produces a "feeling of health through the furtherance of the vital bodily processes, the affection that moves the intestines and the diaphragm; in a word, the feeling of health that makes up the gratification felt by us; so that we can thus reach the body through the soul and use the latter as the physician of the former." Norman Cousins, in *Anatomy of an Illness*, wrote about the ability of laughter to help reduce the inflammation in his joints. His personal experiment called for exercises (for example, through films and books) that encouraged positive emotions. He said, "I made the joyous discovery that ten minutes of belly laughter had an anesthetic effect and would give me at least two hours of pain-free sleep." Later, he went completely off drugs and sleeping pills.

Norman Cousins's story has the backing of scientific research, which illustrates how ascorbic acid, which is produced by laughter, is very helpful in assisting the recovery process.

ARE YOU WILLING TO MAKE RADICAL CHANGES IN ATTITUDES, LIFESTYLES, AND BEHAVIORS?

BEING EFFECTIVE IN DEALING WITH LIFE CRISES SOMETIMES REQUIRES RADICAL SHIFTS IN BEHAVIOR AND VALUES.

Effective people are able to:

- View life crises as creative ways to develop and grow
- Define meaning and a clear purpose in life
- Develop support systems and be open to expressing their fears
- Gather information from a variety of perspectives and be receptive to being creative in using it
- Exhibit creativity, humor, and relaxation

PRINCIPLE 6:
Reduce Stress-Promoting Foods

INCREASE FOODS THAT IMPROVE WELLNESS

It is a very odd thing
As odd as can be
That whatever Miss T. eats
Turns into Miss T.

—WALTER DE LA MARE

The foods that we purchase in restaurants and fast-food outlets—McDonald's hamburgers and French fries, Kentucky Fried chicken, Coca-Cola or Pepsi Cola, ice cream, and apple pie—are very different than what our ancestors ate. Many of these foods are high in fat and sugar. These foods are stressful to our systems.

What is in these foods—the fats and sugars—is only part of the problem. What is not in these foods—the nutrients—is just as important.

THE FOOD WE EAT

Much of our food is a by-product of fertilizers, feed lots, preservatives, chemical supplements, and sterilizers. How good is this for us?

Soil fertilized with manure or compost contains about 50 percent humus, a substance formed when bacteria and fungi interact. This makes the soil rich, dark, and spongy. When the soil is fertilized with chemicals—and sprayed with pesticides and fungicides—most of the bacteria and fungi are destroyed. The resulting soil is organically dead and less spongy and erodes more easily. Nutritional analysis indicates that chemically grown vegetables contain about a quarter of the minerals as organically grown vegetables. As a result, the food that we eat today is not as nutritious as that which we ate many years ago when it was grown naturally.

Chemicals added to our food are, in some cases, detrimental. For example, the hormone DES (diethystilbestrol) was used for years, beginning in the 1940s, to make animals fatter. It was finally banned by the U.S. Food and Drug Administration as a cancer-causing agent. Chloramphenicol was an antibiotic given to beef cattle to stop them from dying of "shipping fever" during the very bumpy, stressful ride to the slaughter house. It causes a fatal blood disorder in some people. DDT and dieldrin are other dangerous pesticides that were very common and are still used in some countries.

The list of dangerous chemicals in our soil is quite extensive and includes heptaclor, alar, PPBs, PCBs, hexachlorophane, phosgene, dioxin, and many others. Pesticides and other chemicals remain in the environment for years, and we continue to be exposed to them long after they have been officially banned.

In some parts of the world, there are regular reports of poisoning from chemicals in the water. In one report of poisoning from pollution in Hong Kong, there were 26 cases of paralytic toxic poisoning involving 130 people, compared to 4 cases involving 15 people in 1992. It is said that the buildup of pollution in Hong Kong waters has caused an almost ninefold increase in the number of illnesses from eating seafood. There have been many similar experiences elsewhere. Problems result from red tides and toxins in the water, and as yet there are no standards to check contaminants in seafood. Worse still are reports of fishermen who are overly eager to placate Asian diners' desire for fresh fish. According to a U.S.–New Zealand report, the increasing demand for live fish in Hong Kong, China, Taiwan, Singapore, and Japan has encouraged fishermen to use cyanide, a poison that is used to execute criminals in the United States. Typically, the fish are revived after a moderate dose of cyanide and kept in pens until picked up by special transport ships. The use of cyanide has become so widespread that it is destroying reef ecosystems.

Several foods are, according to the U.S. Environmental Protection Agency and Academy of Sciences, more likely to have high levels of toxic residues of agricultural chemicals. In order of risk, these foods include: tomatoes, beef, potatoes, oranges, lettuce, apples, peaches, pork, wheat, soybeans, beans, carrots, chicken, corn, and grapes.

Minimizing our exposure involves restricting the quantity of meats that we eat, since these foods contain, on average, about 8 times the amount of pesticides as green leafy vegetables. Milk and dairy products contain about 3 times as much and 14 times as much as grains and roots. When eating vegetables, it is important to wash them thoroughly, and it might be appropriate to remove the skins of apples and pears. Vinegar is a useful solution to use in washing vegetables. Other solutions include eating more organic foods and eating them in combinations that are healthy and not disruptive to the body's chemistry. The most effective plan, of course, is to grow one's own food.

THE STRESS-PROMOTING DIET

STRESS IS A SOURCE OF WEAR AND TEAR ON THE BODY, BUT PROPER NUTRITION IS THE BASIS FOR RESISTING THE ILL EFFECTS OF THIS PROCESS.

Certain foods can exaggerate the stress response. Caffeine, sugar, and salt are examples of foods that can provoke or hinder the body's systems. Caffeine, for example, is a stimulant that can trigger a stress response in the body; the intensity of the response depends on how much you consumed, your body size, and the presence of other nutrients in your body. Caffeine is a sympathomimetic agent, a chemical substance that mimics the sympathetic nervous system stress response, creating fatigue and irritability. Vitamin depletion, sugar, and salt provoke stress in other ways.

TEST 13. THE STRESS-PROMOTING DIET TEST

The following short test will help you analyze your diet. After completing the test, read about how each of the various dietary factors might increase your stress or reduce your ability to handle stress.

Check the most appropriate response to each of the statements below:

1. Coffee, Tea, Cocoa, or Colas
   _____ (a) 2 cups or less a day
   _____ (b) 3 to 4 cups
   _____ (c) 5 to 6 cups
   _____ (d) 7 or more cups a day

2a. Sugar (teaspoons of sugar each day)
   _____ (a) Do not add sugar in coffee, cereals
   _____ (b) Use 3 to 4 teaspoons per day
   _____ (c) Use 5 to 6 teaspoons per day
   _____ (d) Use 7 or more teaspoons each day

2b. Sugar (candies, chocolates, ice cream, sodas, desserts, cookies, etc.)
   _____ (a) Do not normally take any of the above each day
   _____ (b) Normally have one serving of the above each day
   _____ (c) Normally have 2 to 4 each day.
   _____ (d) Normally have 5 or more each day.

2c. Processed foods and flours: I eat:
   _____ (a) Naturally processed foods
   _____ (b) Foods that are enriched
   _____ (c) Small quantities of pastries, pastas, and white breads
   _____ (d) Large quantities of pastries, pastas, and white breads

3a. Salt
   _____ (a) I watch and try to restrict my salt intake and do not eat canned foods, crackers, and other such foods

_____ (b) I normally do not add salt to my foods at each meal, but do not generally watch the salt intake of the foods I eat

_____ (c) I do not add salt to my foods and do eat some canned foods, pork products, snack foods, cheeses, seasonings, and fast foods

_____ (d) I like to add salt to my foods and eat many canned foods, pork products, snack foods, cheeses, seasonings, and fast foods

3b. **Salt intake: I add salt to food at meals (total shakes of a table salt shaker or when cooking the food):**

_____ (a) 0 salt or take potassium chloride.

_____ (b) 4 to 5 shakes per day only when cooking

_____ (c) 6 to 15 when eating or cooking

_____ (d) 16 or more

4a. **Weight and Fat: I am:**

_____ (a) At ideal weight with very little body fat

_____ (b) Near ideal weight with little body fat

_____ (c) 10 to 25 pounds overweight

_____ (d) More than 20 pounds overweight

4b. **Dietary Fat**

_____ (a) No more than 3% to 5% of total calories (for males) or 10% to 12% (for females) from dietary fat

_____ (b) Eat 13% to 16% of total calories (for males) or 22% to 25% (for females) from dietary fat

_____ (c) Eat above 25% of total calories (for males) or 30% (for females) from dietary fat

_____ (d) Eat much more than 50% of total calories from dietary fat

5a. **Smoking**

_____ (a) Do not smoke and never did smoke

_____ (b) Do not smoke, but smoked previously

_____ (c) 10 cigarettes per week or more

_____ (d) 10 cigarettes per day or more

5b.   Air Pollution in City or Work Setting

_____   (a) No air pollution and work in clean setting

_____   (b) Some air pollution but don't work in a sick building (enclosed/no outside air)

_____   (b) Some air pollution and work in a sick building (enclosed/no outside air)

_____   (c) Polluted environment and work setting

5c.   Smoke of Others Around Me

_____   (a) Not at all

_____   (b) Others smoke and they smoke in air conditioned/closed environment

_____   (c) I have frequent interactions with people who smoke

_____   (d) People who I work with or live with are smoking regularly

6.   Alcohol Consumption

_____   (a) Do not drink or drink moderately

_____   (b) Do not generally drink but sometimes go out "on the town"

_____   (c) Have 3 to 4 drinks per day

_____   (d) Have more than 5 drinks each day

Analyzing Your Diet

For each of the questions mark your scores in the following spaces. Scoring: a = 1, b = 2, c = 3, d = 4.

	Individual Scores	**Total Scores**
1. Caffeine	1 ._____	
		_____
2. Sugar and	2a._____	
Processed Foods	2b._____	
	2c ._____	
		_____/3

3. Salt   3a._____

                   3b._____

                                       _____/2

4. Weight and Fat 4a._____

                   4b._____

                                       _____/2

5. Smoking and Air 5a._____

   Pollution   5b._____

                   5c _____

                                       _____/2

6. Alcohol   6 ._____

   Consumption   _____

                   Total Score   _____

Add scores for each of the above items and divide by the number of items. The ideal for each category is a score of 1. A score of 3–4 indicates that the foods you eat may be stress provoking. Add up your total score for all seven categories. A overall score of 6 is ideal. Scores of 16–24 indicate that your overall diet is stress provoking.

Caffeine

CAFFEINE, A CHEMICAL THAT BELONGS TO THE XANTHINE GROUP OF DRUGS, IS THE MOST COMMON OF THE SYMPATHOMIMETIC AGENTS.

Xanthines such as caffeine are amphetamine-like stimulants that can stimulate the release of the stress hormones, increasing heart rate, blood pressure, and oxygen to the heart. Continued exposure can harm the heart tissue.

Caffeine is found in coffee and, to a lesser extent, in tea, cocoa, cola drinks, chocolate, and other foods. Some people drink 5 to 6 cups of coffee a day, with each cup containing between 100 and 150 milligrams of caffeine (per 6-ounce cup), depending on how it is brewed. This extra jolt of energy that people give themselves to keep alert each day triggers the release of stress hormones. Heart rate and blood pressure increase, as does the body's demands for oxygen.

Coffee drinking encourages the body to stay in this superalert state all day long. Anxiety, irritability, diarrhea, arrhythmia (irregular heartbeat), and the inability to concentrate are some of the side effects of excessive coffee consumption. Coffee also stimulates the secretion of pepsin, a digestive enzyme, in the stomach. When the stomach is empty, pepsin and the natural oils in coffee can combine and irritate the stomach lining. Caffeine can increase a person's metabolism as well as increase the possibility of stomach upset or irritation. Obviously, this will have a greater impact on children or people who have low body weight. Overall, this morning caffeine "hit" may not be that desirable.

Decaffeinated coffee has 2 to 5 milligrams of caffeine per cup. However, some such coffee also contains many chemicals, depending on the decaffeination process. Some of the chemicals may be worse for you than caffeine.

Tea, cola beverages, chocolate, and cocoa also contain xanthine stimulants. Six ounces of tea does not contain the irritating oils found in coffee, although it does contain about 90 milligrams of caffeine, as well as other xanthines such as theobromine and theophylline. Various cola beverages (for example, Coca Cola, Pepsi Cola, Dr. Pepper) contain 45 to 60 milligrams of caffeine per 12-ounce container, while a 1-ounce chocolate bar has about 20 milligrams. Some energy drinks are really solutions of caffeine and sugar. Although sodas and chocolate have less caffeine, they are just as undesirable, because they have a lot of calories and little nutritional value.

Processed Flours and Sugars

During stressful times, certain vitamins are needed to assist the body in maintaining the nervous and endocrine systems.

VITAMIN DEPLETION LOWERS THE BODY'S ABILITY TO COPE WITH STRESS BECAUSE IT WILL MAKE YOU HIGHLY SUSCEPTIBLE TO THE SIDE EFFECTS OF B-COMPLEX DEFICIENCIES.

Vitamins B-1, B-2, and niacin are important for the body's processing of glucose to make energy, called carbohydrate metabolism and gluconeogensis. Vitamins B-5, C, and choline are used to produce adrenal hormones, secreted during the stress response.

Deficiencies in B-complex vitamins (vitamins B-1, B-5, and B-6) can lead to anxiety reactions, depression, insomnia, and cardiovascular weakness. The biggest role of the B vitamins is the maintenance and building of the myelin sheath around the nerve cells. This sheath is what conducts the electrical current. Diseases of the central nervous system implicate B deficiency. Vitamins B and niacin deficiencies are associated with stomach irritability and muscle weakness.

REFINED WHITE SUGAR AND PROCESSED FLOUR ARE DEPLETED OF NEEDED VITAMINS.

An average-sized chocolate bar may contain 7 teaspoons of sugar. Iced cake has 15 teaspoons, pies have 10 to 13 teaspoons, and sodas contain 7 to 10 teaspoons. Sugar products are thought to be sources of quick energy, but they also provide empty calories with little nutritional value. When the body processes sugar for energy, it uses B-complex vitamins. Sugar products do not have these vitamins, so the body has to steal them from other food sources. If a person does not obtain sufficient B vitamins from nutritious foods or supplements, the result is a vitamin-B deficiency, with symptoms such as anxiety, irritability, and general nervousness.

Refined white sugar causes the body to draw nutrients from other foods or from storage. Brown and raw sugars aren't much better; they are over 90 percent refined.

Processed flour is also associated with vitamin-B depletion. Flour is processed by using steel rollers to crush the wheat grains into a fine powder, which is then bleached into the common white flour used for baking. We see this bleached flour in breads (even brown breads) and pastas. The process removes at least twenty-two known essential nutrients, including most of the vitamins, vitamin E, and minerals such as calcium, phosphorous, potassium, and magnesium. Because of this processing, the body loses some of the valuable vitamins it might have gained from wheat and flour. In turn, the body must get these vitamins from other foods. Thus, breads can be empty calories that deplete the body of important vitamins. Many processed flour products are enriched with some of the nutrients that are destroyed during processing, although this enrichment process does not restore a food's natural integrity; only a small number of the deleted nutrients are replaced.

Hypoglycemia from Sugar and Processed Flour

Sugar is a basic food for all of us. Our main food consists of carbohydrates, which is sugar in a complex form. Sugar is not the problem; it is the type and amount we consume. Refined white sugar is the most harmful, but brown sugar, honey, and other simple sugars can also cause problems because they raise the blood pressure too quickly.

> **LOW BLOOD SUGAR IS KNOWN AS HYPOGLYCEMIA, AND IT MAY RESULT IN SYMPTOMS SUCH AS ANXIETY, HEADACHES, DIZZINESS, TREMBLING, AND INCREASED CARDIAC ACTIVITY.**

Hypoglycemia has many causes, but dietary behavior is an important factor in many cases. A person who constantly and excessively snacks on sugary foods may be prone to this problem (reactive hypoglycemia). People who consistently skip meals will lower their normal intake (functional hypoglycemia). Hypoglycemia most often results from the cumulative effects of eating refined sugars and flours and may affect nearly 50 percent of the population (24 percent of these cases are severe).

In hypoglycemia, the body removes glucose (or sugar) from the blood faster than it replaces it. A high intake of sugar or processed foods first raises the sugar level in the blood. Quickly assimilated refined carbohydrates, such as alcohol, candy, and soda, send a person's blood sugar level soaring. This drops to an abnormally low level a few hours later due to the action of the insulin from the pancreas. To process these foods, the body needs to draw vitamins (like B-complex vitamins) and minerals from other sources. Excess sugar enters the tissues of the body and is not selectively saved for the central nervous system, which requires blood sugar. The pancreas produces insulin, and this chemical change results in peculiar mental and emotional responses (within one or two minutes). Soon after, the blood-sugar level drops too low and the person begins to feel sluggish and craves more sweets.

A person who cannot get through the day without a break for more food is in a prediabetic state. Over a long period of time, the pancreas may become overworked and sugar diabetes might develop. When blood-sugar levels drop below 60 milligrams of glucose per 100 millilitres of blood, a person is likely to feel fatigued with little energy. Long-term sugar intake, in addition to associated physiological conditions, may be responsible for people continuously feeling hungry. Breakfasts of sweet cereals, coffee (with sugar), and sugary snacks (cookies and candy) may increase this condition. By the middle of the morning, the person will have a low blood-sugar level and resulting feelings of fatigue. This inhibits his or her ability to handle stress and to perform. The same situation may occur in midafternoon or any other time of day after high sugar intake.

SUGAR AND REFINED FLOUR PRODUCTS CAUSE SHARP VARIATIONS IN THE BLOOD-GLUCOSE LEVELS, WHICH DETERMINE YOUR LEVEL OF ENERGY.

The body gets an energy boost from sugar and refined flour products but only for a short time, and then the body reacts as the energy levels plunge. White rice, white bread, and other refined flour products have the same effects.

Alcohol-induced hypoglycemia develops because the drinker forces the liver to metabolize alcohol when it really is trying to make new blood sugar from the nutrients it has available. The brain receives alcohol instead of blood sugar.

It is entirely possible to consume one or two cups of sugar a day and still believe that you have eaten no sugar. Many processed foods contain hidden sugar. For example, bread, canned soups, canned and frozen vegetables, sauces, canned fruits, and fruit juices contain sugar.

The stress associated with sugar consumption is best avoided by eating well-balanced meals and being aware of the sugar content of foods and the way that foods are processed. Your goal is to reduce your intake of processed foods, such as white rice, white bread, and processed sugars.

Sugar and carbohydrates are important in our diets. For example, the brain relies on glucose, which is also known as blood sugar. The brain consumes 24 percent of the body's available sugar and, unlike other organs, cannot switch over to fat and other fuels. The blood can only carry enough glucose to last about four hours and must have a constant replenishment of sugar.

Sugar either comes:

- directly from the bloodstream from foods such as honey and grapes
- from breaking down carbohydrates into glucose
- when other supplies are exhausted, from the liver that converts stored glycogen into glucose and secretes it into the bloodstream

A superstrict fad diet, which excludes all forms of sugar and carbohydrates, does not furnish the body with glucose to process the fats and proteins consumed. As a result, the brain becomes starved for sugar from natural sugar foods, carbohydrates, and liver glycogen (if a person does not eat enough protein and fat to supply liver glycogen).

An additional problem with refined grains is that they contain very little fiber, which is essential in slowing down the release of sugar, in addition to lowering blood cholesterol and helping to eliminate toxins. On a high-fiber diet, foods take about a day to get through the digestive system, while on a low-fiber diet, they may take as long as three to five days. During this extended period of time, the food rots or putrefies.

Salt

Most table salt is a combination of two elements called sodium chloride. The sodium ion causes a retention of water in the body and is partially responsible for regulating the body's water balance. Too much salt or foods high in sodium may result in excessive fluid retention, which, in turn, can result in nervous tension or edema (an abnormal accumulation of fluid). Excess fluid retention could also lead to higher blood pressure. If a person's blood pressure is already high due to stress and anxiety, the increased fluid retention may make it dangerously high.

Those who eat too many salty foods may increase their risk of contracting cancers of the lungs, stomach, throat, and the upper nasal passage. These diseases are very common among the Chinese in Singapore, Hong Kong, Shanghai, and the United States. Salt intake is high in many countries. In Japan and the United States, where the per capita intake of salt is rather high, it may be one of the factors that contribute to high blood pressure.

> **THE BODY USUALLY NEEDS ABOUT 1 GRAM OF SALT TO FUNCTION, BUT MOST PEOPLE, BECAUSE THEY EAT PROCESSED FOODS, CONSUME 4 TO 8 GRAMS PER DAY.**

An average shake of a salt shaker is 100 milligrams. Even if you use no salt at the table at all, however, you are probably eating too much. Most of our salt intake comes from the salt in processed foods. Sodium is used in processed foods to improve taste and enhance preservation. Check the content of some of the foods you buy. Most canned foods (soups, vegetables), pork products (ham, bacon), snack foods (potato chips, french fries, popcorn), cheeses, fast foods, and seasonings (mustard, catsup, soy sauce) are high in salt. For reducing overall salt intake, salt substitutes (potassium chloride) are popular. Natural flavoring substitutes for salt include ginger, mint, cinnamon, chili powder, curry, and many other spices.

The food processing industry is so reliant on the use of sodium that it is difficult to imagine how we would get along without it. Food tastes bland without sodium, so much so that manufacturers are scared to take the risk of sodium-free foods. The best solution for us is to stop adding salt and then monitor the salt content of the foods we buy. As a general principle, foods that are canned, bagged, or preserved are likely to be high in sodium. The best way to avoid sodium is to eat fresh foods that have not been processed.

Fats and Oils

FATS AND OILS CLOG THE BLOOD VESSELS, SLOW DOWN BLOOD FLOW, AND OBSTRUCT IMMUNE CELLS.

Saturated fats are linked to high cholesterol levels in many studies, and they may increase the risk of lung cancer in women fivefold. For some time, the standard advice was to avoid saturated fats and use more unsaturated fats; that is, for example, we might avoid butter, lard, coconut oil, and palm oil and switch to margarine and corn oil. This is not as simple as it sounds.

Saturated fats solidify at room temperature. They are found in meat, cheese, butter, lard, cream, egg yolk, chocolate, palm oil, coconut oil, and milk. Unsaturated fats stay liquid at room temperature. These fats are found in vegetable oils. There are two types of unsaturated fats, polyunsaturated and monounsaturated. Polyunsaturated fats are found in safflower and soybean oil and they were once said to help lower cholesterol. In fact, they may be just as bad as saturated fats. The monounsaturated fats found in olive and canola oils seem to be the most healthy and play a different role in reducing cholesterol.

WHILE ANIMAL FAT IS COMMONLY BLAMED, VEGETABLE OILS CAN BE EVEN MORE HARMFUL WHEN THEY HAVE BEEN HYDROGENATED TO FORM MARGARINE.

Hydrogenation is the process by which natural oils are changed into margarine. It changes the natural oil's unsaturated and essential fatty acids. In the process, the liquid oil is heated to a very high temperature in the presence of a metal catalyst and mixed with hydrogen under high pressure. Hydrogenation is used in the manufacture of margarine and other hydrogenated or partially hydrogenated fats for use in processed foods. The presence of the metal catalyst is worrisome. A completely hydrogenated oil, in addition to being contaminated by a metal catalyst, contains no essential fatty acid (EFA) activity whatsoever.

Partial hydrogenation produces margarine, shortening, shortening oils, and partially hydrogenated vegetable oils. These products contain large quantities of trans-fatty acids and other altered fat substances.

Studies indicate that trans-fats tend to increase the so-called bad cholesterol (LDL) and lower the good cholesterol (HDL). Thus, diets high in margarine and other partially hydrogenated vegetables oils, long touted as a healthy alternative to butter and lard, could raise the risk of heart disease. Thirty thousand heart disease deaths in the United States each year could be blamed on diets high in trans-fats.

Vegetable oils do not contain saturated fats and are cholesterol free, except for palm and coconut oil, which contain mainly saturated fats. Vegetable oils contain high proportions of unsaturated fats and essential fatty acids, like linoleic acid (LA) and linolenic acid (LNA). These acids, found in the oils of nuts and seeds, are important for nutrition and health.

Vegetable oils have certain disadvantages because light, air, and heat can cause them to spoil. The oils oxidize when exposed to light and air, and heating speeds up the process. Heating also produces unstable molecules called free radicals, toxic substances that can lead to atherosclerosis, premature aging of the skin, and cancer.

A GOOD OIL FROM A NUTRITIONAL STANDPOINT MAY NOT BE USEFUL FOR COOKING.

Most oils have already been heated during the manufacturing process. It is preferable, therefore, to use cold-pressed oils, such as sesame oil, which is one of the least easily damaged vegetables oils.

The best oil to use for cooking is olive oil, since it is easy to purchase. It contains only minerals and nutrients and is rich in monounsaturates. Oils should not be overheated. When cooking, place water in a wok before adding the oil, as the Chinese do, or place vegetables in a frying pan before the oil, as some European chefs do. Deep frying is not a good idea.

Additives

Many types of food contain chemical ingredients or additives that are used for preservation, color, improved taste, texture, sweetening, or sterilization.

> **EACH OF US CONSUMES A VARIETY OF CHEMICALS EACH YEAR, PERHAPS AS MUCH AS FIVE TO TEN POUNDS.**

The following table illustrates some of the ingredients in popular food products. Note how often sugar and sodium or salt are included. Also note the types of oils used.

TABLE 10.1 POPULAR INGREDIENTS

Diet Soda: Carbonated water, citric acid, natural flavoring, asparatame, sodium citrate, sodium benzoate (a preservative).

Soft wheat bread: Wholewheat flour, enriched high-protein flour, purified water, vital wheat gluten, granulated cane sugar, bread baker's yeast, 100% pure vegetable oil, vacuum dried salt, soya flour, dough conditioners, vitamin C, calcium, iron, thiamine (vitamin B-1), riboflavin (vitamin B-2), niacin (vitamin-B complex), calcium propionate.

Mayonnaise: Soybean oil, eggs, vinegar, water, egg yolks, salt, sugar, pure lemon juice concentrate, dried garlic, dried onion, calcium, sodium to preserve freshness, paprika, natural flavor.

Pizza sauce: Water, tomato paste, soybean oil, salt, modified food starch, dried onion, sugar, spices, corn syrup, natural garlic flavor.

Dry noodles: Wheat flour, vegetable oil, salt, egg powder, cellulose gum, sodium phosphates, sodium and potassium carbonates, riboflavin.

Nondairy creamer: Glucose syrup, hydrogenated palm oil, sodium caseinate, emulsifier, emulsifying salt, anticaking agent, flavoring, color.

Much of the concern about added chemicals in our foods is based on their possible relationships to various forms of cancer. Chemicals that we eat or that we absorb through water and air can be carcinogens, causing mutations, or alteration in cells. This could lead to cancer. As many as 80 to 90 percent of cancer cases might be correlated with exposure to environmental factors. The food we eat is one factor that might account for 60 percent of the cancers in women and 40 percent in men.

Many additives serve useful purposes to make food safe. Certain "safe" additives, as defined by the Food and Drug Administration in the United States, are put on their GRAS list (generally regarded as safe). The FDA evaluates and approves substances and allows them to be used in foods. Sometimes, because of public outcry and new research, it has to reevaluate its evidence. For example, certain additives once approved that were subsequently banned include sodium cyclamate, some red and yellow dyes, and ethylene glycol. While the GRAS-list substances are probably considered safe, future studies may prove otherwise. This has led many people to search for ways to reduce the amount of chemicals in foods and to use as many natural foods as possible.

THERE IS INCREASING EVIDENCE THAT THE CARCINOGENESIS PROCESS CAN BE REVERSED IF THE CHEMICAL INTERVENTION CAN BE REMOVED OR NEUTRALIZED, ALTHOUGH THE MUTATION IN THE CELLS MAY BE IRREVERSIBLE.

Many types of food contain enhancers, chemical additives, or artificial sweeteners, like MSG (monosodium glutamate), aspartame, sulphites, and tartrazine. These are artificial substances with molecular structures that the immune cells have to break down. The relationship between food and cancer is not clear cut. The possibility that carcinogens may cause harm depends only partially on the presence of carcinogens in food. It also depends on the interaction of many nutrients and nonnutrients.

Smoking

EVERY CIGARETTE SHORTENS THE SMOKER'S LIFE SPAN BY 7 MINUTES, WHICH ADDS UP TO A STAGGERING FIVE MILLION YEARS OF POTENTIAL LIFE THAT AMERICANS LOSE TO CIGARETTES EACH YEAR.

Every minute smoking takes a minute from a person's life, according to calculations from the Centers for Disease Control and Prevention. Smokers need greater intake of vitamins E and C, and so does the person who is exposed to a lot of secondhand smoke. For example, smokers may have 30 to 50 percent less vitamin C in their blood than do nonsmokers.

A person who smokes thirty cigarettes a day receives nearly as much radiation as from an x-ray. Moderate smokers receive the equivalent of 300 x-rays per year. Milk and certain other mucus-forming foods increase the risks of lung cancer for smokers because mucus accumulates in the lungs and traps the tar and smoke particles that are inhaled. Tobacco also causes the body to lose calcium.

There has been a great deal of debate about the harmful effects of smoking and the effects it has on nonsmokers and the offspring of smokers. It took a long time for governments to require manufacturers to attach warning labels to cigarette packages. It took even longer to restrict cigarette companies from advertising and encouraging others to smoke. Cigarettes have been banned from many workplaces and subjected to tax increases. In spite of knowledge about the ill effects of smoking, tobacco sales continue to grow worldwide. While cigarette consumption has decreased in many Western countries, cigarette makers have targeted Asia and Eastern Europe. It is estimated that China will open its market of 298 million smokers to Western cigarette makers.

While smoking may be associated with cancer, it is also a stressor. Tobacco contains nicotine, which, like caffeine, is a sympathomimetic chemical. As such, it is capable of causing adverse reactions in the sympathetic nervous system (heart, blood vessels, and sweat glands). Nicotine may enter the body by smoking tobacco, inhaling the tobacco smoke of others, or by chewing tobacco. This stimulates the adrenals, releasing hormones that cause increased heart rate, blood pressure, and respiration and stimulate the release of fatty acids and glucose into the blood.

Alcohol

Alcohol affects the body's ability to respond to stress. A great deal of alcohol is consumed throughout the world. On average in the United States, every person over the age of fourteen consumes nearly three gallons of absolute alcohol per year, the equivalent of 7.5 gallons of 80 proof whisky or 25 gallons of wine. Considering the fact that many people do not drink at all, those who do may consume much more.

Alcohol does the greatest harm to the liver, as this is the organ that detoxifies and metabolizes all foods, fluids, and other substances. The liver must work hard to deal with the toxicity of alcohol, as it would in dealing with any poison. While the liver is able to deal with many toxic substances, the metabolization process uses up vitamin B-complex and C. Alcohol also adds empty, nonnutritious calories, which must be burned up or turned into fat, and depresses the synthesis of protein. Long-term damage can result in diseases such as cirrhosis of the liver, one of the top ten causes of death.

ALCOHOL IS OFTEN TURNED TO AND RELIED ON BY PEOPLE WHO ARE FACING STRESS. THE COMMON RESPONSE IS TO HAVE A DRINK, "LET OFF STEAM," AND RELAX.

Alcohol steals the nutrition that you might use for repair and growth of the body's cells. Your ability to deal with stress is impaired. It is not conclusive that alcohol is always a substance that is harmful. Individuals who drink moderately (one or two drinks per day) may suffer fewer heart attacks because they feel more relaxed and calm. In addition, moderate consumption of red wine might be associated with lower levels of cholesterol, even in countries whose populations (for example, France) eat foods high in fat and cholesterol. However, most of the alleged benefits of alcohol are related to relaxation; other relaxation methods may be more effective. When doctors talk about a safe level of consumption, they are referring to the ability of the liver to detoxify it. The liver still has to do its work of destroying a toxin or poison.

A STRESS-PREVENTION DIET PLAN: SEVEN STRATEGIES

Sometimes it seems like everything we eat or drink is stress provoking or cancer causing. However, many foods and vitamin supplements help us reduce stress. Indeed, the manner in which we eat these foods is important in reducing stress.

Strategy 1—Adjusting Your Diet During Stressful Times

There are times when your stress level is higher than normal. These may be during exams, winter blahs, or when you have to travel through a number of time zones. They might also be periods when it is especially difficult to be positive.

Because of the serotonin-producing effects of eating carbohydrates, which causes a feeling of well-being, eating foods that produce higher levels of this brain chemical can calm us. Food can be an important tranquilizer for people undergoing stress. How do you eat carbohydrates to reduce stress?

1. Eat one part protein to five parts carbohydrates. Each time you eat protein, you elevate the concentrations of amino acids required for their digestion.

2. Fruits are carbohydrate foods that will relieve stress. Complex carbohydrates provide energy and fiber and are found in fruits, vegetables, whole breads, cereals, and beans.

3. Avoid carbohydates with fats and sugar. The fats and sugars make it harder for the body to produce tryptophan, which is the precursor of serotonin.

4. Examples of carbohydrates that might help reduce stress include:

   - baked potatoes
   - bagels
   - pasta
   - pretzels
   - rice
   - oatmeal
   - zucchini

If you are going to have a stressful morning, you might consider a high-carbohydrate breakfast.

Strategy 2—Reduce the Consumption of Stress-Promoting Foods

To reduce stress-promoting foods, you need to find appropriate substitutes. Here are some suggestions.

Try to reduce your consumption of processed foods. People need more calories if the foods they are eating are less nutritious. For example, people who eat highly refined foods (such as white breads, cakes, and candy) require more food than those who eat nutritious foods (such as whole grain bread).

We tend to overeat when we are presented with a variety of foods. In one study, twice as much ice cream was eaten if three flavors were chosen as opposed to one. In traditional societies, a monotonous diet is the rule, and most meals have a staple carbohydrate (rice, bread, or pasta). People in these societies do not get much variety and do not have a tendency to overeat.

High-fiber foods provide more bulk and a feeling of fullness and satisfaction. Although fiber contains no nutrients, it is nature's way of regulating bowel movements, controlling cholesterol, and eliminating toxins. Refined foods like white bread, which have little fiber, do not provide fullness and satisfaction, so we tend to eat more. Fibrous foods are also more satisfying because they require longer chewing. Chewing stimulates the production of saliva, which is needed to predigest carbohydrates. It also stimulates the pituitary gland.

Getting off the "caffeine trip" may be easier than you think. Since living in Asia for three years, I have become a fan of green teas. Green tea and black tea are both made from the same tea leaves, but they are processed differently. The real difference between them is the processing, much more than the taste. The tea leaf is rich in truly remarkable substances called polyphenols, which may constitute up to 30 percent of the tea leaf. Polyphenols have both antioxidant and anticancer properties. When black tea is made, the tea leaf is crushed and these polyphenols are oxidized by the enzymes within the leaf. The oxidation turns the tea leaf black. Green tea is first dried and heated, which blocks this enzymatic destruction of the polyphenols. It is far more healthy and contains much less caffeine than black tea. You may also wish to try one of the many herbal teas available.

Strategy 3—Recognizing How to Balance the Foods You Eat

A healthy diet helps develop your immune system and reduce the stress you feel. When you eat foods that are hard to digest, this uses up energy you might use for handling stress or developing your immune system.

It is difficult for the body to create the chemicals to break down foods that have different textures and compositions. The enzymes needed to break down and metabolize a steak (protein) are different than those created by the body to work on fruits and vegetables. If we combine certain foods, we are requiring our body to produce different types of enzymes.

Many of us have challenged our bodily systems with the task of digesting an assortment such as beer, hamburger, French fries, salad, and ice cream. That our systems can somehow deal with such a variety of foods and supply nutrients for the body is one of life's miracles. Such combinations remain in the body, stirring around for a longer period of time.

We might visualize a person's digestive system as an old-fashioned furnace that needs fuel to create energy. Any type of fuel might be burned, from wood, propane, coal, kerosene, or heating oil (diesel). We would hesitate to mix these fuels without some knowledge of the furnace and the fuel. The furnace might easily consume wood, although coal might be added when the fire gets burning with proper ventilation. Kerosene, propane, or heating oil would not be advisable combinations. Yet, some people throw kerosene on the fire to get it going, and often cause a dangerous explosion, just as we might expect in the stomach if we consumed ice cream and beer, or hot dogs and cola. There is likely to be a gaseous explosion.

Food combining is based on the discovery that certain food combinations can be digested with greater efficiency. Consider the textures of a diet that includes some green salad with dressing, a steak, some potatoes and carrots, milk, coffee, and fruit or cheese. The production of energy to digest these foods depends on enzymes that are produced throughout the digestive process. They are made of chains of amino acids (the building blocks of proteins). Food enters the digestive system as we chew it into small portions for swallowing. As we chew many of the carbohydrate foods like bread or potatoes, pytalin or other alkaline juices are immediately secreted by the saliva in our mouths. These foods require an alkaline medium in our stomach in order to complete digestion.

Food passes through the esophagus into the stomach, which has many layers of heavy muscle to help the stomach churn like a washing machine. For some foods, expecially protein, the stomach begins making acid digestive juices and mucous to protect the stomach from its own acid.

It is obvious what happens when our body develops both alkaline and acid juices simultaneously to digest both carbohydrates and proteins together. The resulting solution is very weak.

The digestive action in our bodies might become something like a putrefaction or fermentation process, much like you would observe in the fermentation of beer in a brewery. Imagine what happens when we leave a few grams of hamburger in a dark, warm, and moist atmosphere for twenty-four hours. In our stomach, we experience gases, cramps, bloating that results in constipation, foul stools, bleeding piles, and so on. The messy combination of food sits in our digestive system longer, producing toxins that the body has to react to. In some cases, these produce food allergies such as rashes and nausea. Indiscriminate food combining creates a fermentation vat in our stomachs that impairs its proper digestion. Instead, we are creating a breeding ground for all sorts of bacteria. The types of foods and how they are combined can be quite shocking to our digestive system, creating digestive system cramps, pains, noises, and blockages. The quantities of antacids, digestive aids, and laxatives sold may be one manifestation of some of the strains that we put our systems through.

Avoiding specific processed foods is the first step to rebuilding a healthy digestive system. The next step is avoiding combinations of foods that are hard to digest together.

Separating proteins and carbohydrates from each other allows the mouth and stomach to participate more effectively in digestion. Harvey and Marilyn Diamond, in their book *Fit for Life,* illustrated the importance of not eating carbohydrates and proteins together. The sweeter and the more refined the carbohydrate, such as white sugar, the more it retards the digestion of protein. Heavier proteins, such as red meat, will take longer to digest when eaten with carbohydrates. Other interesting introductions to the logic of food combining can be found in John Matsen's *Eating Alive* or Denis Reid's *The Tao of Health, Sex, and Longevity.*

Proteins also do not combine well with many *acidic* fruits like oranges and grapefruit. As a result, grapefruit or orange juice do not combine well with meat and eggs.

Proteins are best eaten by themselves or in combination with subacid fruits (apples, pears, peaches) and raw vegetables. Proteins and carbohydrates might be eaten at separate meals. A breakfast of grains and starches (bread) might start the day, while protein and vegetables might be taken in the evenings. Sandwichs do not generally encourage a healthy combination of foods. In addition, the milk and bread (carbohydrates) combination is also a poor mixture. Potatoes and pastas should not be combined with cheese or meats.

Carbohydrates (starch and sugars) and acidic fruit also do not mix well. Such combinations are found when we put sugar on grapefruit, berries, or juices.

The best way to eat starches (cereals, rice, bread) is to blend them with nonacidic fruit and fresh raw or lightly cooked vegetables. Cereal and fruit go well together. Carbohydrates at breakfast might include toast and cereal. Unfortunately, a mouthful of fluid taken with the cereal or fruit will dilute the saliva that is secreted.

Fats are best eaten with carbohydrates, vegetables, and fruits. Oils on salads are good combinations. Raw vegetable salads each day provide valuable nutrients and enzymes, in addition to bulk. They are best eaten straight from the garden if possible. This is when they have the largest percentage of enzymes and other nutrients.

Many people may find problems digesting acidic fruit, such as grapefruit, pineapples, or oranges, when they are combined with other foods. Indeed, fruit seems to cause a great deal of digestive distress. However, if these fruits are eaten alone and in sufficient quantity, they provide a rich assortment of enzymes, vitamins, amino acids, and energy. They can be cleansing and detoxifying. It is also worth noting that a very nourishing part of fruit is the seeds and white fibers that are often found in the core.

The best way to eat fruit is to specialize in one or two fruit each day, and they should not normally be combined with starch and protein. Sweet and acidic fruits should be eaten at different times, and sugar should not be added at any time.

The principle of food combining suggests that we should guard against eating certain food combinations, such as meat and starch. We might instead recognize that certain food combinations provide a better enzyme structure for digestion. The logic of food combining is one part of an overall attitude about diet and nutrition in which the goal is to eat foods and food combinations that are not toxic and that supply energy at the highest level.

Strategy 4—Regulating Your Eating Schedule to Maintain a Healthy Weight

Many fat people are compulsive and live by the "See Food Diet." Whenever, they "see" food, they eat it.

Eating at least three meals a day is important. Eat when you are hungry rather than starving yourself, but be conscious of what you eat. Be aware of what you are eating when you are hungry. Do not snack on muffins or bread, but drink fluids (water, green tea, juices) and fruit. Skipped meals promote muscle loss and not fat loss, and there is a tendency to overeat later.

The minimum calorie requirement for moderate-sized men is about 1,500 calories (for women, it is 1,200), and these should be distributed throughout the day. Eat like a king for breakfast, a prince for lunch, and a pauper for dinner. Eat before or immediately after exercise because exercise raises the rate at which calories are burned. As a result, the amount of fat deposited is reduced.

Snacks, especially high-fat cheese or cookies, should be avoided. It is especially important to avoid snacks in the evening or other physically inactive periods. Unburned foods is stored as fat.

Strategy 5—Reduce Fat Consumption

The typical Western diet is made up of 40 to 50 percent fat, 300 to 500 mg cholesterol, 25 to 35 percent carbohydrate, and 25 protein. Traditionally, Westerners consume lots of eggs, fatty meat, milk, cheese, ice cream, sugar, refined carbohydrates, coffee, tea, and alcohol. Such diets do not include an abundance of fruits and vegetables.

To lower cholesterol and weight, the balance of foods should be adjusted to 30 percent fat, 65 percent carbohydrates, and 15 percent protein. This can be achieved by eating leaner meats and fewer eggs, sauces, ice cream, and cheeses, while eating more fruits and vegetables.

Several fad fat products have been invented as a way of weaning people off the real thing or to allow you to eat fats and not suffer the consequences. Fat substitute products—like low-fat ice cream, cheeses, milks, and other fat substitutes—do not change eating habits. Fat substitutes do not encourage people to lower their intake of such foods. The solution, it seems, is to go "cold turkey." For example, people who restrict these foods entirely will learn to adjust to new food tastes, just as those on salt-restricted diets learn to prefer less salt.

To reduce weight and cholesterol, a goal might be 10 to 15 percent fat, little or no cholesterol, 70 percent to 75 percent carbohydrate, and 10 to 15 percent protein. This diet is not vegetarian, although it restricts the amount of eggs, fish, and dairy products. It encourages the eating of whole grain foods, fruits, and vegetables.

Some experts encourage people to abstain completely from meats and dairy products as a way of being "fat free." This may be sound advice for people with certain body types or who are seriously overweight. However, fats are important sources of energy and the key to consumption is combining them with compatible foods such as concentrated protein. When taken in appropriate quantities from wholesome, natural sources, you will not be overweight. Some groups of people, like Eskimos, eat raw blubber, and thrive on it. Eliminating fat from the diet is a mistake, as it is the main source of energy, with three times the amount found in sugar and twice as much as protein.

Fats. One gram of fat supplies about 9 grams of calories, while carbohydrates and protein will supply only 4 grams of calories. For this reason, we can get away with eating more carbohydrates and proteins. Fat intake will have a greater effect on weight loss or gain.

Fat is an important source of linoleic acid that is needed for growth and maintenance of the body, and it insulates and protects the body's organs from trauma and cold. Most nutritionists agree that it is important to eliminate more saturated fats and to eat monounsaturated fats instead of polyunsaturated ones. To reduce fat intake to 10 to 15 percent requires a drastic change in habits, but it is a sure way of reducing weight.

The risk of fat consumption has been examined in great detail, perhaps with much more scrutiny than any other nutrient. It has been linked to breast cancer throughout the world, cancers of the gastrointestinal tract (particularly the large bowel), and other cancers. One cannot conclude categorically that dietary fat promotes colon problems, since most of these studies are correlational. However, it may be a very strong contributing factor.

Strategy 6—Getting Rid of Toxins

When you feel ill or under stress, review your diet. Eliminate the foods that are causing you stress, or begin a fast to get rid of toxins in your body.

Toxins are constantly formed during normal body metabolism, when old cells are destroyed or when certain foods are eaten, that are hard to break down. In particular, alcohol, tobacco, caffeine, fats, and salt may be toxic, and certain processed foods and sugars may be difficult to digest. The most obvious form of toxins are chemicals in foods such as artificial colors, flavors, preservatives, emulsifiers, and other additives.

The body has various systems to discharge its waste, including the colon, the bladder, and the skin. Detoxification occurs naturally through regular bowel movements, deep breathing, and perspiration from exercise.

Fasting. Fasting is one of the best ways of cleaning out toxic material from the body. The process gives the body's enzymes "time off" from working on foods so they can devote time to detoxification. During fasting, the body's enzyme system is cleaning up and digesting and eliminating damaged tissues, putrefied proteins, and foods that have been hard to digest.

While fasting reduces the risks of weight-related diseases such as diabetes and hypertension, it also helps clear the body of toxic wastes. About six hours after the last meal, the body starts to use glycogen, which is a carbohydrate stored in the liver and muscles. When there is no food in the stomach, the body stops the process of assimilation and concentrates on getting rid of toxins and other waste products.

Fasting should not be thought of as "starving" or as the first stages of anorexia nervosa, a condition common to some teenage girls who become obsessed with weight control. The goal is health, not weight loss. When weight loss becomes the goal, we are losing sight of the true objectives.

Purifying Foods. Certain foods are known for their ability to purify the body and blood. For example, daikon, or Chinese white radish, is known for its ability to wash out medicines. Daikon removes excess fats and neutralizes the toxins in fish and seafood. The large Chinese black mushroom, shiitake, is often cooked with meat because it removes meat toxins and cholesterol. Chinese tea and Japanese green tea are also used for similar purposes.

Other so-called cleansing foods include lotus root, which dissolves excessive mucus and is used by those who suffer from asthma, coughs, sinus problems, and related ailments. Carrot juice is used for flushing the liver, and the herb burdock is a blood cleanser. Sesame seeds, lemons, and fruits are generally cleansing foods.

Strategy 7—Using Tonic Foods

THERE IS NO SUCH THING AS A LITTLE GARLIC.

Some foods can act like tonics. The magic is to take the tonic that is required for the problem.

Foods can also help us cope with hypertension. If you have hypertension, you might consider three options.

- Eat more foods that can soften the blood vessels, such as kelp, sea grass, mung bean sprouts, and fruits.

- Use vegetable oils such as olive oil. Try not to use animal fats and oils, and reduce your cholesterol.

- Eat more foods that can reduce blood pressure, such as celery, hawthorn fruit, bananas, and persimmons.

A recent book called *Foods That Harm, Foods That Heal* by Reader's Digest is an excellent beginning source to learn more about healing foods.

YOUR NEXT STEP

We are beginning to realize that what we eat can make a difference in the way we handle stress as well as general health. Eating healthful foods need not be complicated or dull. Eating nutritious foods can be a pleasurable experience, made even more so when you begin to feel better at handling the stresses around you. You will be sick less often, have more energy, and you will look better. Work on one strategy at a time. Start with Strategy 1 during the first week. During each of the following weeks, work on another strategy.

PART THREE

FIGHTING BACK THROUGH CONQUERING STRATEGIES

Taming the Dragon

11

PRINCIPLE 7:
Exercise to Reduce Anxiety

USE STRESS-PREVENTION VERSUS STRESS-PROMOTING EXERCISES

Better to hunt in the fields, for health unbrought,
Than fee the doctor for a nauseous draught.
The wise, for cure, on exercise depend;
God never made his work for (humans) to mend.

— EPISTLE TO JOHN DRYDEN OF CHESTERON

Before we evolved into our present sedentary society, and especially during the Stone Age and tribal cultures, physical activity was much more common than today. Physical activity—either by flight or fight—was a natural response to stress. When a Stone Age person saw a saber-tooth tiger, the response was to flee or attack. Either response was a form of physical activity.

WHILE THE HUMAN BODY HAS BEEN CONDITIONED BY CENTURIES OF EVOLUTION FOR CARRYING OUT PHYSICAL ACTIVITIES, OUR PRESENT-DAY LIFESTYLE DOES NOT REQUIRE THEM.

We have gone through dramatic changes over time, and our stressors now call for mental, not physical, reaction. We are expected to respond to job stress with a calm and controlled reaction. For example, police officers, teachers, and administrative assistants are taught to listen and be polite to an unruly and impolite client. In the early stages of our evolution, we responded to such stresses by fighting and fleeing.

IN MOST JOBS, PEOPLE SIT DOWN AND RARELY MOVE ABOUT EXCEPT DURING LUNCH OR COFFEE BREAKS.

A number of years ago, 30 to 40 percent of the tasks carried out by carpenters and factory workers involved some form of muscular activity. Today, as little as 1 percent of a worker's tasks involve moderate or intense physical activity. Most jobs take up a lot less energy. While at work, many work activities require a person to sit and perform eye and hand motions without moving around. After work, the most strenuous activities involve mowing the lawn, washing the car, or weeding the garden.

Many workers spend the majority of their days sitting, standing, or moving their hands from one location to another. Such is the life of the office worker, manager, sales clerk, or other white-collar worker. Blue-collar work has also changed and there are many fewer jobs were strenuous physical labor is required (such as cement work or bricklaying). But even in these jobs, the physical requirements have been reduced. Production systems are automated and workers push buttons rather than shovel, lift, or push heavy objects. Even the work of the farmer has become highly mechanized by tractors, conveyors, and computers. In industrialized countries, we are living a sedentary lifestyle.

While most jobs are requiring less and less physical activity, there is a growing belief that the physical stress of work and life are greater than ever before. No previous generation of people in history has experienced the variety and intensity of pressures, conflicts, and demands placed upon them. To many observers, we are entering an "age of anxiety."

EXERCISE IS ONE OF THE SIMPLEST AND MOST EFFECTIVE MEANS OF STRESS REDUCTION AND IS THE NATURAL OUTLET FOR THE BODY DURING ITS FIGHT-OR-FLIGHT STATE OF AROUSAL. AFTER EXERCISE, THE BODY RETURNS TO ITS NORMAL EQUILIBRIUM, AND THE PERSON FEELS RELAXED AND REFRESHED.

We have the same need for exercise as our primitive ancestors, whose hunting and gathering lifestyle required walking and running several miles every day. Exercise can play an important role in reducing stress. You do not need to be a tennis star or a squash player, but you should develop an exercise program that will be good for your general health as well as for reducing stress.

THE VALUE OF EXERCISE

FEW PSYCHOLOGICAL EMOTIONS ARE MORE FASCINATING TO OBSERVE THAN THOSE EXPERIENCED BY SOME PEOPLE AFTER PHYSICAL EXERCISE.

Many people experience an emotional "high" after climbing a mountain, completing a hike, or winning a game of tennis. This psychological state is full of positive energy. Exercise provides an opportunity for feeling good, being stimulated, and being challenged. It often provides experiences of relaxation or meditation, when the mind looks inward. This can be observed in joggers who focus on their breathing during a long monotonous marathon, or swimmers who concentrate on each stroke by counting laps as they move down the pool, repeating the number of the lap during each length.

As we get older, the body receives a certain amount of wear and tear. In terms of physical activity, age alone does not determine an individual's functioning or how well he or she enjoys life. An unhealthy lifestyle is usually the culprit behind many disabling and immobilizing conditions and serious chronic diseases that afflict elderly people.

EXERCISE, DIET, AND LIFESTYLE CONTRIBUTE A GREAT DEAL TO A PERSON'S PHYSICAL FLEXIBILITY AND ABILITY.

After a person reaches the age of forty-five, and even earlier in some cases, muscles tend to shrink and fat takes over. Reduced muscle mass is almost wholly responsible for the gradual reduction of basal metabolic rate. Exercise and strength training allow a person to maintain physical capabilities for much longer in life. The body's ability to process oxygen in a given time, or aerobic capacity, starts to decline as early as twenty years old for men and thirty for women. A person who is sixty-five years old has a capacity that is only 30 to 40 percent of a young adult. While an older person can maintain aerobic capacity, he or she will have to work harder to do it.

Exercise and Stress

It is not surprising that an unfit person might not handle stress as well as one who is fit and in good condition. When confronted with stress, the body undergoes a number of changes. More oxygen is required, the heart rate increases, muscles tense, and blood pressure increases. These changes occur as the body prepares for its flight-and-fight response.

The goal of exercise is to improve and develop the body's capability to handle stressful events. Regular and adequate exercise increases muscular strength, endurance, and flexibility and relieves chronic muscular tension. It provides a safety valve for stress, helps to shed unwanted pounds, and improves cardiovascular efficiency and metabolism. Exercise will fight both chronic fatigue and insomnia.

Regular exercise provides both a conditioning and a preventive maintenance program. It is a practical and inexpensive preventive program for preventing injury and muscle aches. If the body is conditioned from exercise on a regular basis, normal household chores such as mowing the lawn, weeding the garden, and shoveling snow are less likely to cause injury. In addition, there is less likelihood of mishaps such as backaches, sore muscles, heart attacks, sprained ankles, and so forth.

General Benefits of Exercise

Interest in physical fitness is often motivated by a general interest in health and stress control. Jogging and aerobics have been at the forefront of this interest because they are easy to do. However, other types of exercises are popular as well, such as swimming, bicycling, squash, and tennis. Reasons for exercising include:

- Meeting people and socializing.
- Increasing one's strength and physical endurance. This leads to a more efficient utilization of energy. People who exercise are able to do more without tiring.
- Replacing fat with muscle and increasing muscle tone and posture.
- Reducing weight and improving the absorption and utilization of food.

- Improving appearance through muscle tone and weight loss.
- Strengthening the heart and lungs and improving circulation of the blood, thus lowering blood pressure and decreasing the heart rate. Increasing the flow of red corpuscles, thus facilitating oxygen flow throughout the body.
- Improving the ability to relax and sleep.
- Improving the functioning of the heart and reducing heart disease (the most important reason).

GENERALLY, PEOPLE WHO EXERCISE REGULARLY AND PROPERLY HAVE FEWER HEART ATTACKS THAN PEOPLE WHO DO NOT EXERCISE.

Interest in fitness has grown from the concern that lack of exercise and inactivity are associated with health problems, obesity, and mental disorders (anxiety and depression), as well as coronary heart disease. Exercise is one sure way of mobilizing the immune system and promoting blood circulation. It makes you breathe deeper, increases the body's intake of oxygen, and nourishes the immune cells. Perspiration during exercise is an effective way of eliminating toxic waste from the body so that the immune system is not overtaxed.

People who are in better shape and who are fit seem to perform better in schools and universities. This link was first noted among elementary school students, but the correlation has also been found among high school and college students. The percentage of obese students was also lower among students who achieve higher grades.

DEVELOPING A PROGRAM

Many people who exercise think in terms of improving performance, capability, or stamina, but do not take into account other aspects such as muscle flexibility, posture, balance, and rhythm.

Some runners are heavy on their feet and have poor posture. Cycling often encourages an arched back and poor posture, and some racket sports (squash and tennis) are jerky and not rhythmic. Some people will exercise intensely after a long week of sitting in the office. A good rule to remember is that an effective exercise program to improve health utilizes constant, regular movements.

Heavy exercise may be an important cause of heart attacks in normally sedentary people. Among those who exercised once a week, sudden exercise raised the risk of having a myocardial infarction (heart attack) by 107 times. For those who exercised regularly at least five times a week, sudden violent exercise doubled the risk. The death rate starts to rise very early in life, in the mid-thirties.

Aerobic exercise has become very popular (exercise in which a person uses large quantities of oxygen). Walkathons, jogathons, marathons, aerobic dancing, and other exercises and events are all used to achieve aerobic fitness. The increased consumption of oxygen leads to improvements in the functioning of various organs and bodily systems. This physical activity improves physical fitness and the operating efficiency of the heart, lungs, and muscles (total fitness). Thirty minutes to an hour of light aerobic exercise—brisk walking, jogging, swimming—can be performed three or five times a week. Any activity however that raises your heart rate into your target zone and maintains it there for fifteen to twenty minutes, is considered ideal.

My personal exercise routine once included squash and running, as well as the occasion game of soccer. I used to believe in competitive, strenuous aeorobic activities. My downfall was in trying to do too much for my age. I was a Type A exerciser. Exercise was, for me, a competitive experience. I was a zealot, trying to be twenty years old again. The extra strain of playing squash and running were hard on my body. I have three very seriously deteriorated disks in my back and two that are moderately so. "Grow old gracefully." This was what a doctor told me after I had spent ten days in traction in a Singapore hospital. I overdid it when I was preparing for the Singapore marathon. The message here is that I needed to devise an exercise program more in harmony with my body and my ideal of stress management.

While very strenuous exercise might be appropriate for some people, it can produce strain and increase susceptibility to illness. During intensive exercise, cortisol is produced by the adrenal cortex. Cortisol influences carbohydrate and protein metabolism and helps maintain blood volume; it is beneficial because of its anti-inflammatory and antiallergic properties. In excess, however, the catabolic process continues to break down proteins and/or deprive the myocardium (the muscle tendons of the heart) of potassium and magnesium.

Many people have heart attacks when they begin exercising strenuously after years of physical inactivity. An ECG, a treadmill test, and blood tests can give you a measure of the health of your heart and arteries before you start an exercise program. Certain risk factors make it even more important to see a physician first: high blood pressure, high cholesterol, smoking, diabetes, a family history of heart disease, obesity, age over forty years, or bone or joint aches. You should also see a physician if you have chest pains, fainting periods, or times when you are excessively out of breath, such as walking up stairs.

THE RISK OF A HEART ATTACK DURING OR JUST AFTER HEAVY PHYSICAL EXERTION IS TWO TO SIX TIMES GREATER THAN THE RISK DURING LESS STRENUOUS ACTIVITIES OR NO ACTIVITY.

Regular moderate exercise diminishes the added risk of heart attack during exercise to practically none at all. These findings, based on recent studies published in the *New England Journal of Medicine,* suggest that sedentary people should indeed be careful when beginning an exercise program. Plan to get into shape carefully and gradually.

These studies also provide solid evidence that active, physically fit people have a lower risk. In one study, the chance of a sedentary person suffering a heart attack during or just after heavy exertion was nearly fifty times that of people who usually exercise five or more times a week. Exercising even one or two times a week cuts the risk by 80 percent. In another study, only about 5 percent of the heart attacks occurred during heavy physical exertion; the rest occurred during moderate activity such as driving a car, shopping, or mowing the lawn. But 5 percent is significant when we consider all the heart attacks that occur each year.

The exercise routine I recommend for those of us who are getting older is moderately strenuous, but is more consistent with the ideals of stress management. Vigorous and strenuous exercise is not normally part of a stress management program. The ideals of stress management encourage exercise that is gradual and rhythmic. While strenuous exercise may be good for the heart, lungs, legs, and general health, it does not contribute a great deal to flexibility.

Exercise that encourages regular stretching keeps the muscle tissues elastic, helps prevent injuries, and allows a greater range of movements around each joint. Examples of exercises that encourage flexibility include walking, hiking, and swimming.

I am committed to a program that includes exercise such as hiking, swimming, and biking. These can be performed gradually and are consistent with my goals of stress management while enjoying the outdoors.

Warming up. Warming up and cooling down are extremely important. If you have been sitting, or if you have just completed a meal, imagine what your heart and blood are doing. Your heart is probably pumping around 70 beats a minute, pumping most of the blood and oxygen to the brain and its vital organs. If you have just eaten a meal, then a large amount of blood is diverted to the stomach and intestine to facilitate digestion. Only a small amount of blood will be flowing to the muscles.

When you suddenly begin to exercise without any warmup, most of the blood will still be in the vital organs, as there is not enough time to move it to the muscles. Exercise may cause some microscopic tearing of muscle fibers or stretching of ligaments and tendons. The tissues are not lubricated and are cold and more prone to injury and damage. If you are not fit or are fat, the heart will also demand more blood, which may result in heart pain (angina) if the vessels around the heart are partially blocked.

A warmup is an attempt to take the body gradually from a resting state to the one it will be in during exercise. Such a warmup might last from five to seven minutes and comprise stretching of various joints and muscle groups. This short warmup may be appropriate for a person who wishes to jog for a few miles, but may not be enough for an Olympic runner. Longer warmups for strenuous events should involve a simulation of the actual activity. For example, a baseball pitcher might throw several practice pitches, while a tennis player will perform rallies and serves before the actual game.

The warmup helps raise the temperature of the body and muscle tissue. This sets off several physiological changes that enhance performance and reduce injury. There is a rapid and complete release of oxygen from the red blood cells into the muscle tissue, which allows for greater bursts of energy. The contracting muscles can work more smoothly because the internal fluids thin as they warm up.

The increased body temperature from warming up allows nerve impulses to transmit rapidly, stimulating the muscles to contract. Contracted muscles are also stronger. Warming up also causes a gradual shift in the pattern of blood flow from one part of the body to another. Elasticity of the muscle tissue depends on the amount of blood available, so warm muscles are less injury prone.

When the muscles are warm, the blood vessels are more flexible, and they will dilate, allowing a greater flow of nutrients for energy production. Waste products, such as carbon dioxide and lactic acid, can also be more easily transported.

Warmups can be combined with stretching, breathing exercises, and mind control. While you can focus your mind on the muscle group you are exercising, I try to meditate and relax. Start your warmup with some stretching exercises. Extend your body to its fullest by stretching your muscles to the point where there is mild tension and slowly move onto your tiptoes. Overstretched muscles will tighten due to the activation of the automatic stretch reflex mechanism. The muscles being stretched will contract, causing pain, which is the body's way of preventing muscle injury. If there is pain, stop stretching.

Cooling Down. The cooling-down period aids the circulation of blood in the veins and back to the heart. If there is no cooling-down period, blood may accumulate in the veins, especially in the legs, putting pressure on the heart. Cooling down allows your heart to slowly return to its resting state. If a person must interrupt exercise, he or she should keep moving. This is why you often see joggers run in place when they have to stop for red lights.

YOUR NEXT STEP

The following suggestions will help you keep up your exercise program until it becomes as automatic as eating or sleeping:

- Visualize what you want to attain with exercise. See yourself as already having attained the benefits of exercise. Imagine what you will look like and be able to do at the age of fifty, sixty, and seventy. If you cannot continue the exercise program, you might think of alternatives that will enable you to do so.

- Moderation is important. This means starting slowly until you gain fitness. If you get sick, very sore, or exhausted, you may have overexerted yourself. Exercise should be fun, not torture.

- Set goals for what you might try to accomplish over two weeks. Be realistic about the goals. Display them around the house or office where you can see them everyday.

- Focus on all the rewards of exercise. You will notice that you feel more relaxed, energized, and refreshed, are more able to concentrate, and your sleep has improved.

- Keep records. Records of your daily and weekly progress can be used to keep a check on your weight and blood pressure.

- Try to exercise with others. Get support from your family and friends and communicate your goals to them. Join an exercise class, running club, or fitness center. I joined a swim club, and I also go swimming in the mornings with my wife.

- Choose an appropriate exercise program. The best type of exercise for stress management and health is gradual and rhythmic. What exercise would you enjoy? With whom would you like to exercise?

- Determine how much you want to exercise. Remember the simple acronym FIT. Your exercise program can be described by its Frequency, Intensity, and Time.

    Frequency. The ideal frequency for exercise is three to five times a week.

    Intensity. The intensity of your program is how hard you exercise. This is your target heart rate. Your exercise activity should raise your heart rate (pulse beats per minute) to within the heart rate target zone and maintain it at that level for at least fifteen to thirty minutes, at least three to five times a week. The target zone heart rate (per minute) is:

    200 minus your age for the upper limit

    170 minus your age for the upper limit

    When starting a fitness program, you should attempt to maintain a heart rate close to the target zone lower limit. As your fitness level improves, you may choose to go to a higher rate, but stay within your target zone.

    Time. Exercise should increase the heart rate and maintain it for approximately fifteen to thirty minutes. Examples of ideal activities are walking for thirty minutes, cycling for thirty minutes, or swimming for twenty minutes. Perform these activities briskly.

- Develop a schedule for exercise. The schedule you have for exercise is like an appointment with your doctor. Schedule this appointment three to five times a week.

Your exercise program needs to be combined with diet, relaxation, and stress control. Your exercise program should also recognize your age and general fitness. Competitive exercises are great for recreation and entertainment but not for stress management and general health. My personal recommendations include stretching exercises, walking and hiking, and swimming. I also like biking. Running, jogging, and squash were especially hard on me and that is one of the reasons I would not recommend them as they may impose risks to your health.

12

PRINCIPLE 8:
Use the Power Within You

USE MEDITATION AND RELAXATION TECHNIQUES

Men at some time are masters of their fates:
The fault, dear Brutus, is not in our stars,
But in ourselves, that we are underlings.

—WILLIAM SHAKESPEAR, *JULIUS CAESAR*

Robert Pirsig, in his book *Zen and the Art of Motorcycle Maintenance*, used the word "gumption" to describe what happens when someone connects with quality. A person filled with gumption does not sit around unsure of the future. "He's at the front of the train of his own awareness, watching to see what's up the track and meeting it when it comes. The gumption-filling process occurs when one is quiet long enough to see and hear and feel the real universe, not just one's own stale opinions about it."

If you are going to repair a motorcycle, an adequate supply of gumption is a very important tool. This is the psychic gasoline that fuels the repair process. Technical expertise and shop manuals will help. But during repair and preventive maintenance, there will be tasks that test a person's gumption. A nut might be stripped or a replacement part will not fit properly. These trials and tribulations challenge a person's enthusiasm.

> IT IS VERY DIFFICULT TO EXPECT A MOTORCYCLE, CAR, OR ANY MACHINE TO RUN FOREVER WITHOUT SERVICE AND MAINTENANCE, JUST AS THE HUMAN BODY CANNOT KEEP RUNNING EFFECTIVELY WITHOUT CARE AND ATTENTION.

The body's use of food and energy to repair and regenerate its organs is important. Like a motorcycle, our bodies need maintenance and regeneration to repair the cells and organs that wear down. This wear and tear is greater when we face stressful situations, or when we get older (just like the motorcycle). Our muscles may get sore from exercise, our mental faculties may become tired from too much reading and writing, or we might feel fatigued from staying up late watching a movie.

Stress management reduces the need for excessive maintenance and repair. A person might take steps to reduce his or her stressors by taking on a less stressful job, moving to a less congested city, or taking drugs to calm his or her nerves. It is likely, however, that not all stressors can be avoided. There will always be the problems of life, such as fixing broken televisions, consoling a child after a poor test grade, or paying taxes. Traditional stress management suggests that stress is affected by its component parts—job stresses, personality, and lifestyle. These stressors can be ameliorated, just as a motorcycle mechanic can go beyond the basic procedures of a shop manual.

STRESS MANAGEMENT INVOLVES DERIVING MENTAL ENERGY FROM TECHNIQUES FOR RELAXATION AND MEDITATION.

Some of the meditation techniques in this chapter are rather simple and might be used in crisis situations to reduce stress, while others are more complex and require some commitment to master. Many of the exercises are based on Western practices, while others involve traditional Chinese methods for breathing and meditation. The goal of such exercises is to develop an attitude for health and stress management. Most of these techniques require practice as well as an inner resolve to use them.

FINDING THE POWER WITHIN YOU

Self-reverence, self-knowledge, self-control—
these three alone lead to sovereign power.

—ALFRED, LORD TENNYSON

Many of us admire the person who is able to complete a number of tasks and carry on a busy array of activities. Because our cultural norms encourage productivity, relaxation may be very hard to do, and it may even be stressful. Some people who are instructed to sit and relax may feel quite stressed. They may start to fidget, write notes to themselves, or look for something to do. This is a great pity, because relaxation can be the source of much power, productivity, and energy.

YOU DO NOT HAVE TO BE A WORKAHOLIC.

Most workaholics seem to spend endless hours working, and they often joke about others who come in late and leave early. They talk about how busy they are and bustle around doing a whole range of activities. Worse, the organization will probably promote some of these people ahead of you. The words that unite the Type A workaholics seem to be, "If I get done today what I am supposed to do tomorrow, then the last day of my life will be completely free."

Rest and Regeneration

Everyone takes some time out for rest and regeneration. Most of us will sit or lie down or even take a short nap. All of us rely on sleep as a key mechanism for this process. Sleep is an opportunity to take a break and build up our reserves. Sleep is very beneficial for helping muscles heal and allowing the body to build up its immunities to fight viruses. We may feel tremendously refreshed and invigorated from a good sleep or short nap.

WHILE SLEEP IS A TREMENDOUS MECHANISM FOR RESTORING THE BODY'S MUSCLES AND ORGANS, IT DOES LITTLE TO ASSIST THE MIND TO REST.

Even when we are sleeping, the mind can be fully engaged to such a degree that it may be undergoing more stress than it would during a day at work. Periods of sleep when dreams occur may actually kick the body into high gear. The heart may speed up and blood pressure increase as the body prepares for its fight-or-flight response. The sympathetic nervous system may be in overdrive. During such stages of sleep, this internal turmoil may trigger heart attacks.

Today, scientists explain dreams with one of two theories. These are:

- the mind's way of *taking notes,* and reviewing a day's activity to decide what to file or throw away, or
- the brain's way of becoming a *supermarket* and recharging and restocking its essential chemicals.

The note-taking theory is more recognized and accepted, and it suggests that unpleasant events, doubts, fears, and even happy experiences may reoccur as dreams or nightmares.

With the use of an EEG (electroencephalograph), scientists are able to tell when a person is dreaming and when he or she is sleeping. They are still not sure what the person is dreaming about. From this research, it appears that people sleep in cycles, with the brain at first quiet, then active for a period of time creating dreams. Using instruments to measure eye movement, scientists have learned that the brain does not shut down and rest during sleep. During four or five periods during the night, the eyeballs will suddenly dart left and right quickly as if the sleeper is rapidly reading a book. This eerie phenomenon is known as rapid eye movement, or REM sleep.

During the REM period, the brain suddenly becomes active and the muscles of the body appear to be paralyzed. This is the dreaming state. In this period, a person may be quite tense. The wave of nervous activity that brings on REM sleep starts at the top of the spinal cord. It is closely linked to the region in the brain responsible for sight, which is probably why dreams are so visual.

Healthy people will spend about 15 to 20 percent of their sleep time dreaming. As well as seeing their dreams, many people will feel strong emotions, such as fear and anger. This presents difficulties for those with heart problems. While they might be able to reduce their stress during the day, they might not always be able to stop it at night. A heart-pounding dream can cause blood pressure to rise and release stress hormones for the flight-or-fight response. Angina attacks do occur during sleep. While alcohol, sleeping pills, and some drugs suppress dreams for a while, after they wear off, there is a rush of dreaming. Suppressing dreams can have short-term effects such as irritability, slurred speech, minor visual hallucinations, and poor attention to mundane tasks.

WHAT SEEMS VERY CLEAR IS THAT SLEEP DOES LITTLE TO EASE THE TENSIONS OF THE MIND.

DEVELOPING YOUR PROGRAM FOR BREATHING, RELAXING, OR MEDITATING

There are various types of breathing, relaxing, and meditating techniques. Many of these techniques can help us dissipate the frustrations and anxieties we feel from the day's events or life's pressures. Others can play a valuable role in bringing about long-term changes in attitudes about life and nutrition.

Let me offer you some warnings. As useful as these exercises are, many people find it difficult to fully integrate them in their lifestyles. Very few people who take meditation, yoga, or hypnosis courses practice these techniques on a regular basis. I have taken several such courses, and I am quite skilled in using these techniques to train others or help people use the power of their minds to overcome illness or deal with injuries. Still, I have found it difficult to practice these techniques on a regular basis.

The lesson here is that you may have to work diligently to integrate these exercises into your lifestyle. However, they are extremely important, as they can set the tone for how you handle everything else. To be successful, I recommend that you approach these techniques on an incremental basis. You will have to make choices. Don't try to do everything.

Three sets of exercise are included: breathing, relaxing and meditating, and self-hypnosis. How and when do you practice these exercises?

I recommend that you start out with some breathing exercises. Practice these for a week or so. During the second week, try some of the relaxation exercises. Record the suggestions of the progressive relaxation exercise on an audiotape and listen to it with some nice background music. You might then try a self-hypnosis exercise in the third week.

These techniques can help you develop an attitude that your mind has the power to help you relax and control your life, and helps you focus your stress management.

WHILE OTHERS GET STRESSED, YOU CAN TAKE CONTROL.

I now use these techniques in various ways. I practice breathing several times during the day, sometimes before exercising, making a speech, or after I have been sitting in front of the computer. I practice hypnosis when I get stressed. I also illustrate it in my workshops and have, on several occasions, used it to help others. For example, I recently hypnotized a person who had fainted in a restaurant. While we waited for an ambulance, I helped this person get control of her breathing and body temperature. When the paramedics came, she was well on the road to recovery.

I often meditate when I am in a line or find myself listening to a boring meeting or speech. In short, these techniques are fully integrated into my day. I do not program myself to do them at specific times.

The relaxation technique I now use most is yoga. I usually do some yoga breathing and stretching exercises when I get up in the morning or before I go swimming.

BREATHING EXERCISES

Breathing is essential for life. Proper breathing can directly affect a person's emotional state and can be an antidote to stress. When an insufficient amount of fresh air reaches your lungs, your blood is not properly purified or oxygenated. Waste products that should have been removed are kept in circulation, slowly poisoning your system. When your blood lacks enough oxygen, it is bluish and dark in color, and your complexion suffers. Digestion is hampered. Your organs and tissues become undernourished and deteriorate. Poorly oxygenated blood contributes to anxiety, depression, and fatigue and makes each stressful situation many times harder to cope with. Proper breathing habits are essential for good mental and physical health.

Breathing exercises help people relax or release tension. They are very quick and easy to do and can be carried out almost anyplace. For example, before giving a speech, one is often advised to take a deep breathe and recite a confidence-building phrase such as, "take charge," or "feel good." Breathing exercises are part of many relaxation techniques and are often combined with other methods of concentration.

THE LAMAZE METHOD TEACHES EXPECTANT MOTHERS TO CONCENTRATE ON AN OBJECT AND DEVELOP A BREATHING RHYTHM.

When the pains of childbirth increase, mothers are encouraged in the Lamaze method to intensify their concentration by more intense breathing (panting). Breathing exercises provide an introduction to many relaxation programs; often a body position coinciding with relaxation is suggested. Most Asian techniques encourage keeping the backbone straight. This is best accomplished in a standing or sitting position. If the person wishes to lie down on his or her back, it is important to bend the knees.

There are different types of breathing exercises. Generally, the goal is to breath in through the nose and out through a small gap in the mouth. The focus will be on both inhaling and exhaling. Some methods emphasize exhaling. In Chinese medicine, we are exhaling the negative "qi."

Dynamic Breathing (Bhastika in Yoga)

This exercise not only cleanses your lungs, it also stimulates and tones up your entire breathing apparatus and refreshes your whole body.

- Sit or stand up straight using good posture.
- Inhale slowly and deeply through your nose and at the same time push the abdomen out.
- Hold this breath for a few seconds.
- Exhale the air slowly through the mouth and at the same time pull the abdomen in.
- As you continue the exercise, breathe in and out more quickly with a "bellows" sound, pushing the abdomen in and out. The movement of the abdomen and the breathing process should be synchronized and the speed increased. Then, the rhythm should be slowly decreased.

Relaxing by Exhaling

Exhaling releases tension and can be practiced at will as a means of relaxing. The Chinese believe that we should focus on exhaling only.

- Sit or stand up straight.
- Don't think about inhaling—just let the air come in naturally.
- Concentrate on exhaling slowly. Simply allow the air to return.
- Repeat this procedure eight to twelve times whenever you feel the need to experience the feeling of relaxation.

Alternative Nostril Breathing (Nadi Shodana Pranayama in Yoga)

This exercise sometimes is used to end a yoga session. Sit in a comfortable position with your back straight. Place the index and second finger of your right hand on the center of your forehead and your thumb on one nostril and your third finger on the other.

- Close the right nostril with the thumb and inhale through the left nostril. Retain the breath for a moment, and then close the left nostril and exhale through the right.
- When fully exhaled, breathe in through the same nostril. That is, inhale through the right nostril (hold momentarily). Exhale through the left. Allow about eight seconds for inhaling and exhaling and four seconds for holding.
- Continue the exercise for five minutes.

Complete Breath Standing (Hasta Uttita Pranayama in Yoga)

This is a breathing exercise that usually begins a yoga session.

- Stand with feet together and your arms at the side with palms facing the thighs and your spine straight.
- Slowly start breathing in, and begin raising your arms to the side. When your arms are at shoulder height, roll your arms at the shoulder so that your palms are facing upward. Continue to raise your arms until they touch on top of your head. As you do this, you are moving to a position where you are standing on your toes.
- When the palms touch above your head, you have fully inhaled, and you are standing on your toes. For a moment, hold your breath in and balance on your toes.
- Begin to lower your arms to the side and begin exhaling slowly. Unroll your arms at the shoulder (when they are at shoulder height) and continue to lower them until they are at your side. As you do this, the soles of your feet move toward the floor.
- For a moment before beginning the next sequence, the body should be limp. Repeat the process for a least five cycles.

In many cases, these exercises can be performed on a regular basis as part of a daily sequence of mental or physical routines. For best results, perform the exercises two or three times a day until your breathing habits change. You might practice these exercises just before you begin a new work task or new activity. Taking four or five exhaling breaths at odd times of the day is also refreshing. Dynamic breathing and exhaling exercises can be performed quickly and can be used when you are sitting in a traffic jam, standing in line, or waiting in a doctor's office. They are also a useful way to begin meditation and self-hypnosis.

> **THE VALUE OF BREATHING EXERCISES IS IN CHANGING YOUR BREATHING HABITS SO THAT YOU ARE FULLY REALIZING THE ENERGY (QI) AND OXYGEN THAT WILL REPLENISH THE BODY.**

It is best to set aside a specific time for breathing or other meditation exercises. According to Chinese theory, the best time to practice these exercises are from: 11 P.M. to 1 A.M. (Zishi), 11 A.M. to 1 P.M. (Wushi), 5 A.M. to 7 A.M. (Maoshi), 5 P.M. to 7 P.M. (Youshi), and from 3 A.M. to 5 A.M. (Yinshi). During these periods of day, the vital energy is flowing to different parts of the body. Other practitioners suggest that the best time is in the morning; this allows you to focus the mind in a constructive and healthy way for the day ahead.

RELAXATION AND MEDITATION

Muscle relaxation is based on the premise that the body responds to anxiety-provoking thoughts and events with muscle tension. This physiological tension, in turn, increases the subjective experience of anxiety. Deep muscle relaxation reduces physiological tension and is incompatible with anxiety.

When a person is tense, upset, or angry, there is a tendency to unconsciously tighten the muscles. You may grit your teeth and tighten up your muscles in your shoulders. This can result in a stiff neck, headache, muscle cramps, or back pain. If a person spends a great deal of the day feeling stressed or emotionally upset, he or she is also putting muscles in a tense and "working" state. Muscles that are working and tensed will become fatigued.

When you do not have time to recuperate from emotionally and physically stressful events, your body chemistry becomes imbalanced and your mood is disturbed. The goal of muscle relaxation exercises is to normalize your physical, mental, and emotional processes. The tension in your muscles will affect the tension in your mind.

Muscle relaxation exercises are designed to release some of the built-up tension and to increase relaxation. The dissipation of muscular tension is often associated with improved mental relaxation and calmness.

The following are a group of muscle relaxation exercises that can be used by themselves or in association with other exercises.

Tense and Release Exercise

Each muscle or muscle group is tensed from five to seven seconds then relaxed for ten to thirty seconds. This procedure is repeated at least once.

- Clench your right fist tighter and tighter, studying the tension as you do so. Keep it clenched and notice the tension in your fist, hand, and forearm. Let the tension inside you go. Feel the looseness in your right hand, and notice the contrast with the tension. Repeat this procedure with the right fist again, always noticing that as you become more relaxed you are less tense. Tell yourself, "Breathe calmness in, breathe tension out."

- Repeat the entire procedure with your left fist, then both fists at the same time.

- Next, try this technique with forearms and biceps.

- Wrinkle up the forehead. At the same time, press your head as far back as possible, roll it clockwise in a complete circle, reverse. Now wrinkle up the muscles of your face like a walnut: frowning, eyes squinted, lips pursed, tongue pressing the roof of the mouth, and shoulders hunched. Let the tension go and feel the looseness. Repeat this again. Let the tension go and feel the calmness.

- Arch your back as you take a deep breath into the chest. Hold. Feel the calmness. Take a deep breath, pressing out the stomach. Hold. Feel the calmness.

- Tighten your buttocks and thighs. Flex your thighs by pressing down your heels as hard as you can. Feel the calmness and feel the difference.

- Now curl your toes downward, making your calves tense, feel the tension. Let the tension go. Bend your toes toward your face. Feel the calmness again.

- Feel the heaviness throughout your lower body as the relaxation deepens.

- Relax your feet, ankles, calves, shins, knees, thighs, and buttocks.

- Now let the calmness spread to your stomach, lower back, and chest. Let go more and more.

- Experience the calmness deepening in your shoulders, arms, and hands. Deeper and deeper.

- Notice the feeling of looseness and relaxation in your neck, jaw, and all your facial muscles.

Progressive Relaxation

You can visualize each muscle group and tell yourself to relax it. Relaxed muscles feel loose, heavy, limp, and calmn.

Close your eyes. With your eyes closed, imagine that you are looking at the ceiling. You might experiment with your position and move your head slightly backwards, focusing your eyelids toward the ceiling. Let them relax. In your mind, command them to relax. You should begin to feel your eyelids quiver and palpitate.

In your mind's eye, focus on the backs of your eyelids. Tell your eyelids to let their tension go. Tell them to go loose and limp and heavy, so heavy that you do not want to open them. When they feel totally loose and calm, test them by seeing how heavy they really are. Gently try to open them.

With your eyes closed, take the feeling of calmness and looseness you have in your eyelids and move it down through your body. In your mind's eye, think of your cheekbones and tell them to let their tension go. Feel the looseness. Try to see your cheekbones and feel them let the tension go. Think of your chin and tell it to relax. Let it go loose and limp.

Think of your throat and tell it to relax. Let it go loose and limp. Think of your chest cavity and tell it to relax. Let it go loose and limp. Think of the diaphragm at the top of your stomach and tell it to relax. Let it go loose and limp. Think of your stomach and tell it to relax. Let it go loose and limp. Try to see each body part.

In your mind's eye, think of your pelvis and tell it to let the tension go. Try to see it and let it go loose and limp. Think of your thighs and tell them to go loose and limp. Let it go loose and limp. Think of your knees and tell them to feel the calmness. Let them go loose and limp. Think of your skin and tell it to let the tension go and feel the calmness. Let it go loose and limp. Think of your ankles and tell them to relax. Let tension go and feel the calmness. Think of your toes and soles of your feet. Let your mind focus on the various parts of your feet and feel them let the tension go, first the left foot, and then the right. Now in your mind's eye, move up to the back parts of your ankles and tell each part to let the tension go.

Think of your calf and tell it to let the tension go. Let it go loose and limp. Think of your chin and tell it to let the tension go. Let it go loose and limp. Think of your bottom and tell it to let loose of its tensions. Let it go loose and limp. Think of the backs of your knees and tell them to feel calmness. Let them go loose and limp. Pay special attention to your backbone and try to picture the structure from its base to its connection at your neck. Picture each vertebrae and move up each one, telling each to let the tension go and feel good. Slowly move up your back, breathing in and out, slowly and deeply.

Think of the back of your head and the brain cavity within. Tell them to feel good and let the tension go. Now, move your mind's eye down your arms, first to your shoulders and then to your biceps. Tell them to relax.

Think of your elbows and tell them to let their tension go. Think of your wrists and tell them to feel heavy with calmness. Let them go loose and limp. Think of the palms of your hands and tell them to go loose and limp, letting the tension go.

Move your minds' eye down to your fingertips and tell them to be heavy with calmness. Let them go loose and limp.

Repeat this exercise two more times.

Other Ways of Using Your Mind to Relax

Another method of relaxation involves visuling various parts of your body and repeating statements to enhance relaxation, warmth, and restfulness. You can do this exercise sitting or lying down. If you lie down, your head should be supported and your knees should be bent. Your toes should be pointed slightly outward, and your arms should rest comfortably at your sides.

- Concentrate on the part of the body to which the phrase is directed. Begin with, "My right arm is heavy." Repeat this two more times.
- Proceed to the left arm, right leg, left leg, neck, and shoulders.
- Concentrate again on the part of the body to which the phrase is directed. This time, the phrase is, "My right arm is warm." Proceed to the rest of the body as above. This exercise increases peripheral blood flow, relaxes the blood vessels, and promotes self-healing physiological changes.
- Repeat the phrase, "My heartbeat is calm and regular."
- Repeat the phrase, "My breathing is calm and regular." This exercise prompts slow, deep, regular breathing.
- Mentally repeat, "My forehead is cool." This is done primarily for its psychological effect, which is to combine deep relaxation with alertness.
- The exercise ends with the phrase: "I am refreshed and alert."
- Take a deep breath and stretch.

Biofeedback

Biofeedback enables people to gain control over some bodily functions previously thought to be involuntary. It is basically the conscious monitoring of internal body states. By watching and/or listening to sensitive recording machines (or simple home devices), you can learn to control many internal body processes. In biofeedback training, you use the information about the body process to learn how to change that process voluntarily. With a little instruction and daily practice, almost anyone can learn to regulate pulse rate, body temperature, muscle tension, and other internal processes.

Biofeedback instruments monitor selected body systems that can be picked up by electrodes and transformed into visual or auditory signals. Any internal change instantly triggers an external signal, such as a sound, a flickering light, or readings on a meter. When you are hooked up to the biofeedback equipment, you can see and/or hear the continuous monitoring of your selected body functions. Biofeedback training allows you to take this information about your body states and use it to modify or change them. You will be able to apply your increased awareness of tension to your daily life. You learn to say, "I am aware of feeling tension now and I need to relax."

Biofeedback is more difficult to get involved with because the equipment is expensive. It is, however, very effective. It is now possible to buy some equipment (such as blood pressure monitors and thermometers) cheaply.

MEDITATION AND SELF-HYPNOSIS

The many demands of modern society create a habit of directing the great majority of our thinking and behavior outward. We tend to resolve problems by thinking consciously. Our minds are a chaotic array of memories, images, fantasies, and feelings related to our everyday experiences. We normally seek to resolve this stress by consciously finding external resolutions to problems. The remaining techniques in this chapter help you focus on your inner self, or your subconscious.

Meditation

Almost all of us have found ourselves in a meditative state at one time or another. You may have been looking into a campfire, watching the ocean's waves, or listening to some music. During this state, your mind was not thinking of anything at all, except it was concentrating intensely.

This is what meditation is like. It is a process of helping the mind concentrate on one thing, rather than the many things that we are normally thinking of at once. It is an intense concentration in which we encourage the mind to focus on taking control and being relaxed and at ease.

Sports stars often use their minds in a similar fashion to focus their bodies intensely on making a jump or on lifting some weights. In these cases, the athlete is using the power of the subconscious to perform. Afterwards, many will describe themselves as being in an altered state. They often are heard saying, "I was in another world," or "I cannot imagine what possessed me, I was superhuman." This partially explains why some athletes excel during competition.

MEDITATION WORKS TO HELP YOU USE YOUR INNER POWER, THE SUBCONSCIOUS, TO ASSIST IN RELAXATION AND BUILDING CONFIDENCE.

Meditation is effective in creating a state of deep relaxation in a relatively short time. The body's metabolism is slowed as oxygen consumption, carbon dioxide production, respiratory rate, heart rate, and blood pressure are decreased. In addition, lactic acid, a substance produced by the metabolism of skeletal muscles and associated with anxiety and tension, is reduced.

Meditation is successful in the prevention and treatment of high blood pressure, heart disease, and strokes. It has proved helpful in curtailing obsessive thinking, anxiety, depression, and hostility. It improves concentration and attention span.

Many of the popular meditative forms are based on Eastern philosophies. Most of us have heard of TM, or Transcendental Meditation. This is often associated with visions of long-haired yogis, gurus, or masters who are working with their bands of devoted followers. This school of meditation uses mantras, chants, or affirmations to focus the mind and to slow down the active beta brain waves into slower, more creative, more peaceful alpha and theta waves. These are the levels that induce harmony with the subconscious by shutting out the outside world and focusing inward on feelings, thoughts, ideas, or on the body's internal organs.

The TM school in the Western world is best known for its leader, Maharishi Mahesh Yogi. Those who enroll in the school are assigned a personal mantra, a word or sound to concentrate on and help shut out distractions. You can choose your own mantra if you wish, or you may want to use phrases to assist you in relaxing. For example, the following phrases are helpful during meditation: "breathing calmness in and tension out," "feeling good," "feeling calm," "letting the body go loose and limp," and so forth.

Some meditative schools recommend slowing down the brain-wave frequency by becoming more aware of your breathing. For example, you might focus on your breath and periodically repeat the statement "breathing calmness in and tension out." You can also use a countdown procedure, starting with the number 50. For example, in your mind, think of the number 50 while breathing calmness in, exhale, 49, inhale, breathing calmness in. If you lose track of the numbers, just pick some random number and continue on.

Many meditation techniques are like hypnosis or self-hypnosis. However, in hypnosis, we use the power of visualization to help change behavior and build confidence. Both techniques have the same objective of slowing down the brain waves, focusing intense concentration, and using the power of the subconscious.

THE BEST WAY TO PRACTICE MEDITATION OR SELF-HYPNOSIS IS TO DO IT AT A REGULAR TIME EACH DAY.

Some of us practice meditation only when we feel really tense, as a mechanism for getting rid of our frustrations. While this will have some benefits, it takes practice to concentrate. For example, after practicing meditation for thirty consecutive days, you will find the level of concentration much easier to achieve. If the objective is to keep stressful incidents from bothering you, in addition to harnessing the power of the subconscious, then meditation and self-hypnosis are best thought of as a long-term strategy.

Meditation is best practiced by sitting in a chair or on the floor with your backbone erect. Your head usually does not need support. If you sit on a chair, make sure that your feet are flat on the floor.

A successful meditation exercise requires a comfortable chair, an uninterrupted space, and a commitment to sit down and enjoy ten to twenty minutes. Stretch your arms, take a deep breath and exhale quickly.

Sit down in a comfortable chair and place your feet flat on the floor with the small of your back against the back of the chair. In a self-hypnosis exercise, put your hands on your legs or the armrests of the chair and do not let your hands touch each other. Some meditation exercises suggest that you maintain contact between your thumb and index fingers or between your thumb and your smallest finger. This helps you concentrate and direct the flow of your energy through your body.

Take a deep breath and hold it. Now, exhale. Take another deep breath and hold it for five seconds: 5, 4, 3, 2, 1. (Each count should last for more than one second.) Exhale deeply by pushing the air from the bottom of your lungs.

Put your head back against the back of your chair or in an upright position facing backwards (a high-back chair is desirable, although it is not necessary).

The following is a popular form of meditation throughout the world. It is good for achieving deep relaxation and for learning self-discipline.

- Go to a quiet place and center yourself. You might begin by using a breathing exercise and relaxation technique. Then, assume the posture of your choice, either sitting in a chair or on the floor with your backbone straight. Release the tension in your body and relax. Close your eyes, or gaze at a spot that is about four feet in front of you. This spot might be on the top part of the wall or on the ceiling.

- Breathe in through your nose and out through your mouth. Inhale, exhale, and pause. Breathe in an easy and natural way. Become aware of your breathing.

- As you inhale, say silently to yourself, "breathing calmness in." Each time you exhale, say, "breathing tension out."

- When thoughts or perceptions take your attention away from your breathing, let go of them quickly and return to recognizing your breathing. You may also wish to start a countdown from the number 50. Breathe in and say "50," and then exhale. Breath in and say "49," and exhale. When you reach the number 1, focus your thoughts on your breathing.

- Try this for ten to twenty minutes at a time.

- Each time you complete this exercise, do not get up for a few minutes. Rather, sit quietly with your eyes closed. Take time to appreciate the effects of meditation.

Meditations Used by Those Who Practice Yoga

Meditation, according to yoga gurus, is the "gathering of our wandering thoughts to a concentrated inner thought or focus." The goal is to expand awareness.

Yoga enthusiasts believe that yoga assists in realizing one's purpose in life. Each exercise is used to help understand how the mind and body are interconnected to establish a healthy lifestyle. In this pursuit, meditation is to the mind what the yoga exercises are to the body.

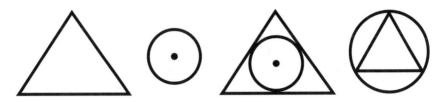

To assist the process of visualization, yoga practitioners use a yantra, which is a geometrically shaped object that is inserted within some symmetrical form. Examples are a triangle, a circle with a dot in it, a circle with a dot in an inverted triangle, a triangle in a circle, and others. The whole shape represents completion, harmony, or integration. Everything is contained in the circle. The inner object is a symbol of the inner spirit within the outer spirit's supreme nature. The point in the center is "bindhu," or everlasting. Other geometrical forms have corresponding meanings. The following steps are used in observing the circle with a dot in the center (yantra meditation 1).

- Place the yantra in front of you and look at it for two minutes.
- Start looking at the point on the circumference and move your sight around the circle. Move your sight to the center when your eyes reach the starting point. Continue doing this for two minutes.
- After two minutes, close your eyes and visualize the yantra. Remain comfortably seated and concentrate on breathing at the same time. You should try to reconstruct the circle and place a dot in the circle. Hold this position for three minutes.
- Lie down and remain in that position, concentrating on abdominal breathing.

Yoga enthusiasts use a variety of yantras in their meditations. They also meditate using a candle, following similar steps to those outlined above.

A SELF-HYPNOSIS EXERCISE

YOU CAN SIGNIFICANTLY REDUCE STRESS WITH SOMETHING ENORMOUSLY POWERFUL: YOUR IMAGINATION.

It is hard to will yourself into a relaxed state, but you can imagine calmness and looseness spreading through your body, and you can envision yourself in a safe and beautiful retreat. All your thoughts become reality—you are what you think you are. For example, if you think sad thoughts, you feel unhappy. If you think anxious thoughts, you become tense. To overcome the feeling of unhappiness or tension, you can refocus your mind on positive, healing images.

Visualization, guided imagery, and hypnosis are effective ways of using the imagination to treat many stress-related and physical illnesses, including headaches, muscle spasms, chronic pain, and general or situation-specific anxiety.

HYPNOSIS IS A WAY TO USE YOUR IMAGINATION TO CREATE RELAXATION.

You can read the following exercise into a tape recorder, and then experience it. Or, you might practice this as a routine.

We are going to start with relaxing your eyelids, and then we'll move through the rest of your body. First, take a deep breath and hold. Count 5, 4, 3, 2, 1. Now exhale. Take another deep breath and hold. Count 5, 4, 3, 2, 1. Now exhale.

Close your eyes and become aware of the noises in the room around you. Be aware of the noises outside. Recognize them but tell yourself that you want to shut them out for a period of time to relax and regenerate. This is your time to relax and give your brain a rest.

As you breathe in, practice breathing deeper and deeper. With each breath you take tell yourself, "I am breathing calmness in and tension out."

With your eyes closed, focus your eyes on the ceiling of the room. Yes, you are looking at the ceiling with your eyes closed. Focus your mind on your eyelids. Let them go loose and limp. They may even feel like they are flickering.

In your mind's eye and with your eyes closed, focus on your eyelids. Let them go limp and heavy. Think of your eyelids and command them to relax. Feel them relax and enjoy this feeling.

Now, let your eyelids feel loose and limp. Tell them to let their tension go. Feel it go. Could you let them go loose and limp? Feel it. Want it to happen. Tell it to happen. Make it happen.

They'll feel very loose and heavy, as if they are hard to open. Yes, that's it. Let them be as tired as you can possibly imagine them.

You might want to test how heavy they are now. Testing now, I'd like you to see how heavy they are. Test their heaviness by trying to open them. Great! See how hard it is to open them?

We are going to let this feeling go down through your body. In the next few minutes, I will be asking you to open and close your eyes three times and each time you do, you are to make the feeling go down your body. I'd like you to transfer the feeling that you now have in your eyelids down to the rest of your body. What you are going to feel is complete calmess, a feeling of looseness.

Now open your eyes and close them and let the feeling go down through your body. Let the feeling go down through your body from your eyes to your cheeks, down through your chest and stomach and upper body, right down to the bottoms of your feet. Let the feeling go up through the backs of your legs to your backbone and to the back of your shoulders and then down your arms to your fingertips.

Now rest for a moment and repeat this exercise two more times. You'll notice that your whole body feels loose and limp. There may even be a tingle at the tips of your fingers. If it is not there, concentrate for a moment and focus your mind's eye on your right index finger and tell it to go loose and limp. Tell it to relax and let its tension go. Let it feel completely at rest and good. Tell it to happen, want it to happen, and let it happen. Feel your fingertip tingle.

The neat thing is that you have just commanded your fingertip to go loose and limp and tingly. You have exhibited control over it. Just as you can control your fingertip, you also have the power to control the rest of your body and tell each body part to let the tension out and calmness in. You can do this anytime you feel tense.

In your mind, picture a white board or a television screen and try to see the numbers 99, 98, 97, 96, and 95. Try to focus on one number at a time. First focus on 99. When you see it clearly, tell it to slowly disappear and disintegrate. As it does, let the feeling of calmness move down through your body, not twice as long but twice as calm and relaxed. Let it swirl away, let it catch a cloud and disappear. Watch it get fainter and fainter.

Think of the number 98, and let it disappear, and as it does let a feeling of calmness go down through the rest of your body.

Think of the number 97, and let it disappear, and as it does let a feeling of calmness go down through the rest of your body.

Let all the numbers disappear and disintegrate, and as they do, let a feeling of calmness go down through the rest of your body.

Let your mind go for a walk. Imagine yourself leaving the area where you live. Leave the daily hassles and the fast pace behind. Imagine yourself going across a valley and moving closer and closer to a mountain range. Imagine yourself in a mountain range. You are going up a winding road. Find a place on the winding road to stop. Find a path to walk up. Start walking up the path. Find a comfortable place to stop on the path. At this place take some time to examine all the tension and stress in your life. Give the tension and stress shapes and colors. Look at them down on the side of the path.

Continue walking up the path until you come to the top of a hill. Look out over the hill. What do you see? Find an inviting, comfortable place and go there. Be aware of the sights, smells, and sounds. Be aware of how you are feeling. Get settled and gradually start to relax. You are now feeling totally relaxed. Experience being relaxed totally and completely. Pause for three to five minutes. Look around at your special place once more. Remember, this is your special place to feel good and relax, and you can come here anytime you want to do so.

Come back to the room and tell yourself that this imagery is something you have created, and you can use it whenever you want to feel relaxed.

In returning to your normal state and today's life, counting from 1 to 5, you are:

1. Feeling completely refreshed; every muscle in your body feels loose and limp.

2. Your mind is calm and free of tension. Each time you breathe, you are breathing calmness in and tension out.

3. Feeling confident and self-assured. Tell yourself that you are proud of what you are.

4. When you open your eyes, you will feel rested and ready to take on the day with an attitude of calmness and feeling of satisfaction.

5. Open your eyes and stretch your fingers in front of you. Flick them and say, "wide awake" three times.

Changing the Script for Self-Hypnosis

There are many ways to change and adapt the above script for different purposes. Normally, a person would only complete one journey during his or her hypnotic induction. For example, you may wish to go to your special place and think about your future or plan your day. You may wish to focus on a specific problem that has been of concern to you. The following inductions might be used for imaging your future or past.

The Future

I'd like to give you a chance to see where you are going to be five years from now. It's the year 1997. Think of what is happening in the year 1997. Go to the year 2002. You have the same job. Think of what is happening in the year 2002. It is September 15; you are visiting a fifth-grade class. Who are you? What are you doing?

- Who is the teacher?
- What is in the room?
- What are they doing?
- How is the teaching taking place?
- Is the teacher happy?
- Are the students happy?
- What are they discussing?
- Are they smiling?
- What are people saying?

The Past

I'd like to give you a chance to see where you were many years ago.

- Think of a little boy (or girl) five years old.
- What's he (she) doing?
- What's he (she) feeling?
- Let the feelings come to the surface.
- Find a little boy (girl) three years old.
- What's he (she) wearing?
- What's mom saying?

- Where's mom?
- Let the feelings come to the surface.
- Find a little boy (girl) two months old.
- What's he (she) doing?
- Find a little boy (girl) just being born.
- Where's the baby?
- What's he (she) feeling?

Using Music

Listening to music is a good way to improve your concentration and visualization. You can pick a musical selection that you like and then take the steps of induction. Choose a piece that you find peaceful and soothing when you want to listen to music for relaxation. Make a half-hour tape of uninterrupted relaxing music that you can play daily, or just when you wish to use music to relax. Repetition of the same music that helped you to relax in the past carries with it a positive association that is likely to be beneficial in the future. After you are completely relaxed, listen to the music and give your own interpretation to it.

CHINESE PRACTICES

Chinese breathing, relaxing, and meditating techniques have a long history. Comments on the importance of breathing and using one's genuine energy to ward off disease can be found in *The Yellow Emperor's Canon of Internal Medicine,* which was written in the Warring State Period (fourth century B.C.). Since that time, there have been many valuable improvements to these exercises. After the founding of the People's Republic of China, breathing exercises were explored very systematically. An analysis of several clinical observations and scientific experiments provided a body of evidence to illustrate that they were useful in reducing the problems associated with high blood pressure, peptic ulcers, gastritis, and some cancers.

The Chinese method of breathing exercises *(qigong)* is integral in the search for longevity, keeping fit, strengthening body resistance, and preventing and curing disease. The breathing exercises are called *daoyin* (directing extremities), *tuna* (exhalation and inhalation), and *lianqi* (training of vital energy). The exercises are directed at using *qi* (vital energy) from the air breathed in to harness and strengthen the original *qi* (the genuine and spiritual part of us). When the original *qi* is strong, it can act as a powerful force in conquering disease and achieving good health. As a result, traditional Chinese medicine relies on training to strengthen the original *qi* and its growth.

The Western exercises presented in the previous sections of this chapter are specialized. There are exercises to assist breathing, relaxation, and meditating. The Chinese breathing exercises are integrated and directed at achieving muscle relaxation, mental quietude, and spiritual stability. They act on the body as a whole. It is necessary to control one's mental activities and emotional reactions to achieve a comfortable and quiet state. This helps strengthen the body's resistance and prevent and conquer disease.

Western technologies have proven to be quite useful in evaluating the effect of breathing exercises on the nervous, cardiovascular, digestive, respiratory, and endocrine systems. For example, after exercising, patients show a weakening of reaction in the sympathetic nerve, while that of the parasympathetic is strengthened. Breathing exercises promote blood circulation by dilating the capillaries and strengthening the pulse. The patient's heartbeat slows down when inhaling deeply, and there is an increase in blood volume during deep exhaling. The digestive system develops a greater rhythm during certain exercises, resulting in improved digestion and absorption. A more thorough analysis of the effects of these exercises is available in various sources.

A CHINESE BREATHING EXERCISE

There are three parts to any breathing exercise:

- adjusting the body (posture)
- adjusting the mind
- adjusting respiration (breathing)

Adjusting the Body

There are various postures for the body, although the most popular is the standing position because it helps generate the internal vital energy. In the standing position, the body is straight with the feet shoulder-width apart, toes pointed slightly inward, and knees slightly bent. The head and neck are erect. The chest is relaxed and the body's posture represents three points on a straight line from toe to head. The tip of the tongue should gently touch and lick the top palate of the mouth. The anus is raised and the buttocks are drawn in. The shoulders are relaxed. Eyes should look straight forward into infinity when starting the exercise, and they should be closed afterwards.

The three points on a straight line position links three acupuncture points—*Baihui* at the top of the head, *Fengshi* at the fingertips, and *Yoong Chuan* (or Yongquan) at the base and midpoint of each foot. The inner vital energy can easily be started once the body is in this position.

The inner energy will ascend from the *Du* channel (the back midline channel on the top of the backbone) when breathing in. It will ascend from the *Dazhui* acupoint (located under the seventh cervical vertebra) and up to the top of the head (*Baihui*).

Touching the top palate of the mouth with the tongue is equivalent to building a bridge for the energy to pass for *Baihui* and to descend in the *Ren* channel in the front of the body just below the skin line. It will descend to the middle *Dantian* (chest area near the heart). The vital energy will sink to the lower *Dantian* (located in the stomach area).

Adjusting the Mind

After adjusting the posture, it is possible to gradually begin the meditation and breathing exercises. The first step is to concentrate the mind and begin a state of meditation; try to rid the mind of distracting thoughts and relax the inner and outer parts of the body.

- The deeper one gets into meditation, the greater the therapeutic effect. Meditation is achieved by concentrating the mind on a certain point. You might focus on the three points on a straight line. Or, you might concentrate on your respiration. There are various ways to encourage a meditative state.

- Point concentration: You can focus your mind on a point in the body such as the Dantian point (just below the umbilicus).

- Free breathing: Concentrate on the in-and-out movements of your abdomen. Focus on your breathing but do not direct it.

- Counting while breathing: One round of respiration, exhaling and inhaling, is called *xi*. Count the number of *xi* silently from one to ten to one hundred, or until you reach a seeing nothing, thinking nothing state, and thus meditation.

- Reading silently: Read some simple material or phrases such as "silent and relaxing."
- Listening to breaths: Concentrate on the sounds of your breath, but hear nothing. It is better to hear nothing to get into a meditative state.

After a time, you should direct the turbulent air (along the *Ren* Channel) by descending from head to toe. To do this, let your mind focus on:

- The *Baihui* point at the top of your head,
- next, relax your *Jianjing* point on each shoulder,
- then, relax your breasts,
- then, your hips,
- then, your knees,
- then, the *Yoong Chuan* (*Yongquan*) point on each sole.

The whole body should be relaxed at this point. If it is not, repeat the exercise again.

After relaxation, focus your eyes to the front and let the eyelids fall naturally. Close the eyelids. Move in your mind's eye down to the abdomen as if you are looking at the umbilicus (or 1.97 inches above the umbilicus). This is called "concentrating one's idea at *Dantian*." It is regulating the *head* (mind). The *Dantian* is the "hub" of all connecting channels and the spot of generating and storing vital energy. Sticking your concentration at this point increases your immunity to disease.

Having generated the inner vital energy, let it move along the channels naturally.

Adjusting the Respiration (Breathing)

Generally, the exhaling and inhaling motions should be of the same force. Weaker people, who have a stronger *Yin*, require more inhaling than exhaling. Stronger people have shorter exhaling motions. The ideal respiration is to inhale and exhale equally.

While inhaling, the air is taken to *Shanzhong.*

While exhaling, the air sinks to *Dantian.*

While inhaling, one should focus the mind on the *Dantian* acupoint and repeat silently the word *Dantian.* While exhaling, one should relax and think of words like "loose, quiet, natural" or "quietness." The repeated movement of air (*qi* or vital energy) between *Shangzhong* and *Dantian* can clear the Ren channel and is the first phase of "cultivating the essence of life and change it into vital energy." The goal is to fill *Dantian* with an abundant of vital energy.

YOUR NEXT STEP

People will be just about as happy as they
allow themselves to be.

—ABRAHAM LINCOLN

Get started by setting aside a day for yourself, with no television or other interruptions. Go to someplace you enjoy and start practicing these techniques.

Eastern practitioners like to get in touch with nature. They want to capture the energy, or qi, of the environment.

PART FOUR

ENRICHING YOUR LIFE THROUGH CHANGE

Making the Dragon Work for You

13 Your Personal Plan for Taming the Dragon

That's why it's time for a change

—T.E. DEWEY

The principles of stress management, diet, exercise, and relaxation outlined in the previous chapters do not demand self-denial and a boring lifestyle. With a little creativity, it is easy to get started on a program that you will find interesting and healthy. You can now begin a program for change and improve your ability to handle and prevent stress.

WHAT DO YOU VALUE MOST?

A STRESS MANAGEMENT PHILOSOPHY STATEMENT IS JUST ONE TOOL FOR DEVELOPING THE BELIEFS AND VALUES BY WHICH YOU WANT TO LIVE.

Like organizations that have cultures of service and sales excellence, a person can develop beliefs and values that are less stressful and more healthy for living. Your philosophy statement articulates the values you feel are most important. Beliefs are more theological and describe the meaning of life. They are a statement of your fundamental truths. Values are more philosophical and are assumptions of what is worth pursuing in life.

First, you should articulate a philosophy of realistic, credible, attractive, and desirable values and preferences. It can be described in terms of your values toward life and should be articulated in relationship to work and social life, exercise and fitness, diet, and your general life attitude.

Envisioning what you might wish to do in life is very easy. However, it is much more difficult to break with the negative beliefs and self-defeating behaviors that may be making it difficult to realize this vision.

Set aside three or four hours and find a quiet place to read the following chapter. You should search for a place where you will not be interrupted so you can work out the steps you will take to develop a program that focuses on your diet, stress, and lifestyle.

> *The seats on the train of progress all face backwards;*
> *you can see the past but only guess about the future.*
>
> —E.G. BORING

In your quiet place, you should get into a comfortable position and, if possible, relax and meditate. Close your eyes and begin the procedures outlined in *Principle 8: Use the Power Within You.* Begin by relaxing various parts of your body and using the self-hypnosis countdown procedure to achieve a deep state of relaxation.

In your relaxed state, picture yourself at a dinner where you are being "roasted." There are several people there that you know, including your spouse and closest friends, who are going to tell stories about you.

Four speakers are offering their thoughts on what they feel you have accomplished.

The first speaker is your boss. He or she will talk about the way you have designed and managed your work, as well as the way you are an example for others. Have you worked hard? Are you challenged? Are you productive, satisfied, stressed, or enthusiastic?

The second speaker is a colleague who regularly exercises with you. What are some of the things that he or she might say you believe in? Do you exercise a great deal? Do you overdo it?

The third speaker is your husband or wife, who will comment on your personal habits. He or she will talk about the types of foods you eat at each meal, the stress-promoting things you ingest (additives, caffeine, alcohol, nicotine), and the principles you use to maintain a balanced diet. What are some of the comments that your husband or wife might make?

The final speaker is a friend who is aware of your general life attitude. What are some of the things he or she says you believe in?

After you have finished your meditation exercise, jot down some of the things said about you in relationship to:

The Stresses You Exhibit in Life and in Your Job

_____

_____

The Stresses and Benefits of Your Personal Program of Exercise

_____

_____

The Stresses and Benefits of Your Personal Eating Habits

_____

_____

The Stresses and Benefits of Your General Life Attitude

_____

_____

SOME PEOPLE SEEM DESTINED TO BE STRESSED IN EVERYTHING THEY DO.

I recently purchased a new car, and as I was standing in the car lot talking to the salesperson, the dealership manager was moving hurriedly to his vehicle. The salesperson caught the manager's attention and sought to introduce him to me. The manager walked briskly over to us, and he seemed to want to demonstrate that he was a busy person. He looked quickly at his watch before grasping my hand in a stern handshake. He was at least thirty pounds overweight, was out of breath from walking, and had Type A and anxiety written all over him. I shook his hand slowly and jokingly said, "You seem to be a very busy person in a hurry." He said he was on his way to the doctor and was late for his appointment.

This manager seemed to have a lifestyle of working hard, feeling anxious, overeating, not exercising, and possibly being hypertensive. Most doctors would encourage this manager to slow down and rethink his lifestyle.

Unfortunately, most suggestions would go unheeded as a person such as this truly believes he has to work this hard. I believe that this manager does not want to be in this state, but is caught up in beliefs that are ill defined or contradictory. This manager has an ineffective paradigm, or a system of related self-reinforcing beliefs that are self-defeating. The beliefs may be logical to the manager, but they are inconsistent and ineffective.

We might ask this manager to define what other people say about him and then to outline his values toward stress and exercise. He might say he wanted to be healthy, in shape, slim, and less tense. He might also indicate that he had to work long hours to keep the business vibrant, that he often had to have business lunches and take customers out for drinks, and that he found it difficult to schedule exercise at a convenient time. You may find this true of yourself.

Before reading any further in this chapter, write down some of the values you have. Review the principles and strategies in the previous chapter.

What are the values you seek in relationship to the way you wish to deal with the stress of your work, your career, and life?

_____

_____

_____

Write down some values you want in your new relationship to exercise.

_____

_____

_____

Write down some things you want to do in regard to diet and nutrition.

_____

_____

_____

Write down some of the values you want to have in relationship to relaxation.

_____

_____

_____

In looking at these values, develop a philosophy statement for yourself.

A PHILOSOPHY STATEMENT DESCRIBES THE VALUES YOU FEEL ARE DESIRABLE OR PREFERABLE AND THE NEW BELIEFS YOU NEED FOR FULFILLING THIS VISION.

A philosophy statement contains underlying values and beliefs, such as those reflected in the family-like values of some Japanese organizations. The following is an example of a statement of one religious organization's beliefs. A next step is to define the values flowing from these beliefs.

- Of all the environmental influences in our lives, the most powerful ones are personal relationships.
- Of all relationships, it is the family relationship that leaves the deepest impressions and has the greatest effect on us.
- Fundamental to the work of society is honoring and respecting each person: adults and children needing our services; staff and volunteers working in our programs; board and society members providing direction for the organization; professional colleagues in other agencies and in government departments; benefactors who donate money, goods, and services in support of the center's work.

A good strategy is to develop a philosophy statement that contains your values and then think about it for a week or two. You might even talk to some of your friends about the values and beliefs they have. This thinking and discussion should help you develop a philosophy statement that is brief and inclusive of your values and beliefs for a positive future.

WHAT IS YOUR VISION OF WHAT YOU WANT TO BE?

Articulating Your Vision of How You Manage Your Stress

A home renovation metaphor illustrates how your life philosophy can be useful in creating a novel and nonroutine vision of the way you will manage your life and control your stress. When renovating a home, the builder must assess the technical features of the present structure—its foundation, bearing walls, electrical facilities, and plumbing system. The builder must pinpoint the problems to resolve and define the needs and values of the homeowner.

A person's philosophy statement is only one perspective on renovating a home. A successful and thoughtful renovation emerges from someone's vision of what the renovation might look like based on architectural ideas, trends in construction, and new materials available. The vision, a creative idea, is "tailored" to the present structure and the values of the homeowner. The final changes emerge from the initial sketches to the more detailed architectural plan, which is submitted to the building inspectors and engineers. A plan for construction helps the builder implement the envisioned design.

Look again at the comments made by the four speakers. What future direction or vision is hinted at by these statements?

> YOUR VISION IS AN IDEA OR A DIRECTION, BUT IT HAS SUFFICIENT DETAILS, JUST LIKE THE ARCHITECT'S VISION OF A NEW HOUSE HAS SOME VERY DETAILED SKETCHES.

Your vision evolves from a definition of your values and the possible things you might do that are quite different from what you do now. For each of the values you have identified, what opportunities are there for you to do something different to fulfill these values?

Your vision should evolve from your values. What ideas do you have for changing the various aspects of your life so that they recognize your new values? Compete the following statements.

I want to be more _____ in handling stress in the future at work. What would this require me to do?

_____

_____

I want to be more _____ in using exercise to handle my stress and improve my health. What would this require me to do?

_____

_____

I want to be more _____ in changing my diet to help me reduce stress and improve my health. What would this require me to do ?

_____

_____

I want to be more _____ in relaxing and enjoying life so that I can manage stress. What would this require me to do?

_____

_____

Articulating your vision statement is both an art and a science and should be viewed as a trial-and-error process. Successive definitions of the vision have to respond to inhibitors such as your willingness to change your existing personal style, beliefs, values, and habits of eating, exercising, working, and so forth. The home renovator has a similar problem. He or she has a vision of what is ideal, but is faced with dealing with the way the present house is designed, the cost of renovation, values, and future plans.

The philosophy and vision statement assist you to articulate the values and beliefs you want to realize in work, exercise, diet, and relaxation.

WHAT IS YOUR MISSION IN LIFE?

ONE OF THE MOST IMPORTANT GOALS IN DEVELOPING A MISSION STATEMENT IS TO HELP YOU TO CRYSTALIZE A PARADIGM THAT IS IN BETTER HARMONY WITH THE DESIRED VALUES AND BELIEFS OF HAVING A HAPPY LIFE AND EFFECTIVELY MANAGING STRESS.

We can sharpen our focus so that we are participating in activities that we truly value. A personal mission statement describes your purpose in life. It is your justification for existence. Most of us fumble along in life as we react to the many events and opportunities we face. We learn to think of this as a rather random process that is shaped by luck and opportunities. If we accept this logic, we must believe that the manager of the car dealership was destined to overwork, feel anxious, overeat, not exercise, and be tense.

Every person has his or her own opportunity to shape some part of the world with which he or she interacts. This shaping affects friends and family as much as it does oneself. We can determine how we work and relax as well as what we eat and drink. We can find effective substitutes or alternative ways of doing things to respond to the threats around us. Each of us has an internal set of standards that we live by in work, diet, exercise, and so forth. They are revealed by value statements such as, "I really should exercise more," "I should take more time off," "I wish I could relax," "I eat too much." If only we could live the values that we felt were important, we would be better off. The task is to be comfortable with the way we are or to realign our paradigm of life.

A mission statement requires the identification of your key stakeholders, or the persons or groups that place a claim on your resources, time, or outputs. The key to success for most people and organizations is the satisfaction of stakeholders. A complete understanding of the stakeholders' needs is necessary for judging and evaluating success. It illustrates which of your resources and skills are most in demand and others which are most needed. Analysis will help clarify whether you should have a different mission and set of strategies for different stakeholders.

The mission statement is not something which you can write on the spot. Its creation usually requires some thought and discussion with other people. To help provoke this thought process, respond to the following questions:

What: What makes you distinct?

Who: Who are the stakeholders that you must satisfy?

Why: Why do we have the goals and motivators we have?

Where: Where do we do our main activities (work and leisure)?

How: How are we carrying out these activities?

How do we carry out the activities of work (production and adaptation)?

How do we carry out our nonwork activities (entertainment, relaxation, exercise, eating)?

What do you do at work and when you are not at work? This can be expressed in terms of needs met and what makes you distinct. It can be stated by the products, services, or requirements you supply. For example, you may work as electrician to assist home contractors and you may be a husband and father and provide companionship to your spouse and guidance to your children. You may be an important source of support and inspiration for your colleagues and friends. This method of stating what you do allows you to look for new ways of meeting needs; it expands your range of possibilities.

Who are some of your key stakeholders or people that you feel you have to respond to to be effective? In your organization, these might be clients, superiors, and influential people. In your nonwork life, these might be your spouse, children, relatives, important friends that you value, or other key people. It is most important to identify those people who serve as your mentors are your protégés. This clarifies the people to whom you have to relate.

Why do you do what you do? This may be related to survival and include the need for finances, public image, leadership, or some other broad objective. This part of the mission statement provides qualitative criteria for assessing your success.

Where do you do your key business?

How and **Where** production occurs are statements of the mechanical aspects of production. This provides a description of the facilities and equipment. It also indicates how you respond to key stakeholders. Your mission statement describes the unique goals setting you apart from others.

The statement refers to what you are in "business" for, or the purpose of existence. It is your *raison d'être,* your "reason for being."

WHAT IS THE STRESS THAT YOU FACE?

The most important visions of developing a healthier lifestyle are those that help you respond to the immediate stress you may have. Based on the previous chapters, you should be aware of your personality, work habits, and general lifestyle.

Summarize the prime stressors associated with your work, exercise, diet, and relaxation profile.

After listing these stressors, define why they might be occurring. For example, you may feel that you are overweight because you find yourself in situations where you are overeating or eating the wrong kinds of foods. You may have business lunches that encourage you to eat restaurant meals (which are often very fattening). Or, you may find you are a constant nibbler with a "see food" habit of eating all the time. You might want to relax more with meditation but never seem to have the time. You might want to exercise but never seem to find the time to do it.

There are a number of questions that you should answer to analyze the types of stressors you are encountering.

- Are these stressors caused by other people, your own mental model (paradigm), or some situation completely beyond your control (sickness of others, traffic delays)?
- What assumptions or values are these stressors based on?
- Are these assumptions true and are they consistent with your philosophy, mission statement, and vision?

Prime stressors at work or based on your personality	WHY?
Example: I dislike my colleagues.	**Example: I have high expectations of my fellow workers. They do not live up to these expectations.**

Prime stressors from exercise (heart rate, blood pressure, general physical stamina, and so on.)

WHY?

Example: Overexertion.

Example: I have high expectations of myself. I tend to overdo exercise.

_____

_____

_____

Prime stressors from dietary habits (overweight, high cholesterol, general physical ability, and so on.)

WHY?

Example: Overeating.

Example: I arrive home famished, and head for the fridge and eat sandwiches before dinner.

_____

_____

_____

Prime stressors from inability to relax and refocus (sleeplessness, general self-esteem and confidence, and so on.)

WHY?

Example: No time to relax.

Example: My family life keeps me too busy.

_____

_____

_____

Many of us are very perplexed about the next step to take in rethinking new work habits, diet improvements, or relaxation or exercise programs. Our values and beliefs constrain us, even though we know what we want to do.

Many people will never actively begin a program of change and, at best, will adopt a philosophy of "moderation." In theory, moderation seems faultless, as it suggests that we can gain the advantages of being healthy and still eat some of the foods that we know to be high in fat. Or, we can still smoke a few cigarettes and not have to quit smoking; or we might still eat a moderate amount of cancer-causing and stress-provoking foods.

You might believe that your body can deal with some putrefaction from the digestion of foods, some hypertension from caffeine, some sugar, which plays havoc with your blood-sugar levels, and some fat, which clogs up your blood vessels. While our systems are able to deal with some poisons, it is not clear how much this inhibits the body in preventing illness. If the bodily systems are so busy fighting toxins, can they muster enough energy to effectively combat diseases? Will the body have the needed energy to fight off the additives in milk, chlorinated water, plastic fumes, and so on?

The philosophy of moderation means different things to many people and the continued use of some very harmful habits and foods. As a result, one person might moderate his or her drinking habit to five drinks a day and smoke half a pack rather than a whole pack of cigarettes. Another person might continue to eat sugar and foods to which he or she is allergic. In these cases, "moderation" is an excuse to continue to practice some very unhealthy habits.

MAKING AN ACTION PLAN

There are probably certain stressors causing the most problems for you and with which you most need to deal with. Often, these are the ones where there is a gap between what you really want to do but seem unable to do, because of habits and beliefs. For example, you may really want to lose weight or quit smoking but never seem to be able to do it. You might begin the week with a diet but find yourself indulging in some very fatty foods at a Christmas party. You may find yourself unable to alter a very stressful and hectic work schedule.

ONE OF THE MOST EFFECTIVE RULES FOR TAKING ACTION IS TO DO IT ONE STEP AT A TIME. PICK ONE STRESSOR AND WORK ON IT.

Your Action Plan

YOUR ACTION PLAN IS A TENTATIVE COURSE OF ACTION, PLOTTED IN A SEQUENCE OF STEPS. IDEALLY, YOUR PLAN IS A WRITTEN SET OF NOTES WHICH INCLUDE YOUR MISSION, PHILOSOPHY, VISION, AND THE KEY STRESSORS TO WHICH YOU WANT TO RESPOND.

The word *planning* has many different meanings, ranging from military plans to sequential steps. In conventional planning, defining goals or objectives is usually performed at the beginning of the process; it is the step on which all other steps are based, not the product of those steps. It the crucial point of the whole process.

Changing your lifestyle is no small task. It is a revolutionary change. Many effective change processes implement revolutionary plans in incremental ways and recognize people's needs at the time. They illustrate a grand design and the steps along the way. This form of planning can be compared to a sports analogy, in which one identifies actions that get the "ball rolling." It is a sports strategy of winning "one point at a time, one game at a time." The idea is compatible with studies on technological innovation indicating that small, rather than large, changes play a key role in reducing production costs. Small steps form the basis for a consistent pattern that attracts people who want to be allied with the venture. They encourage rewards because it is difficult to argue with the success of small victories. The action plan can be structured in the following manner:

- Divide the year into time segments.

- Name each segment as you would the chapters of a book. Each chapter can be outlined in terms of the activities to be done during implementation; for example, Segment I—Key Stressors and Your Vision of How to Respond to Them; Segment II—Implementation of Steps; Segment III— Keeping on Track and Dealing with Resistance.

- Each chapter should include some benchmarks or criteria on which you will judge your success (for example, losing 10 pounds).

Pick One or Two Main Stressors to Start With

Whenever you try to change some of your habits, there will be a number of factors that enhance or assist the implementation. There will also be a number of factors or events inhibiting the change.

All changes enter into a field of interacting forces, much like a force field. The interacting positive and negative forces are in a state of equilibrium, and they are relatively stable within themselves. There are a range of positive and negative forces, each restraining each other.

Certain laws of physics explain this. For example: *A body will remain at rest when the sum of all the forces operating upon it is zero. A body in motion will remain in motion until it is acted upon by another force.* As changes are introduced, they create stress and strain, disrupting the normal equilibrium. External or internal factors (stimulus) disrupting this equilibrium are countered by forces restoring it as closely as possible to its previous state. There is a tendency for systems to adjust, to seek balance in the light of change.

This equilibrium principle is best exemplified by observing the physiological functioning of the body, as when adrenaline and white corpuscles immediately respond to injury or illness, or when the body's internal thermostat assists in helping to adjust to changes in temperature through shivering or sweating. In organizations, there is a constant inertia, or resistance to new changes affecting individual habits and group norms. This does not mean that organizational systems are never modified by change, but they continually try to adjust to it.

In one example, Carol Duncan wished to reduce the feelings of stress and overwork that she had in working in her organization. She was very stressed about her task of making presentations and workshops to a group of managers on a weekly basis. She spent hours preparing for the lectures and generally did a commendable job. However, there were sometimes comments on her evaluation form that irritated and antagonized her.

Carol had been used to getting her way in most of the discussions and debates. Some staff members felt that they let her have her way just to appease her. On the other hand, she worked hard and was motivated to do a good job.

Carol became especially angry with the way her department and the organization in general was run. She hated inefficiency and managers who tended to make decisions without acknowledging the accepted procedures and policies. While she agreed with the policies used for selection and evaluation, she became irritated when the director hired a new staff member and awarded her a contract and salary without involving other members of the selection committee. In the months that followed, Carol made several attempts to discuss the issue. Confrontations with the director were fruitless, so she decided to file a grievance. The grievance process dragged on, and she became frustrated. Four months after the dispute started, Carol took a four-month stress leave.

Carol's values indicated that she had a desire to live a healthy and unstressful life. She was very conscious of her diet and had spent many hours getting advice on how to meditate and relax. She had joined a hiking club in an effort to change her lifestyle.

Her vision of herself at work was to be a person who was recognized by her colleagues for her achievements. She desperately wanted to be liked. However, the grievance process put her in a situation where she had alienated herself from the rest of the department. She was spending endless hours discussing her frustrations with the process, and her stress was, if anything, getting worse.

Table 13.1 illustrates the force field affecting Carol's desires to change. Among the forces helping the chances of reducing stress were her desire, some supportive colleagues, and her general ability to do a good job. These helpful forces are called *facilitating forces*.

Among the forces that hurt the chances of her work becoming less stressful (called *impeding forces*) were not liking and not being liked by some people in the department, a stress-prone personality, a lack of self-esteem and confidence, insecurity, and a lack of experience.

As in the movement of bodies in physics, the balance of facilitating and impeding forces determines the possibilities of change or reducing stress, even though the "body" being acted on is not tangible (the behavior of a group of people). As in physics, the forces need not be of the same magnitude. The result, illustrated in Table 13.1, is a series of opposing forces of varying strengths (represented by varying lengths). Attempts to induce change by removing or diminishing opposing forces will generally result in a lower degree of tension. An important restraining force that requires removal in our example is Carol's stress-prone personality and her lack of self-esteem.

TABLE 13.1 CAROL'S FORCE FIELD EXAMPLE

The change is: Trying to live within her vision of a satisfying and non-stressful work life.

FACILITATIVE FORCES		IMPEDING FORCES
	|	
Some supportive peers	|	Not liking some people in the department
———>	|	<—————
	|	
Desire to reduce stress	|	Personality profile of being anxious, perfectionist, Type A, aggressive/hostility
——————>	|	<—————————————
	|	
Works very hard and is generally competent in workshops and writings	|	Lack of self-esteem, Lack of confidence, Insecurity, Lack of experience
————————————>	|	<——————————————
	|	
	|	
	|	
	|	
	Present State	

ATTACK THE NEGATIVE FORCES FIRST.

Changes accomplished by reducing the restraining or negative forces are likely to be more stable than changes induced by additional or stronger driving forces. Removing restraining forces avoids a push for a return to old behaviors and ways of doing things. If changes come about only through the strengthening of driving forces, the forces supporting the new level must be stable. For example, many work groups are stimulated toward new ways of working together, only to find former behaviors and habits reemerging shortly after return to the day-to-day job. If the change started by the enthusiasm of learning and working together is to continue some other driving force must be ready to take the place of the initial stimulation.

The importance of dealing with the restraining or negative forces first was underlined for me some years ago. I felt the need to be more cheerful and to have a more positive disposition. The restraining forces against accomplishing this were some of the people with whom I was associated. They were negative, angry, and hostile toward others and the organization where we worked. The solution was obvious for me. Reducing the restraining forces involves spending less time with people who are negative and hostile. I can reverse the direction of this restraining force by encouraging myself to spend more time with people who are positive and enjoyable.

One efficient way to enhance change is to reverse the direction of one of the restraining forces. If Carol, in our example, can be persuaded to recognize that many of her difficulties come from her lack of self-esteem, lack of confidence, and insecurity, she might take on a different attitude toward her co-workers. This negative force is based on incorrect assumptions. There is no reason for her to feel insecure, as she is a very competent person. Thus, the removal of a powerful restraining force (lack of self-confidence) becomes an additional, strong driving force (high self-esteem) in the direction of change.

A group or organization stabilizes its behavior when the forces pushing for change are equal to the forces resisting change. Kurt Lewin called the result of this dynamic balance of forces the "quasi-stationary equilibrium." In our example, the equilibrium is represented in Table 13.1 by the midpoint between the two arrows.

■ Carol's stress is at its present level because of a balance of organizational and individual needs and forces. Thus, change will only occur if the forces are modified so that the system can move to and establish itself at a different level in which the driving and restraining forces are again equal. The equilibrium can be changed in the direction of establishing a less stressful life by:

- Strengthening or adding forces in the direction of reducing stress
- Reducing or removing some of the restraining forces which encourage stress
- Changing the direction of the forces

Identifying Possible Actions

IN GENERAL, ACTIONS ARE THINGS THAT RESOLVE STRESS.

The selection and development of possibilities for action are simplified by listing numerous proposals. The choice of the most feasible action possibilities is an opportunity to "flesh the proposal out."

Initial proposals may be vague and much larger in scope than is necessary. It is useful to find some experiences in which it is possible to check these ideas out. This is a kind of "pilot work," as used by nautical people when a pilot is taken on board a ship to guide it through uncharted waters. This kind of pilot work is not the scientific firming up of procedures before one carries out research. Rather, this piloting process seeks to guide the ideas and principles into other waters. This involves talking to others, looking for examples in other settings, and seeing if the idea is relevant at "sea."

Actions may take the form of individual or group training, counseling sessions, or time off for other activities, as dictated by the action plan. The pattern and pace of specific actions will vary according to the sequence in the general action plan.

Carol was able to identify a number of actions that might help resolve the stress she felt in her organization.

- Closing her office door and coming into the office less. This was based on the principle of "out of sight and out of mind" reasoning. However, she later discovered that she found it even less stressful to come in and begin relating to people she trusted.

(**Principle**—Discuss the organizational issue openly.)

- Spending more time with people who are confident and positive. Spending less time with Type A people who are aggressive and angry.

  (**Principle**—One of the biggest stressors we have is other people.)

- Developing a close personal relationship with a mentor and discussing how to resolve some of the issues at work.

  (**Principle**—Never take on organizational issues by yourself.)

- Becoming constructively involved in changing the procedures in the organization. Forming a committee to identify and resolve some of the difficulties in applying the procedures.

  (**Principle**—Focus on dealing with anger and hostility in a constructive manner.)

- Taking on a positive mental framework and developing self-confidence.

  (**Principle**—Recognizing and accepting the value of what we have and what we have to offer. Recognizing that our confidence comes from our self-esteem and need not be based on the recognition of others.)

- Meditating.

  (**Principle**—Recognizing that meditation can help us get a vision of our true selves.)

- Exercising.

  (**Principle**—A healthy body is associated with a healthy mind.)

ONE USEFUL STEP IS IDENTIFYING CRITERIA TO JUDGE THE ACCOMPLISHMENT OF YOUR VISION.

Identifying criteria to judge your success is not a rigid definition of the level of change expected based on currently existing measures. Rather, the criteria identify the standards you can use to focus their development. This is a way of articulating what one really wants to obtain when the change has been implemented. That is, what will your actions look like when it is finished?

At some stage in the change process, it may be appropriate to summarize the major outcomes and results of the change effort. What are some of the positive aspects of what is happening? What are some of the difficulties?

During your attempt to change, it is also appropriate to think about the overall effect of your efforts. Many actions are like pebbles thrown into a lake. A small intervention (a pebble) in a large system (a lake) can have far-reaching effects (sending ripples to the far shore). A small operation may have effects that reverberate to other aspects of the program of change. An important element of any reevaluation is the summary and discussion of what you are doing with others. When people are asked for their views, they are usually interested in seeing how others responded.

SINCE YOU ARE THE ONLY ONE THAT YOU CAN REALLY CHANGE, THE BEST ADVICE TO GIVE TO SOMEONE IS TO CHANGE YOURSELF.

SUMMARY

The above process of change encourages you to take a direct part in planning and directing your future. The process will not naturally reduce your level of stress, as this often hinges on your commitment. A first step is to write down your philosophy statement, mission, and vision. You also need to know what actions you might try to take to resolve the stressors you are experiencing. An important aspect of this process is to start working on one stressor and discussing your progress with someone you value. When you are getting some satisfaction with that, continue trying to focus on others.

ONE OF THE SUREST WAYS TO ASSIST THE CHANGE PROCESS IS BY INVOLVING OTHERS IN HELPING YOU IDENTIFY YOUR STRESSORS AND YOUR STRATEGIES FOR RESPONDING.

14 Begin a Process of Self-Renewal

The truth is cruel, but it can be loved
and it makes free those who have loved it.

—GEORGE SANTAYANA

Any changes—whether dietary habits, exercise routines, or lifestyles—are difficult to implement. Favorite habits are hard to break, even if there is ample evidence of the need to do so. This is why so many people have difficulty in quitting smoking and drinking.

Change—such as reducing the stress from your organization, job, interpersonal relationships, life, diet, and general lifestyle—requires an in-depth look at yourself. This may involve confronting and re-prioritizing who you are and what you want to do.

Change is very hard. Imagine the difficulty you might have in quitting smoking. What if you were told to accept Christian prayers and principles in school when you were a Muslim (or vice versa)? Imagine the difficulties that many people have had in accepting changes demanded by the women's movement. While behaviors may have changed, some people still maintain beliefs they have held since they were children.

Changes are even difficult when we desire them. Perspective 16 reflects some of the best programs that try to help people change. These are well-renowned programs for improving diet and health, ways of working, and organizational effectiveness. Complete this short exercise.

PERSPECTIVE 16. HOW SUCCESSFUL HAVE WE BEEN IN CHANGING OURSELVES?

Take a piece of paper and jot down your answers to the following questions. You are asked to indicate your best guess at the success of some programs in terms of getting people to accept the change.

Over the last thirty years, there have been many books and programs which help people lose weight. We all know of various fad diets that never seem to work. Some of the best programs are those that help people change their habits and behaviors.

- What percentage of people take off the weight they planned to take off when they entered the best programs for managing diet?
- What percentage of these people kept this weight off over a one-year period?

Over the last ten years, public and private agencies have encouraged people to be more conscious of their health and diet.

- What percentage of Americans are classified as overweight today?
- What percentage of heart patients stop smoking when their doctors tell them to quit?
- What percentage of heart patients stop smoking when they are on their deathbed?

One of the biggest antismoking projects by U.S. researchers was a $45 million study by the National Cancer Institute. The program involved an intense educational campaign in twenty paired communities in the United States and two in Canada. One community in each pair ran the campaign, called the Community Intervention Trial.

- How successful was the program in comparison with the control groups?

Public agencies and medical doctors have issued a number of health recommendations to women about the importance of breast self-examinations.

- What percentage of women performed a breast self-examination over the last year?

The answers to these questions illustrate how unsuccessful we have been in initiating change.

- Only 5 percent to 7 percent of Weight Watchers were able to take off the weight they projected to take off.
- Only ½ of 1 percent kept it off for two years.
- It has been estimated that 34 million Americans are obese and another 34 million border on being so, according to the National Institute of Health. In a society that has become obsessed with fitness and the appearance of slimness, there are tremendous health and social pressures on those who are overweight, according to the *New England Journal of Medicine*.
- Only 6 percent of patients quit smoking when their doctors told them to quit.
- Only 43 percent quit smoking when they were finally on their death beds.
- The modest success of the program was 3 percent higher than the control group for moderate smokers, according to the National Cancer Institute.
- Only one of nine women do breast self-examinations, according to the National Cancer Institute and the Canadian Cancer Society.

The exercise in Perspective 16 should illustrate one thing: Change is very difficult. Even some of our best programs for change are not all that successful in changing dietary habits, smoking habits, and ways of working.

FIRST STEPS IN THE PROCESS OF SELF-RENEWAL

The eight principles of stress management in this book embody many fundamental strategies for personal health and well-being. These principles are basic, common sense and integrate science and personal well-being. The strategies within each principle allow you to begin focusing on a process of renewal.

First of all, review the principles and the strategies associated with them. Identify those strategies that are most important for you to work on.

Principle 1: Change the Dragon Within You: Develop a Positive Disposition

In other words, know yourself and how your personality may affect the way you deal with stress. The most damaging elements of the stress-prone personality are anger, hostility, anxiety, and low self-esteem. A positive disposition includes a sense of humor and cheerfulness to replace anger and hostility. High self-esteem and low anxiety contribute to your self-worth and confidence.

> *Humor acts to relieve fear.*
> *Rage is impossible when mirth prevails.*
>
> —WILLIAM FRY, M.D.

Humor and cheerfulness not only make you easier to live with and more enjoyable to be around, they widen your support system and circle of friendship.

Some people allow themselves to be soured on life and the people around them and are angry about the injustices they have faced. This disposition sets in motion a cycle in which they view new things in the same way. Anger and blame become the way these people interact with others.

The most powerful evidence of the benefits of being cheerful and full of humor comes from the immunity it gives you in handling the stress around you. It sets in motion powerful reactions within your system. Angry and hostile people are more likely to suffer from heart disease and other ailments. Cheerful and humorous behavior is a powerful antidote for pain and a less stressful lifestyle.

TAKING CONTROL OF YOURSELF INVOLVES UNDERSTANDING WHO YOU ARE AND FEELING COMFORTABLE WITH THAT.

Taking control of yourself involves reducing your anxiety. Reduce your anxiety through exercise, meditation, and support systems.

Anxiety means fear. It may be fear of criticism, of not doing well, or fear of not getting ahead. Younger people (under thirty) generally have more anxiety. It is common for them to try to get ahead in life, find a new job, or seek to advance in their careers. Anxiety is also high for those going through a midlife crisis, when questions about their progress in life become more central. They seem to believe that time is running out.

Taking control also involves developing a sense of self-worth. Stress attacks one's self-esteem more than anything else. When you are stressed and overloaded, you begin to have self-doubt.

People who are most immune to stress are those who learn to recognize and be proud of what they have and what they can do. They are competent people within their worlds, and they are proud of their accomplishments. A person with high self-esteem does not perceive an attack on his or her work as an attack on his or her value. When John, an architect, was criticized by the city engineer for the architectural design he had chosen, he responded by saying, "You have given me valuable feedback, which might help me revise my design. I will respond to this feedback as part of the process of developing a better design. I also have to meet with other groups to get their feedback."

He viewed the criticism as feedback, just one step in the process of developing a consensus of what the building should look like in this community. He had dealt with many engineers and city council members before and knew that they all have a perspective, and sometimes, they just want to be heard.

Self-esteem is often connected with anxiety. People who are anxious often have low self-esteem. They are fearful of criticism and have no sense of pride in their own accomplishments.

Principle 2: Control Your Organization: Don't Let It Control You

Find meaning and direction in the organization for which you work. Your desire to fulfill yourself in your organization and career is a dominant stressor. This principle illustrates the importance of managing yourself in a stress-promoting organization.

SATISFACTION IN YOUR ORGANIZATION AND LIFE IS HIGHLY CORRELATED.

People who are able to manage their stress and well-being find meaning in being involved and committed to something beyond themselves. The most common outlet to provide meaning is the organization you work for or your life pursuits and ideals.

Organizations that are overloading can be as destructive of a person's efforts to find meaning in life as those that do not help an individual focus his or her career or future. The organizational hierarchy may play an important part in generating stress and poor health. People who are at lower levels in the hierarchy die sooner after retirement and are more stressed and dissatisfied throughout their careers.

Should you take this to mean that you should go around with a hopeless attitude saying, "I'll never get ahead. The organization I work for is impossible. There is no way that they will ever recognize how they are stressful to their people"? While you may never stimulate your organization to change, you might take action to focus what you are doing within defined priorities. You might consider refocusing your career. You might identify social objectives or begin working with an idea. The point is that you must begin to develop ways to find meaning in your organization or life if you want to reduce stress and enhance your well-being.

HAVING A CLEAR GOAL IS ONE OF THE MOST IMPORTANT THINGS YOU CAN DO WHEN WORKING IN AN AMBIGUOUS ORGANIZATIONAL ENVIRONMENT.

Not having a goal or vision of where you are going is like playing a football game and not knowing where the goalposts are. You would never know which way to run or what you should do to score.

Organizations sometimes make people feel like they are playing a football game without goalposts. Goals are never defined, are vague, and change quickly. By the time you finish the project you are doing, it is no longer important.

Daphne worked as an engineer in a transportation department that was responsible for the construction and maintenance of highways. The priorities for highway construction and maintenance were different depending on which political party was in power. One government privatized the maintenance service. This decision was reversed a year later, only to be reversed again two years later.

Daphne described herself as being completely frustrated. At one time, she helped administer the maintenance services before losing her responsibilities and being assigned a number of temporary projects. She began, at the age of thirty-two, to anticipate a future goal to which she would strive in her work. She became a specialist in roadbed maintenance methods. "I may never know it all, but it comforts me that my research will help others do a better job in maintaining highways. Whether the government or private sector is responsible for maintenance, I now feel my work is focused on something." Daphne could not count on her bosses to help focus her job and career. She learned that the best way to handle an ambiguous environment was to define goals for herself.

Principle 3: Establishing Winning Relationships

Conflictive relationships are an ever-increasing cause of stress both on and off the job. While conflictive relationships are harassing and stressing, healthy relationships can invigorate and help us prevent or deal with stress.

TRUST AND SUPPORT ARE KEY ELEMENTS OF A STRESS MANAGEMENT PROGRAM.

Trust and support can be developed in several ways. On the job, they are associated with supervisors and colleagues who value and trust each other. If there is one thing akin to cancer in an organization, it is the breakage of trust. A breakage of trust is not generally repairable, as it more often continues to deteriorate rather than mend. Like a cancer, you might cut some of it out and infuse it with protective drugs to arrest it, but it always has the potential to reoccur. When it does reoccur, the stakes are higher.

Support systems grow from a trusting environment in which supervisors and colleagues can help each other. Jane worked as a manager in a hospital where she was in charge of training and organizational development activities. One of her tasks related to designing programs to reduce stress and improve well-being. What she noticed in one of her programs is that while people privately expressed a great deal of stress, they did nothing about it. They were unwilling to admit to their supervisors and others that they were stressed. Trust and support is cultivated by an ability to be open. It is probably the characteristic that is most associated with an ability to adapt and change. If we are open to the trust and support of others, we have made an important first step in being open to feedback.

Whether married, cohabiting, or being with friends, people who are healthier and satisfied with life are visibly more affectionate. They care for others and do not exploit them. They help others.

These people also spend more time on relationship building. They say things such as, "Relationships are most important to me," "Even though we are millionaires, all we really have is each other," "When I work on a job, the most important thing to me is relationships, much more than the task," "It is the relationships that keep us together."

Supportive relationships help deal with stress. They also help us focus our lives and careers. It is for this reason that relationships are one of the most important factors in reducing stress.

Principle 4: Enrich Your Job

Find learning and growth on your job. Our jobs can be full of learning and growth or boring and monotonous. Imagine working at the hamburger grill at a fast-food restaurant. How long do you think you would enjoy your job without a change?

John Rhodes worked at a fast-food restaurant for over a year. His first weeks were interesting because he learned new things. The managers at the restaurant were conscious of the fact that the jobs in fast-food restaurants could be boring and unstimulating.

To keep John Rhodes and others interested and committed, the managers believed that jobs had to be designed so that there was learning and growth. To do this, workers were assigned a variety of tasks and rotated through various jobs in the restaurant. They also had the opportunity to learn new skills in supervision and customer relations.

LEARNING IS ONE OF THE MOST IMPORTANT ELEMENTS IN ANY JOB.

We can take active steps to make sure that we can learn new things in the jobs we do, even when managers do not actively seek to improve the jobs of the people in their organizations. Our self-directed learning might involve part-time courses, or even a willingness to take on new assignments.

Principle 5: Control Life's Trials and Tribulations

No one is protected from the crises of life. The most common quality of those who are more effective in dealing with life's crises is the way they handle the uncertainty and trauma they face. They use the experience to propel themselves forward rather than hold them back.

The only sure way to reduce the stress of life is to reduce the number of stressful situations and crises you face. This is an avoidance strategy.

AVOIDANCE IS LIKE LIVING IN A COCOON SEPARATED FROM LIFE.

The capacity to respond effectively to life's trials and tribulations can be learned. Those that are more successful recognize that life crises cannot be avoided. Rather, they become involved with them and challenge them. They learn from each life stress and are more effective in responding to the ones they face later on.

The capacity for responding effectively is associated with other factors as well. These people have lives that have meaning and direction. They talk openly about the stress they encounter, and they are able to gather information and insights that challenge their conventional thinking. They are more positive and creative, and they use humor as an outlet for their frustration. They also take time out to relax.

Principle 6: Reducing Stress-Promoting Foods

While stress is a source of wear and tear on the body, proper nutrition is the basis for resisting the ill effects of this erosion process.

CERTAIN FOODS CAN EXAGGERATE THE STRESS RESPONSE.

Caffeine, vitamin depletion, sugar, and salt are examples of foods and nutrients that can provoke or hinder the body's systems. Much of our food is a by-product of fertilizers, feedlots, food preservatives, chemical supplements, and sterilizers. How good is this for us?

What is in these foods—the fats and sugars—is only part of the problem. What is not in these foods—the nutrients—is just as important.

Terry was informed by his doctor that he had diabetes and that he would have to reduce the sugar and fat in his food. He gave up many things, such as ice cream, cream, desserts, cookies, and many other foods that had been responsible for his weight of over 235 pounds on a six-foot frame. In less than three months, he lost 30 pounds, just by eating much less fat and minimal sugar.

Terry is full of enthusiasm for his new constitution and diet plan. He almost sounds like a preacher when he talks about what happened to him. He is positive and full of energy. Perhaps Terry would be in even better health if he had started earlier. Why did Terry have to learn that he had diabetes before he began to change his lifestyle?

WHILE CERTAIN FOODS ARE MORE STRESSFUL FOR YOUR BODY TO HANDLE, OTHERS CAN HELP YOU RESPOND TO STRESS. THEY CAN GIVE YOU ENERGY AND ACT AS HEALING FOODS.

A nutritional plan has two facets. You should first think about reducing stress-promoting foods.

- Reduce your consumption of stress-promoting foods that contain caffeine, salt, and additives. Quit smoking and be cautious about alcohol use. Try to reduce your consumption of processed foods.
- Reduce your weight. People who are leaner often live longer.
- Lower the fat content of the food you eat. The typical Western diet is made up of 40 to 50 percent fat. Many health specialists suggest that, to lower cholesterol and weight, the balance of foods should be adjusted to include a maximum of 30 percent fat, 65 percent carbohydrates, and 15 percent protein. Twenty to 30 percent fat may be still too high. If you are serious about lowering weight and cholesterol, you should try for 15 to 20 percent of fat in your diet.
- Check to see that the food you eat contains the appropriate vitamins and minerals. Vitamin supplements should be considered.

The many fad diets available seem to promise fast solutions. My experience with such diets has not been promising. Generally, weight loss has been minimal and cholesterol levels have dropped moderately by only 5 to 15 percent. A more effective way to reduce weight and cholesterol is to eat 10 to 15 percent fat, little or no cholesterol, 70 to 75 percent carbohydrate, and 10 to 15 percent protein. This diet is not vegetarian, although it restricts the amount of eggs, fish, and dairy products. It encourages the eating of whole grains, fruits, and vegetables.

A nutritional plan for enhancing wellness includes the following:

- Balance your food combinations. Develop a plan that recognizes healthy food combinations.

- Certain foods are terrific for enhancing wellness. Our Western diets are composed of a higher proportion (four to one) of acidic foods to alkaline foods. Since are bodies are mainly alkaline, we should reverse this so that we take in a higher proportion of alkaline to acidic foods.

Principle 7: Exercise to Reduce Anxiety

Exercise is one of the most effective strategies for reducing stress. On the other hand, certain exercise programs can be counterproductive. An effective exercise program helps you deal with the stress you encounter.

Bob, a teacher, was always about 10 to 20 pounds overweight and would be heavier if he did not maintain an active exercise program. He played squash at least once a day, and sometimes played soccer with his students.

At the age of forty-eight, Bob decided to try to run a marathon, or at least a half marathon. He consulted his doctor and began a training program of triweekly runs and a weekly 10 kilometer run.

After a few months of training, he felt some pain originating in his lower back and traveling down to his left knee. He rested for a few days, but persisted with his training. He was not listening to his body.

After a week, the pain became more intense. He went to his doctor, who gave him some muscle relaxants. The pain became so great that Bob went to the hospital where he stayed under traction and drugs for over ten days. Bob could not walk properly for over a year, and to this day, he still has numbness in his left leg.

It is quite clear that some exercise programs may be more harmful than they are helpful. Bob is an example of a person who, with a large body frame, was not suited for vigorous running and jogging. Running and jogging may be hard on the body, just as squash and football can be.

> MODERATION IS IMPORTANT IN THE DESIGN OF ANY EXERCISE PROGRAM. IT IS BEST TO HAVE AN EXERCISE PROGRAM THAT YOU CAN DO WHEN YOU ARE NINETY.

Bob is now swimming and hiking. He learned the lesson the hard way.

Fit individuals feel less strain and can perform at peak levels with a lower heart rate. The value of exercise is well documented for increasing the body's capability to undertake or respond to stressful tasks, from heavy physical work to the mental stress of handling difficult people. There is no question that the physically fit person can outrun a person who is not in shape. Just as a fit individual is more capable of running up stairs with less strain, he or she is more capable of responding to interpersonal stress.

> **EXERCISE IMPROVES A PERSON'S MENTAL CAPACITY TO DEAL WITH MANY OF LIFE'S EVENTS.**

The exercise habit sets in motion a way of living. People who exercise usually smoke and drink less and have better eating and sleeping habits. The direct benefit is improved cardiovascular performance, which enhances our ability to perform. A most important indicator of overall health is cardiovascular endurance.

Exercise can also reduce stress by acting as a mental diversion and a release or outlet for emotions or physical tensions. It produces a state of relaxation caused by the effects of reduced electrical activity to the muscles. People who walk and elevate their heart rates to 100 beats per minute show significantly less electromyographic anxiety, whereas tranquilizers do not produce the same effect.

Exercise may encourage the release of endorphins, the body's natural opiates, which act like morphine to produce narcotic effects, including calmness. During exercise, plasma levels of noradrenaline increase; this may reduce feelings of depression. In addition, moderate rhythmic exercise, between five and thirty minutes duration, often produces a tranquilizing effect. In studies of chronically depressed individuals, aerobic exercise was also more effective than a placebo or no treatment and was also more effective than other treatment programs such as psychotherapy or meditation and relaxation.

Principle 8: Using the Power Within You

Meditation gives your mind a rest. It also helps you utilize your subconscious. It helps you focus your mind on being proactive in handling stress.

The underpinning of our industrialized society is based on doing something. We see these in terms such as the *Protestant work ethic* or the *Asian work ethic*. If there is one thing that seems to unite Western and Eastern cultures, it is the science of doing something more effectively or efficiently. The word *productive* has many useful connotations: constructive, efficient, energetic, resourceful, useful, moneymaking, remunerative, well-spent, and worthwhile. The meanings of this word are almost antithetical to those describing relaxation: amusement, diversion, enjoyment, leisure, loosening, and slackening.

> **RELAXATION TECHNIQUES ARE RESTORATIVE AND PREVENTIVE AS WELL AS ALLOWING PEOPLE TO REST AND TAKE SOME TIME AWAY FROM LIFE'S STRESSFUL ACTIVITIES.**

Relaxation techniques act in the same way that preventive maintenance screens out dirt and metal fragments from a motorcycle's engine. Relaxation techniques assist in diffusing or purging the buildup of impurities, frustrations, and stress. They also prevent stress buildup, while providing a clean slate for fighting off stressors.

Breathing, relaxing, and meditating are the most powerful tools we have in realizing our full potential and managing our health and stress. However, it is most difficult to practice them regularly, as many of us do not have the discipline or the time to develop a program. It is so easy to put them off, especially when we get busy, which is also the time we need them most. The best way is to start your day with these activities. Get up at a time when no one else is around. Turn on some enjoyable music and meditate. Then, plan your day.

These principles and strategies are not laws. They are rules of thumb that are based on Western science and emerging practice as well as common sense. Review the principles and strategies that are most important for you. Review the chapters associated with them. Then, reread the previous chapter and implement your personal stress management action plan.

References and Notes

Chapter 1: Stress: A Dragon in Disguise

Cooper, C., and Cartwright, S. *Managing Workplace Stress*. New York and London: Sage Publications, 1997. This is a recent review of workplace stress.

Cox, T. *Stress*. Baltimore: University Park Press, 1978. Most definitions of stress deal with three aspects: stimulus definitions, response definitions, or stimulus response definitions. A stimulus definition treats stress as some characteristic, event, or situation in the environment that in some way results in a potentially disruptive consequence. In this situation, stress is an external event as perceived. Response definitions of stress suggest that there may be an internal response, which may manifest itself in a variety of visible ways. The stimulus response definition suggests that stress is a consequence of the interaction between the environmental stimulus and the idiosyncratic response of the individual.

Ornish, Dean. *Reversing Heart Disease*. New York: Ballatine Books, 1990. This popular book offers suggestions on how heart disease might be stopped by changing your lifestyle. It offers suggestions for relaxing, reducing stress, and improving diet.

Payne, R.L. "Individual differences in the study of occupational stress." C.P. Cooper and R. Payne, (eds.), *Causes, coping, and consequences of stress at work*. Toronto: John Wiley & Sons, 1988, 209-231. The paper provides an illustration of how individual differences affect how we respond to occupational stress.

Selye, Hans. *The Stress of Life*. Revised edition. New York: McGraw Hill, 1984. This is a completely revised and updated version of the classic book, which was originally published in 1956. This classic book on stress is by the person who formulated the entire theoretical concept.

Figures on workplace violence are based on Bruce Blythe, president of Crisis Management International, at an annual meeting of the Risk and Insurance Management Society, New Orleans. According to the U.S. National Institute for Occupational Safety, we are witnessing an increase in the incidence of workplace violence and murder since 1980 when 605 workers were victims of workplace murder. Workplace violence is growing as an issue, according to our research.

Chapter 2: Myths Associated with Stress

McGrath, Joseph E. "Stress and behavior in organizations." In M.D. Dunnette (ed.), *Handbook of Industrial Psychology*, Chicago: Rand McNally, 1976. In this book, McGrath illustrates the inverted U-shaped curve.

Peterson, M.F., et al. "Role conflict, ambiguity, and overload: A twenty-one-nation study." *Academy of Management Journal*. 1995 38: 429–462. The authors illustrate that role stresses varied more by country than by personal and organizational characteristics.

Pritikin, Nathan with McGrady, P.M., Jr. *The Pritikin Program for Diet and Exercise.* New York: Bantam Books, 1979. One of the most famous diets for dealing with coronary heart disease was developed by Nathan Pritikin. This book provides an overview of this diet, in addition to furnishing several diet suggestions.

Ten warning signs of stress include: intestinal distress, rapid pulse, frequent illness, insomnia, persistent fatigue, irritability, nail biting, lack of concentration, increased use of alcohol and drugs, hunger for sweets. See *The Ten Toughest Jobs*: The National Institute on Workers Compensation: American Institute of Stress.

Chapter 3: How Stress Kills

Edwards, Jeffrey R. "A cybernetic theory of stress, coping, and well-being in organizations." *Academy of Management Review*, 1992. 17: 238–274. The article presents an integrative cybernetic theory of stress, coping, and well-being in organizations and offers a number of propositions for future research.

Ganster, D.C., and Schaubroeck, J. "Work stress and employee health." *Journal of Management*, 1991. 17: 235–271. This article reviews and summarizes the literature on work stress with particular emphasis on the effects of work characteristics on employee health. The article makes recommendations for how researchers might get beyond using less reliable self-report information.

Fletcher, B. *Occupational Stress, Disease and Life Expectancy.* Chichester, England: Wiley, 1993.

Kahn, R.L., Wolfe, D.M., Quinn, R.P., Snoek, J.D., with Rosenthal, R.A. *Organizational Stress: Studies in Role Conflict and Ambiguity.* New York: John Wiley & Sons, 1964. This is a classic study concerned with the consequences of two kinds of organizational stress: role conflict and role ambiguity. This research marked the beginning of several research studies.

Matteson, M.T., and Ivancevich, J.M. *Managing Job Stress and Health.* New York: Free Press, 1982. This book provides a comprehensive discussion of work in addition to providing an overview of health and exercise.

Pelletier, K.R. *Mind As Healer: Mind As Slayer.* New York: Delta, 1977. This author defines the role of stress in four major types of illness: cardiovascular disease, cancer, arthritis, and respiratory disease.

Russek, H.I., and Zohman, B.L. "Relative significance of heredity, diet, and occupational stress in CHD of young adults." *American Journal of Medical Sciences,* 1958. 235: 266–275. This is one of the many original studies that assisted us in developing an understanding of the role of diet and occupational stress in coronary heart disease. That is, CHD is more than heredity, it is also affected by diet and occupational stress.

Sempos, C.T., Cleeman, J.I., Carroll, M.D., et al. "Prevalence of high blood cholesterol among U.S. adults." *Journal of the American Medical Association,* 1993. 269: 3009–3014. The results suggest that, while tremendous progress has been made, approximately 29 percent of the U.S. adult population requires dietary intervention for high blood cholesterol.

Steffy, B.D., and Jones, J.W. "Workplace stress and indicators of coronary heart disease risk." *Academy of Management Journal,* 1988. 31: 686–697. The present study evaluates the effects of perceived job stressors, job dissatisfaction, and recent stressful life events on five separate biochemical indicators of stress.

Young, T.K., Moffatt, M.E.K., and O'Neil, J.D. "Cardiovascular diseases in a Canadian Arctic population." *America Journal of Public Health,* 1993. 83: 881–887. This paper provides a comprehensive epidemiologic review of cardiovascular diseases of the population of Canada's Northwest Territories and provides a descriptive baseline for future studies. The indigenous population of Indians and Inuit had a lower risk for all diseases of the circulatory system compared with the national population; however, the risk among women approached the Canadian national rate.

Chapter 4: Principle-Centered Stress Management

Borysenko, J. *Minding the Body; Mending the Mind.* Reading: Addison Wesley, 1987. This book illustrates the importance of our perception and attitude in responding to stress.

Brady, J. V. "Ulcers in executive monkeys." *Scientific American,* October 1958: 199, 89–95. This research, popularly known as the executive monkey studies, illustrates the importance of environmental control in reducing ulcers in monkeys.

Lapin, B.A., and Cherkovich, G.M. *Environmental Changes Causing the Development of Neuroses and Corticovisceral Pathology in Monkeys, Society, Stress, and Diseases,* ed. L. Levi. London: Oxford University Press, 1971. Vol. 1, 266–279.

Rosenbaum, M. "The three functions of self-control behavior: redressive, reformative, and experiential." *Work and Stress,* 1993. 7: 33–46. Redressive self-control is directed at controlling responses such as anxiety and pain. Reformative self-control facilitates the adoption of new behaviors, such as quitting smoking, while experiential self-control includes mechanisms such as relaxation and openness to new experiences. It is suggested that highly resourceful people possess a repertoire of behaviors for responding to stress.

The story of the U.S. navy off the coast off Newfoundland was reported in the Memorial University campus paper and the Royal Victoria Yacht Club Mainsheet.

Chapter 5: Principle 1—Recognize the Dragon Within You

Blau, G.J. "Locus of control as a potential moderator of the turnover process." *Journal of Occupational Psychology*, 1987. Fall: 21–29. Taking control of one's life is often said to be important in reducing stress and its organizational impacts. This paper uses this concept in studying its relationship to organizational turnover.

Burns, David. "The perfectionist's script for self-defeat." *Psychology Today*, 1980. November: 34–51. This article introduces perfectionism as a personality trait that may be associated with a stress-prone personality.

Diamond, E.L. "The role of anger and hostility in essential hypertension and coronary heart disease." *Psychological Bulletin*, 1982. 92: 410–435. This study illustrates how anger and hostility may be an important dimension in understanding hypertension and coronary heart disease.

Ellis, A. *Humanistic Psychotherapy*. New York: McGraw Hill, 1973. This author illustrates a rational approach to personal change.

Friedman, M., and Rosenman, R.H. *Type A Behavior and Your Heart*. New York: Fawcett Crest, 1974. This classic book introduced the concept of the Type A personality who is psychologically predisposed to a stressful lifestyle and prone to coronary heart disease.

Friedman, M., Roseman, R.H., and Carroll, V. "Changes in serum cholesterol in blood clotting time in men subjected to cyclic variations of occupational stress." *Circulation*, 1958. 17: 852–861. This is one of the first studies that helped to illustrate the importance of personality in understanding serum cholesterol.

Friedman, M., and Ulmer, D. *Treating Type A Behavior—and Your Heart*. New York: Fawcett Crest, 1984. This book is based on a project designed to modify Type A behavior.

Froggatt, K.L., and Cotton, J.L. "The impact of Type A behavior pattern on role overload-induced stress and performance attributions." *Journal of Management*, 1987. 13: 87–98. This article illustrates a controlled laboratory experiment to investigate the effects of Type A behavior patterns. The results suggest that Type A people may seek out stressful situations and that their performance differs from Type B people.

Holt, P., Fine, M.J., and Tollelfson, N. "Mediating stress: survival of the hardy." *Psychology in the Schools,* 1987. 24: 51–58. This study explored variations in personality characteristics, termed *hardiness,* among female elementary school teachers who had differing levels of burnout despite high levels of occupational stress.

Markovitz, J.H., Matthews, K.A., Kannel, W.B., Cobb, J.L., and D'Agostino, R.B. "Psychological predictors of hypertension in the Framington study." *Journal of the American Medical Association,* 1993. 270: 2439–2443. The results indicate that anxiety levels in middle-aged men (but not women) are predictive of later incidence of hypertension.

Rotter, J.B. "Generalized expectancies for internal and external control of reinforcement." *Psychological Monographs,* 1966. 80: 609. This is one of the original articles that illustrates the logic behind the locus of control concept, an idea that suggests that some people who are less stressed have a higher internal locus of control. They feel they can take personal responsibility for controlling many of the life events which that affect them.

Chapter 6: Principle 2—Control Your Organization: Don't Let It Control You

Cooper, C.L., and Marshall, J. "Occupational sources of stress: A review of the literature relating to coronary heart disease and mental ill health." *Journal of Occupational Psychology,* 1976. 49: 11–28. This article is well recognized for illustrating the importance of stress in coronary heart disease.

Fox, M.L., Dwyer, D.J., and Ganster, D.C. "Effects of stressful job demands and control on physiological and attitudinal outcomes in a hospital setting." *Academy of Management Journal,* 1993. 36: 289–318.

Latham, Gary P., and Locke, Edwin, A., 1979. "Goal setting—A motivational technique that works." *Organizational Dynamics,* Autumn. This is one of the original articles illustrating the importance of goal setting in improving motivation and productivity. Gary Latham and Edwin Locke have continued this research to corroborate these ideas.

Chapter 7: Principle 3—Establish Winning Relationships

Fisher, R., and Brown, S. *Getting Together.* Boston: Houghton Mifflin, 1988.

Fisher, R., Ury, W., and Patton, B. *Getting to Yes.* (2nd edition). New York: Penguin Books, 1991. This is a very popular and practical book that focuses on developing integrative solutions to problems.

Fusilier, M.R., Ganster, D.C., and Mayes, B.T. "The social support and health relationship: Is there a gender difference?" *Journal of Occupational Psychology*, 1986. 59: 145–153.

LaRocco, J.M., House, J.S., and French, J.R.P. "Social support, occupational stress, and health." *Journal of Health and Social Behavior*, June 21, 1980.: 202–218.

Manning, M.R., Jackson, C.N., and Fusilier, M.R. "Occupational stress, social support, and the costs of health care." *Academy of Management Journal*, 1996. 39: 738–750.

Sarason, I.G., Levine, H.M., Basham, R.B., and Sarason, B.R. "Assessing social support: The social support questionnaire." *Journal of Personality and Social Psychology*, 1983. 44: 127–139.

Ury, W. *Getting Past No.* London: Business Books, 1991.

Chapter 8: Principle 4—Enrich Your Job

Arsenault, A., Dolan, S.L., and Van Ameringen, M.R. "Stress and mental strain in hospital work: Exploring the relationship beyond personality." *Journal of Organizational Behavior*, 1991. 12: 481–493. This study focuses on the relationship between job stressors and mental health in hospital work, adjusting for differences in personality traits.

Burke, R.J., and Greenglass, E.R. "Psychological burnout among men and women in teaching: An examination of the Cherniss model." *Human Relations*, 1989. 42: 261–273. This investigation examines psychological burnout among 833 men and women.

Cooley, M. "Computerization—Taylor's latest disguise." *Economic and Industrial Democracy.* Beverly Hills: Sage, 1980. 1: 523–539. The author makes the suggestion that computerization is ushering in many of the negative industrial designs that Frederick Taylor introduced in scientific management. The scientific management movement, which is identified with Taylor, is known for its nonhuman principles of work design.

Maslach, Christina. *Burnout—The Cost of Caring.* Englewood Cliffs, N.J.: Prentice Hall, 1982. This classic work introduces burnout and illustrates how an individual loses his or her power to cope and to function.

Schaubroeck, J., Ganster, D.C., and Kemmerer, B.E. "Job complexity, "Type A" behavior, and cardiovascular disorder: A prospective study." *Academy of Management Journal*, 1994. 37: 426–439.

Wolpin, J., Burke, R.J., and Greenglass, E.R., "Is job satisfaction an antecedent or a consequence of psychological burnout?" *Human Relations*, 1991. 44: 193–209. This study considers the relationship between psychological burnout and job satisfaction.

Terkel, Studs. *Working.* New York: Avon Books, 1974. This book provides some insight into what people say about their work. The author begins the book by suggesting that work is, by its very nature, about violence to the spirit and to the body. It is about ulcers, as well as accidents and many other negative affects.

Test 10 is reprinted with permission from the the Job Diagnostic Scale, based on Hackman, J. R., and Oldham, G. *Work Redesign.* Menlo Park: Addison Wesley Longman, Inc., 1980. Used with permission from the publisher.

Chapter 9: Principle 5—Controlling Life's Trials and Tribulations

Cousins, Norman. *Anatomy of an Illness.* W.W. Norton and Company, 1979, p. 39. This is the story of Norman Cousins and how he changed his attitude and beliefs when he was diagnosed as having one chance in five hundred of surviving. He was diagnosed as having a serious collagen illness. Collagen is the fibrous substance that binds the cells together. These connective tissues were disintegrating.

Kant, Immanuel. *Critique of Pure Reason.* New York: MacMillan and Co., 1929.

Levinson, Daniel L. *The Season of a Man's Life.* New York: Ballantine, 1978.

Sheehy, Gail. *New Passages.* New York: Ballantine Books, 1995.

Sheehy, Gail. *Passages.* New York: E. P. Dutton and Co., 1976.

Test 13 is reprinted with the permission of the publisher from Holmes, T.H., and Rahe, R.H., "The Social Readjustment Rating Scale." *Journal of Psychosomatic Research,* 1967. Vol. 11: 213–218. Pergamon Press, Ltd. by Elsevier Science, Inc., 655 Ave. of the Americas, New York, NY 10010. The social adjustment rating scale became popular to illustrate that some environments were more stressful than others. It does not take into account that individuals handle stress differently.

Chapter 10: Principle 6—Reduce Stress-Promoting Foods

Chen, J., and Gao, J., 1993. *The Chinese Total Diet Study in 1990. Part II. Nutrients.* The study was carried out by the Institute of Nutrition and Food Hygiene, Chinese Academy of Preventive Medicine, Beijing.

Cowmeadow, Oliver. *Introduction to macrobiotics.* London: HarperCollins, 1987. Macrobiotics is about balance and harmony and is based on the underlying ancient unifying principles of yin and yang. Using this philosophy, the author offers several ideas for cooking and eating.

Criqui, M.H., Heiss, G.C.R., et al. "Plasma triglyceride level and mortality from coronary heart disease." *The New England Journal of Medicine,* 1993. 328: 1220–1225. The death rates of coronary heart disease in both men and women increased with triglyceride levels, although other factors were associated. Serum triglyceride levels alone do not predict coronary heart death.

Diamond, Harvey, and Marilyn Diamond. *Fit for Life.* New York: Warner Books, 1987.

Enstrom, J.E. "Cancer and total mortality among active Mormons." *Cancer,* 1978. 42: 1943. This article illustrates that certain populations have a different risk of cancer.

Erasmus, U. *Fats That Heal: Fats That Kill.* (Second printing). Burnaby, Canada: Alive Books, 1993.

Huard, Pierre, and Wong, Ming. *Chinese Medicine.* London: World University Library, 1968. A basic introduction to Chinese medicine.

Hunninghake, D.B., Stein, E.A., Dujovne, C.A., et al. "The efficacy of intensive dietary therapy alone or combined with lovastatin with hypercholesterolemia." *New England Journal of Medicine,* 1993. 328: 1213–1219. The reduction in LDL cholesterol produced by diet was small in this study, and its benefit was possibly offset by the accompanying reduction in the level of HDL cholesterol.

Jenkins, D.J.A., Wolever, T.M.S., Rao, A.V., et al. "Effect of blood lipids of very high intakes in diets low in saturated fat and cholesterol." *New England Journal of Medicine,* 1993. 329: 21–26. This study suggests that very high intake of foods rich in soluble fiber lower blood cholesterol levels even when the main dietary modifers of blood lipids—namely saturated fats and cholesterol—are greatly reduced.

Johnson, C.L., Rifkind, B.M., Sempos, C.T., et al. "Declining serum total cholesterol levels among U.S. adults." *Journal of the American Medical Association,* 1993. 269: 3003–3008. The results document a continuing decline in serum cholesterol levels among U.S. adults.

Kaptchuk, Ted J. *Chinese Medicine: The Web That Has No Weaver.* Longdon: Rider and Company, 1983. This best-selling authoritative book defines the underlying principles of Chinese medicine and shows how they are applied in practice.

Kim I., Williamson, D.F., Byers, T., and Koplan, J.P. "Vitamin and mineral supplement use and mortality in a U.S. cohort." *American Journal of Public Health,* 1993. 83: 546–550. This review paper found no evidence of increased longevity among vitamin and mineral supplement users in the United States. Considering the wide use of such supplements, this study questions the cost-effectiveness of vitamin therapy. While other studies might not contradict this one, they suggest that the "jury may still be out" on the benefits of vitamin supplements.

Kinsley, M.M., 1947. "Sludged blood." *Science*, Nov. 1947. Some of the original ideas of toxemia emerged from Dr. John Tilden who was trying to unravel the question of what causes disease in the early 1900s. In offering an alternative to the germ theory, he wrote a book, *Toxemia Explained*, in which he said diseases arise when toxic matter in the body could not be sufficiently eliminated. Since that time, there have been other reports in medical science. For example, it has been observed that when sick people fasted and recovered from their illnesses, their blood became less sticky. Very healthy people do not have sticky blood.

Klag, Micheal J., Ford, Daniel E., Mean, Lucy A., et al. "Serum cholesterol in young men and subsequent cardiovascular disease." *The New England Journal of Medicine*, 1993. 328: 313–318. The increased risk of cardiovascular disease associated with high serum cholesterol in middle-aged persons has been clearly established. This study indicates there is a link between serum cholesterol levels measured in young men and clinically evident premature cardiovascular disease later in life.

Lee, M., Manson, J.E., Hennekens, C.H., Paffenbarger, R.S., et al. "Prevalence of high blood cholesterol among U.S. adults." *Journal of the American Medical Association*, 1993. 270: 2823–2828. The results suggest that body weight and mortality were directly related. Lowest mortality was observed among men weighing, on average, 20 percent below the U.S. average of men of comparable age and height.

Lu, Henry C. *The Art of Long Life: Foods for Longevity*. Malaysia, Pelanduk Publications, 1990. This books shows how familiar foods from the supermarket can help you build up your immune system. The author has also published *Legendary Chinese Healing Herbs* and *Chinese System of Food Cures*.

Matsen, Jonn. *Eating Alive: Prevention Through Good Digestion*. Vancouver: Crompton Books, 1987. This book offers ideas for balancing foods so that they are more easily digested. Hundreds of cartoon illustrations show you that disease is a result of inefficient digestion due to nutritional and/or emotional stress.

Morioka, N., Sze, L.L., Morton, D.L., and Irie, R.F. "A protein fraction from aged garlic extract enhances cytotoxicity and proliferation of human lymphocytes mediated by interleukin-2 and concanavalin A." *Cancer Immunology Immunotherapy*, 1993. 37: 316–322. This study reveals that an aged garlic extract has very high immunostimulatory activity.

Newberne, P.M., Schrager, T.F., and Conner, M.W. "Experimental evidence on the nutritional prevention of cancer." in T.E. Moon and M.S. Micozzi, *Nutrition and Cancer Prevention*, New York: Marcel Dekker, Inc., 1989. 33–82. This is one of the many early studies that highlights the role of nutrition in the prevention of cancer.

NIH Consensus Development Conferences." Triglyceride, high-density lipoprotein, and coronary heart disease." *Journal of the American Medical Association*, 1993. 269:

505–510. This panel reviewed various findings and offered a consensus report which suggests that, among other things, there is an association between triglycerides, HDL cholesterol, and coronary heart disease. HDL may prevent the entry of cholesterol into the process of atherogenesis or even remove cholesterol from atherosclerotic lesions, so-called reverse cholesterol transport.

Passwater, R.A. *Supernutrition*. New York: Pocket Books, 1975. This popular book introduces an effective vitamin therapy program. Some people suggest that this was one of the first popular introductions to the idea that vitamins are important in antioxidant therapy.

Reader's Digest. *Foods That Harm: Foods That Heal*. Montreal: Reader's Digest, 1997. This is a well-illustrated book on the healthy and less healthy aspects of the food we eat.

Reid, D. *Guarding the Three Treasures: The Chinese Way of Health*. London: Simon and Schuster, 1993. The three treasures of Taoist medicine—essence, energy, and spirit—are the physiological and psychological components of health. The "way of the Tao" is the way of harmony with nature, a dynamic balance with yin and yang.

Reid, D. *The Tao of Health, Sex, and Longevity: A Modern Practical Approach to the Ancient Way*. London: Simon and Schuster, 1989. The author provides an introduction to Taoist principles and combines his research in offering preventive approaches for fighting off disease. Breathing exercises and other aspects of health are explained and illustrated.

Rimm, E. B., Stampfer, M.J., Ascherio, A., et al. "Vitamin E consumption and the risk of coronary heart disease in men." *New England Journal of Medicine*, 1993. 328: 1450–1456. The data does not prove a causal relationship, but it provides evidence of an association between a high intake of vitamin E (more than 60 IU per day) and lower risk of coronary heart disease. Further studies are being carried out.

Shi Jizong, and Chu Feng Zhu. (translated by Shi Jiaxin) *The ABC's of Traditional Chinese Medicine*. Hong Kong: Hai Feng Publishing Company. 1992. This book illustrates how a Chinese medical doctor might diagnose and treat several common illnesses.

Stampfer, M.J., Hennekens, C.H., Manson, J.E., et al. "Vitamin E consumption and the risk of coronary heart disease in women." *New England Journal of Medicine*, 1993. 328, 1444–1449. Although these data do not prove a cause-and-effect relation, they suggest that among middle-aged women the use of vitamin E is associated with a reduced risk of coronary heart disease. Further studies are being carried out.

Syland, E., Funk J., Rajka, G., et al. "Effect of dietary supplementation with very-long-chain n-3 fatty acids in patients with psoriasis." *New England Journal of Medicine*, 1993. 328: 1812–1815. Dietary supplementation with very-long-chain n-3 fatty acids (found in fish oil) was no better than corn oil supplementation in treating psoriasis.

Veith, Ilza (translator). *The Yellow Emperor's Classic of Internal Medicine*. Malaysia, Pelanduk Publications, 1992. This book was published by arrangements with the University of California press. This is the first classic of Chinese medicine. In fact, the whole history of Chinese medicine can be said to be nothing more than a series of footnotes on this Nei Ching fundamental text. This book was copyrighted in 1949.

The Centers for Disease Control and Prevention (CDC) in Atlanta counted 418,690 U.S. deaths in 1990 that were attributed to smoking (20 percent of all deaths in the U.S. that year). They compared the number of cigarettes the dead smokers had puffed with the number of years they lost, based on average life expectancy for Americans. 1993. "Each cigarette shortens a smoker's life by seven minutes."

A $1 million study was carried out in the U.S. Agriculture Department's Human Nutrition Research Center in Beltsville, Maryland. This was reported on in 1992. "Margarine raises cholesterol levels, U.S. study shows." Another study in *The New England Journal of Medicine* in 1990 showed that such trans-fatty acids raised the harmful elements in cholesterol while lowering the protective elements.

Chapter 11: Principle 7—Kill Anxiety with Exercise

Hinkleman, L.L, and Nieman, D.C. "The effects of a walking program on body composition and serum lipids and lipoproteins in overweight women." *Journal of Sports Medicine and Physical Fitness,* 1993. 33: 49–58. The findings suggest that moderate exercise alone may not be a sufficient stimulus to affect body composition and serum lipid profiles favorably in overweight women.

Marcus, B.H., and Simkin, L.R. "The stages of exercise behavior." *Journal of Sports Medicine and Physical Fitness,* 1993. 33, 83–88. Understanding the stages of exercise behavior could yield important information for enhancing rates of participation in physical activity.

Martinsen, E.W., Medhus, A., and Sandvik, L. "Effect of aerobic exercise on depression: A controlled trial." *British Medical Journal,* 1985. 291: 109.

Ohkuwa, T., and Itoh, H. "High-density lipoprotein cholesterol following anaerobic swimming in trained swimmers." *Journal of Sports Medicine and Physical Fitness,* 1993. 33: 200–202. This study demonstrates that anaerobic swimming induces an increase in HDL cholesterol metabolism, suggesting that the anaerobic exercise per se was one reason for the elevated HDL cholesterol levels.

Paffenbarger, R.S. Jr., Hyde, R.T., Wing, A.L., et al. "The association of changes in physical-activity level and other lifestyle characteristics with mortality among men." *New England Journal of Medicine,* 1993. 328: 538–545. The data illustrates that beginning moderately vigorous sports activity, quitting cigarette smoking, maintaining normal blood pressure, and avoiding obesity were separately associated with lower rates of death from all causes and from coronary heart disease among middle-aged and older men.

Sandvik, L., Erikssen, J., Thaulow, E., Erikssen, G., Mundal, R., and Rodahl, K. "Physical fitness as a predictor of mortality among healthy, middle-aged Norwegian men." *The New England Journal of Medicine*, 1993. 328: 533–537. Physical fitness appears to be a graded, independent, long-term predictor of mortality from cardiovascular causes in healthy, middle-aged men. A high level of fitness was also associated with lower mortality from any cause.

Simonsick, E.M., Lafferty, M.E., Phillips, C.L., Mendes de Leon, C.F., Kasl, S.V., Seeman, T.E., Fillenbaum, G., Herbert, P. and Lemke, J.H. "Risk due to inactivity in physically capable older adults." *American Journal of Public Health*, 1993: 1443–1450. The findings suggest that physical activity offers benefits to physically capable older adults, primarily in reducing the risk of functional decline and mortality.

Van Doornen, Lorenz J.P., and De Geus, Eco J.C. "Stress, physical activity, and coronary heart disease." *Work and Stress,* 1993. 7: 121–139. Apart from its beneficial effects on resting levels of blood pressure and cholesterol, fitness is believed to reduce the impact of psychological stress. The study revealed that fit people showed a consistently favorable cardiovascular profile under stress.

A statement by the American College of Sports Medicine suggested that walking, running, and other aerobic exercise lowers the blood pressure by an average of 10 points. The sports group reviewed more than forty studies on blood pressure.

Chapter 12: Principle 8—Use the Power Within You

Benson, H. *The Relaxation Response.* New York: Morrow, 1975. This is an excellent book on relaxation exercises.

Bodhidharma is the author of two classics which have been very important to the *Qigong* martial artists and monks: *Tendon Changing Classic (Yi Jin Jing)* and *Marrow Cleansing Classic (Hsi Sui Jing)*. For an English translation, see Yang, Jwing-ming. *Muscle/Tendon Changing and Marrow/Brain Cleansing Chi Kung.* YMAA, Jamaica Plains, 1989.

Men Den, tr. *Wujishi Breathing Exercises.* Revised by Tin Shen. Hong Kong: Medicine and Health Publishing Co, 1986. This book provides an introduction to breathing exercises.

Jagadish, K.R.I. *Health Through Yoga and Diet.* Phil Ang: Singapore. 1992. The author is affectionately called "Jag." He is a teacher in Brunei who has dedicated his life to his students and patients. This book is a comprehensive guide to yoga and health.

Koh, T.C., "Tai Chi Chuan." *American Journal of Chinese Medicine.* Vol. IX, 1, 15. This author provides an introduction to the role of Tai Chi Chuan in Chinese medicine.

Pirsig, R.M. *Zen and the Art of Motorcycle Maintenance.* New York: Bantam Books, 1974. He suggests that the Greeks used a similar word, *enthousiasmos* (the root of enthusiasm), which means filled with *theos* (God or Quality).

Yogi, Maharishi Mahesh. *Science and Being and Art of Living: Transcendental Meditation.* New York: Signet Books, 1963. This is the classic book that is the definitive introduction to transcendental meditation.

Beta waves are what the brain is normally producing when we function on a daily basis. Alpha waves are related to a more "aware" state of relaxation. Theta waves are produced when we become drowsy. They are produced during deep meditation and may be associated with creative thoughts. They are described as the subconscious. Delta waves are produced during sleep and might be described as sleep or other unconscious states.

I was introduced to yoga and meditation through Noela Murphy in 1991. I worked with her when I was in Singapore during 1991-1994. Noela introduced me to her mentor, Jagadish, or "Jag." He is known throughout the region as a healer and yoga guru. I visited this kind and inspirational individual at his home in Brunei at No. 2, Simpang 884-25, Kilanas, Begawan 2780, Brunei, Darussalam. Fax (02) 240627.

More information about biofeedback can be obtained at most university hospitals. In addition, you might contact: *Biofeedback Research Society*, University of Colorado, 4200 E. 9th Avenue, Denver, Colorado, 80220.

The self-hypnosis exercises are provided by Allan Stibbard of Alandel Systems. During 1990, I worked with him in learning how to use hypnosis in Victoria, British Columbia.

Chapter 13: Your Personal Plan for Taming the Dragon

Collins, J.C., and Porras, J.I. "Building your company's vision." *Harvard Business Review,* 1996. Sept-Oct, 65-78.

Cunningham, B. *Action Research and Organizational Development.* Westport, Conn: Praeger.

Chapter 14: Your Personal Plan for Renewal

Covey, S.R. *The Seven Habits of Highly Effective People.* New York: Simon and Schuster, 1989.

Index

About the Author

BART CUNNINGHAM, Ph.D., is currently involved with a number of workplace initiatives focused on managing stress and improving workplace wellness.

Dr. Cunningham works in a number of related areas concerning stress and wellness: stress and satisfaction related to organizational design, shift scheduling, managerial skills, crisis management, human resource management, technological change, job design, and internal working relationships. He has developed crisis management training programs for municipal governments in Southern California and has assisted with the implementation of new structures and schedules in police departments in the Victoria and Vancouver areas. He has consulted with a range of federal and provincial organizations in Canada, such as the Attorney General Ministry, Coordinated Law Enforcement Unit, Justice Development Commission, Department of Indian and Native Affairs, and the Atomic Energy Commission. He has also worked with the National Productivity Board in Singapore to assess the implementation of quality-related approaches and with the government of Brunei in developing mechanisms for improving methods of resolving conflicts. Dr. Cunningham has also worked with several leading private-sector organizations, such as the Luscar Sterco Coal Mine, the Canadian Imperial Bank of Commerce, and a wide range of small entrepreneurial organizations.

Dr. Cunningham completed a doctoral degree at the University of Southern California in management and administration and was a Visiting Scientist at the Tavistock Institute of Human Relations in London, England. He is a director in the Center for Organizational Research and Effectiveness and is a professor in the School of Public Administration at the University of Victoria, Canada. From 1991 to 1994, he was at the Nanyang Business School at Nanyang Technological University in Singapore, where he was the research director of the Enterprise Development Center. Most recently, he taught at the Czech Management Center and the University of the Philippines. He has published over fifty academic articles and has completed the books *Action Research and Organizational Development* (Praeger) and *Quality of Working Life* (Labour Canada).